Advance Praise for

DEBUNK THIS!

"*Debunk This!* is a must-read for all conservatives eager to master the art of debating liberals. Palumbo's book will equip you with knowledge on virtually every political topic to effortlessly win arguments with your know-it-all lefty friends and enemies."

—KRISTIN TATE, *The Hill*, Author of *How Do I Tax Thee?*

"Matt Palumbo lives up to his reputation as one of the best liberal myth busters in the conservative movement. In *Debunk This!* Palumbo conveniently puts them all in one place and simplifies the wonky data to make it digestible for any and all readers. Looking to dominate your next debate? Look no further."

—WILL RICCIARDELLA, *The Washington Examiner*

"Matt has produced one of the best resources I've found for anyone interested in wasting their time arguing with know-nothings on twitter."

—PHIL LABONTE, All That Remains

"If there's anyone who could convince a socialist like me that the ruling class has the absolute right to accumulate unconscionable amounts of wealth at the expense of everyday American workers, it would be Matt Palumbo."

—CARL GIBSON, *The Guardian*, *Houston Chronicle*

"Socialism has failed everywhere it's been tried, and Matt demolishes the tired liberal myths that try to resurrect it."

—PHIL KENNEDY, Founder, Kennedy Financial

"Matt Palumbo has an exceptional ability to critically analyze political and economic myths in a way nobody else can quite match. In his latest book, *Debunk This!*, Matt looks at some of the most commonly misunderstood political and economic ideas peddled by the American left. From misconceptions about welfare and inequality, to downright lies about hate crimes, Matt Palumbo expertly takes down the modern left's main, fake arguments. This book doesn't 'own the libs.' It totally and utterly destroys the falsehoods perpetuated by the mainstream press and 'progressive' activists."

—JACK BUCKBY, *Poland Daily*

DEBUNK THIS!

Shattering Liberal Lies

MATT PALUMBO

A POST HILL PRESS BOOK

Debunk This!:
Shattering Liberal Lies

ISBN: 978-1-64293-304-8
ISBN (eBook): 978-1-64293-305-5

Cover art by Cody Corcoran

Post Hill Press
New York • Nashville
posthillpress.com

Published in the United States of America

For my parents.

Contents

Foreword

BY DAN BONGINO

It's hard to believe that it's already been nearly six years since Matt Palumbo and I crossed paths.

The year was 2013, and the Clinton Labor Secretary Robert Reich had just released a new documentary largely critical of modern capitalism called *Inequality for All.* An article authored by Matt popped up in my Twitter that purported to prove Reich's "inequality for all" is really "disinformation for all," which I had to give a read.

Those who've followed Matt's column on which this book is based already know that he possesses a unique ability to explain the supposed logic behind liberal policies with as much ease as he has in making mincemeat out of them, with plenty of snark to boot.

I remember Googling Matt's name after reading his takedown of Reich, assuming he was probably a middle-aged academic, not a nineteen-year-old publishing what was one of his first articles ever. Admittedly surprised at his age, I made an effort to reach out to Matt on Twitter (who later joked he didn't know who I was—but assumed I was important due to the blue check mark next to my name), and the rest is history.

Since then, Matt has always been my go-to researcher, or as those on the show know him, my "resident fact-checker."

The phrase "fake news" didn't even enter the nation's lexicon until the 2016 election, and ironically it was coined by the left to explain away why it was they weren't successfully influencing voters against Trump. The liberals in the media must've been projecting, because never have we accomplishments—even when he pursued policies as president that would achieve the opposite of whatever he's taking credit for.

The last section of the book contains essays on gun myths, particularly those spread by the media. Whether it be the claim that Australia eliminated mass shootings by banning all guns or that mass public shootings "simply don't happen" in other countries, this chapter has a refutation.

As a collection of individual essays, there isn't any "grand takeaway" you'll experience at the end of this book, but you will accumulate countless pieces of ammunition to shoot down liberal lies.

ECONOMIC MYTHS

For me personally, politics and economics have always been interchangeable. Conservatism's philosophical underpinnings of limited government and personal responsibility have always appealed to me, but economics has always been the way I quantify and objectively evaluate political policies.

Seldom do politicians think the same.

As Thomas Sowell puts it, "The first lesson of economics is scarcity: there is never enough of anything to fully satisfy all those who want it. The first lesson of politics is to disregard the first lesson of economics."

It's easy to understand the appeal of the kind of Santa Claus economics the modern left is pushing, especially to those who don't believe they'll be ponying up to fund it. I've long joked that the problem with conservative policies is that they work in practice but not in theory.

Due to the left's increasingly glowing attitude toward socialism, I begin this chapter with the lengthiest essay in the entire book, which is an extensive economic analysis of the Scandinavian nations. Due to their generous welfare states, they've become the latest "go-to" success story for socialism. While the typical essay in this book averages around a thousand words, the wide-ranging Scandinavian essay is longer, tackling everything from the massive taxes on the middle class and poor needed to fund such "social democracies" to the drag on their economies their massive governments have had, how their college students still have crippling student loan debt despite "free" college, and much more.

Once all the myths about those supposed socialist successes are debunked, I turn my attention toward Venezuela and the damage control the left is attempting to pretend it isn't a "real" socialist country.

While it's difficult to lie about the reality of failed nations like Venezuela, it's much easier to lie about history. Did we used to tax the wealthy at 90 percent, and the economy boomed? So goes one liberal claim. Did Ronald Reagan's tax cuts rack up a massive deficit, only to be finally fixed by President Bill Clinton and his surplus? It's easy to see how one could come to such a conclusion, but the reality is much more complex.

The modern claims I tackle aren't much better and only exist because a sympathetic media allows them to. If you've ever heard that illegal immigrants pay taxes just like the rest of us, that the Trump tax cuts were "for the rich," or that red states take the most welfare dollars, you can blame an uncritical media and pundits who ought to know better.

Of course, I shouldn't fault my political opponents, as without their incompetence this book wouldn't exist.

Scandinavian "Socialism"

Whereas Venezuela is commonly cited as an example of socialist failure by many critics of socialism, the Scandinavian nations of Sweden, Denmark, and Norway are often referenced by socialists as supposed socialist success stories.

During one of the 2015 Democratic primary debates, the self-identified socialist Senator Bernie Sanders said that "we should look to countries like Denmark, like Sweden and Norway, and learn from what they have accomplished for their working people." During a town hall event in 2016, Bernie said:

> *When I'm talking about democratic socialism, I'm not talking about Venezuela, I'm not talking about Cuba, I'm looking at countries like Denmark and Sweden. And you know what goes on in those countries? All of the kids who have the ability and desire go to college. And you know how much it costs? It is free. They have child-care systems which are outstanding. They have public educational systems which are extremely strong. The retirement benefits for their elderly are much better than they are in the United States.*

Ironically, in 2011 Sanders posted an article to his website that argued "these days, the American dream is more apt to be realized in South America, in places such as Ecuador, Venezuela and Argentina."[1] He's also consistently praised Cuba in the past.[2]

That aside, these alleged new models of socialism are worth exploring.

Why Do People Call Scandinavia "Socialist"?

It must first be clarified that the Scandinavian countries are not socialist. They are capitalist countries that impose excessive levels of taxation on their citizens to fund a wide array of social programs. Those programs include:

- "Free" government-funded health care through single-payer health care systems.
- Generous government-funded maternal and paternal leave.
- Heavily subsidized higher education, free of tuition to all students (and in Norway, to international students as well).
- Generous paid sick leave.

And all these programs are extremely popular when you poll American voters on them—but that's meaningless. Anything that appears "free" polls extremely well—until the public realizes what they have to pony up for "free." If you polled the opinion of the nation's twelve-year olds on a "free Xbox" policy, would you expect anything less than 100 percent support?

The large welfare states of Scandinavia are not without their cost. In 2017, all three countries had levels of taxation exceeding half of every dollar earned. Taxes as a percent of GDP were:[3]

- 50.7 percent in Sweden
- 53.5 percent in Denmark
- 54.7 percent in Norway

For reference, in the US, taxes at all levels of government averaged 26 percent of GDP in 2016 (and have since been cut).[4]

Listen to Bernie's rhetoric and you'd get the impression that it's "millionaires and billionaires" ponying up most of those funds—but they aren't in Scandinavia. While the Tax Foundation found that in 2017 the top 10 percent of American households paid 70.6 percent of the federal taxes, there is no Robin Hood in Scandinavia.[5]

In America, an earner isn't subject to the top tax bracket of 37 percent until they earn over $500,000.[6] While an American would need to earn eight times the average income to be subject to our top tax bracket, the figures are only 1.5 times average income in Sweden, 1.6 in Norway, and 1.3 in Denmark.[7] Their top tax brackets are 57 percent, 39 percent, and 60 percent, respectively (including payroll taxes).

So, how would America's tax system look if it were more like Scandinavia's?

- If the US tax code were as flat as Denmark's, someone earning roughly $70,000 would face a top marginal tax rate of 46.3 percent.[8] That's simply the first layer of taxation, as all Scandinavian countries have a 25 percent value-added tax (VAT) on purchases (the equivalent of a sales tax).
- Even *after accounting for the dollar value of transfer payments and other government benefits,* a single-income couple earning the average wage with two children will pay an average personal income tax rate of 22 percent in the *Nordic* countries (counting government transfers as a negative tax), as compared with a rate of 14.2 percent in the United States. Across all family types, the average American family earning the average wage would pay $2,000–$5,000 in taxes each year (net of the value of any transfer payments) than a *Nordic* family. Note that this comparison is of *Nordic* countries (Scandinavia plus Finland and Iceland).[9]

Since Scandinavia has redistributive welfare states, it would make sense to count transfers as "negative taxes" to give a more honest representation of what citizens are paying net of benefits they receive. Even with that adjustment, taxes are 19 percent higher *at a minimum.*[10]

And despite all the "freebies" in Scandinavia, Americans consume much more overall. According to an analysis of Organisation for Economic Co-operation and Development (OECD) consumption data by the White House, average consumption per person is:[11]

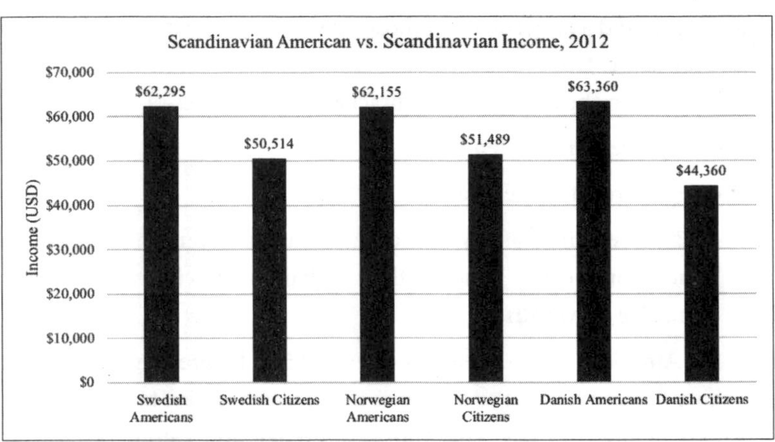

Source: Census Bureau, *Gallup*

The figures for households of Americans with Scandinavian ancestry in 2012 are as follows:[19]

- Norwegian American $62,155 (21 percent higher)
- Swedish American $62,295 (23 percent higher)
- Danish American $63,630 (43 percent higher)

Additionally, the US Census listed a group identifying themselves as "Scandinavian Americans," who earned a median household income of $67,421 in 2012.[20] The median household income of all Americans in 2012 was $51,371.[21]

When it comes to those on the bottom of the income distribution, the poverty rate among Swedish Americans is lower than native Swedes.[22]

And the real kicker? These figures are not adjusted for differences in taxation. Not only do Scandinavian Americans far outperform Scandinavians economically, but they also get to keep a larger chunk of a larger pie.

Scandinavia Is Wealthy Despite Their Welfare States, Not Because of Them

Few disagree that there should be a safety net for when hard times come unexpectedly—but there's a difference between a safety net and a hammock.

In Scandinavia, it's clear which they have.

Despite being one of the healthiest nations in the world, in the early 2000s, 10 percent of Sweden's entire workforce was on paid sick leave at any given time.[23] And why wouldn't they be when the government would pay 80 percent of their salary? The average number of sick leaves taken per Swede per year more than doubled when the government increased the percentage of salary they'd pay from 75 percent to 80 percent. The paid sick leave system has since been reformed and tightened.

In Denmark, roughly 9 percent of the workforce (in 2012) was on disability,[24] and in Norway (in 2016), while the unemployment was below 3 percent, 20 percent of the working-age population was on either unemployment or sick leave benefits.[25] Both countries lack the sick populations to justify such figures—as does every other country.

Scandinavia is rich today—but in spite of their generous government policies, not because of them. As economist Nima Sanandaji noted in the case of Sweden:

> *From 1870 through 1936, Sweden was the fastest growing economy in the world. But after 1975—when the Swedish state began to expand in earnest—Sweden's economy noticeably slowed, falling from the 4th richest in the world to the 13th by the mid 1990s.*[26]

Charted below is GDP growth in Sweden (and Denmark) and per-capita income in Sweden relative to other advanced countries.

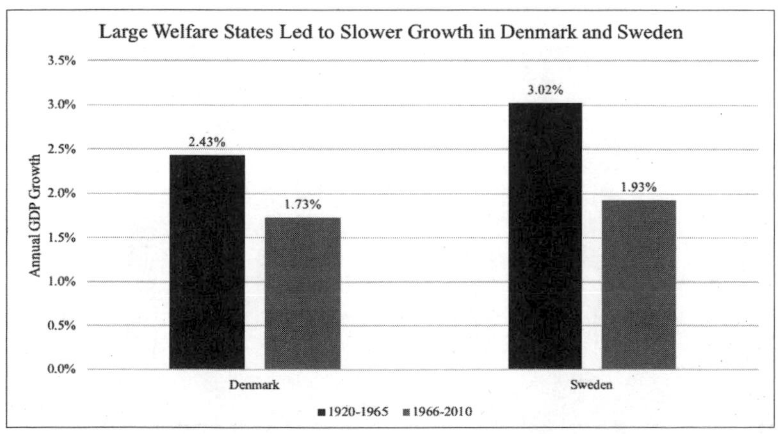

Source: Reform Institutet

Economic Performance in Sweden Has Improved as Their Government Has Shrunk

Sweden's historical economic growth spurt came during a time when they had low taxes and small government, and the brakes began to halt the growth once they created the welfare state they're known for in the mid-1970s. Although their government is still massive, Sweden did implement reforms relatively recently in the mid-1990s that have scaled back the size and scope of their government. And as it turns out, when it comes to government, smaller is better.

Consider the following.

From 1975 to 1995, Sweden's GDP growth was half that of all other OECD countries, and a full percentage point lower than the EU15 countries. After 1996, Sweden has outperformed both groups of nations.[27]

Accompanying that surge in growth was a shrinking public sector.

In the 1990s, more than one out of every five government employees lost their job. It's no secret that government workers are (on average) less efficient than private sector workers, and the reallocation of workers from public to private sector gave the economy a much-needed jolt.

Swedish workers personally saw the benefits of that growth. From 1976 to 1995, Swedish incomes rose only 0.7 to 0.8 percent per year. From 1996 to 2011, the rate of growth nearly quadrupled.

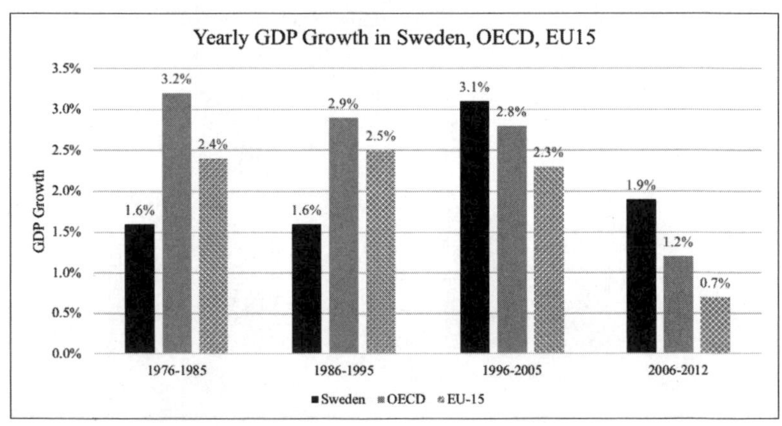

Source: Reform Institutet

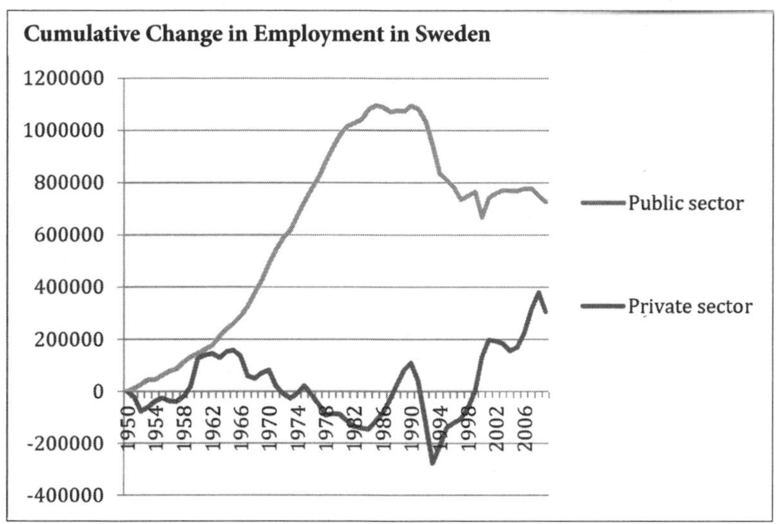

Source: Reform Institutet

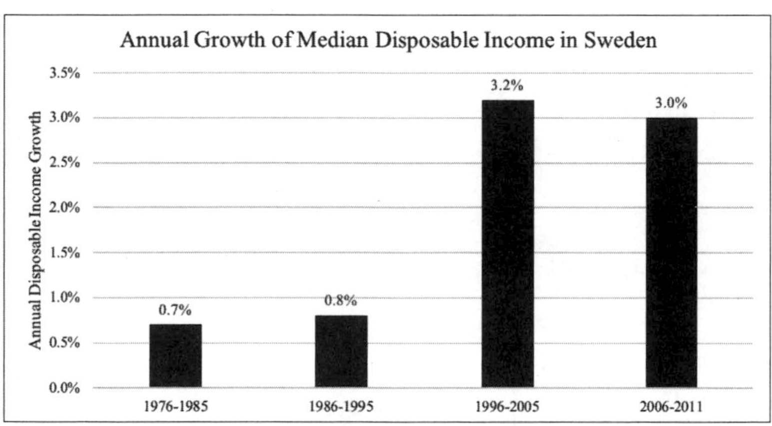

Source: Reform Institutet

As did Swedish incomes relative to the average of all other advanced nations. You can see the reversal in trend once Sweden enters their "welfare state era" and their "reform era." Though taxes remain high and their government is still massive, they made a move in the right direction—with visible benefits.

Source: Professor Olle Krantz

And speaking of the government's finances, in 1994, Sweden's national debt totaled 80 percent of GDP, which has since been cut in half. The catalyst? A 1997 fiscal rule requiring a budget surplus of 2 percent (which was later lowered to 1 percent).[28]

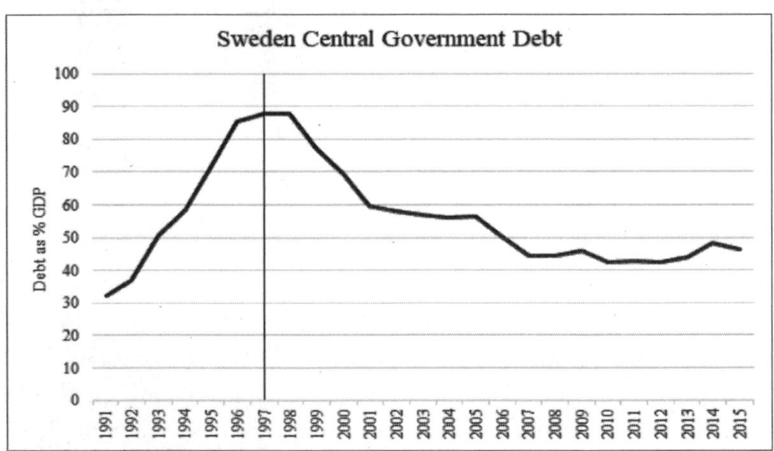

Source: Reform Institutet

That's in comparison with America's national debt exceeding 105 percent at the end of 2018. There is significant evidence that debt exceeding 90 percent of GDP begins to have noticeable negative effects on the economy, and Sweden was able to reduce their debt under that threshold by making major cuts in government spending.[29]

Income and Wealth Inequality in Scandinavia

One of the main benefits touted by advocates of the large Scandinavian welfare states is levels of income inequality among the lowest rates in the world. But just like their general prosperity, the relative income equality of Scandinavia predates the welfare state.

According to one study of income inequality in Sweden in particular, during the period between 1903 and 2004:

> *Starting from levels of inequality approximately equal to those in other Western countries at the time, the income share of the Swedish top decile drops sharply over the first eighty years of the twentieth century. Most of the decrease takes place before the expansion of the welfare state and by 1950 Swedish top income shares were already lower than in other countries.*[30]

And income inequality isn't the only kind of inequality. The Scandinavian nations have plenty of wealth inequality. In the United States, the top 1 percent owns roughly 35 percent of all the wealth. In Sweden, the top 1 percent controls roughly 25–40 percent of total wealth.[31] High-income taxes have proven unsuccessful at alleviating that "problem." According to one study, the share of the richest Swedes who inherited their wealth is around 66 percent, with only the remaining one-third being entrepreneurs.[32] In America, most of the wealth is self-made, while in Sweden, it's generational.

Why? Perhaps because high taxes don't hurt wealthy people as much as they hurt people in the process of becoming wealthy.

Social Program Performance—"Free" College

In the age of endlessly rising college costs and mounting student debt, it's no wonder that the concept of so-called "free college" has been

of bright young people cannot afford to go to college, and that millions of others leave school with a mountain of debt that burdens them for decades. That shortsighted path to the future must end."[37]

Having made such past comments, Sanders would probably be just as shocked as I was to learn that there is student debt in Scandinavia despite the lack of university tuition, and a lot of it. Although tuition is free, room and board are not. Paradoxically, offering free tuition seems to have incentivized students to be more likely to rack up debt by moving out early. While it's becoming more common for American students to save money by living at home and attending a two-year community college, there's less incentive to do so with "free" tuition.

- In 2015, Swedes who borrowed to attend college had an average $17,266 in debt.[38]
- In Norway, the average student graduated with 280,000 NOK in debt in 2016.[39] That amounts to roughly $32,000.
- For contrast, the average student debt for someone graduating in America's class of 2015 was approximately $30,100.[40]

Student debt levels in Norway are on par with America (despite the almost nonexistent ROI on a Norwegian college education), and Swedes have roughly half as much debt, but only in nominal terms. Interestingly, while having less debt per student that takes out debt, more Swedish students graduate with debt than Americans.

In 2004, 85 percent of Swedish students graduated with debt, compared with 50 percent of US students.[41] While Swedes have less debt per capita, the reduced ROI on a Scandinavian college education relative to an American one means that American students graduate with average debt-to-income ratios of 57 percent, compared to 79 percent in Sweden.[42]

In other words, relative to income, American students do indeed have less debt than Swedes and Norwegians.

Social Program Performance—"Free" Health Care

According to Senator Sanders, "our high-priced health care system leaves millions overlooked, and we spend more yet end up with less."

One key metric that Scandinavia performs poorly on relative to the US is cancer survival rates. *The Lancet*'s CONCORD-3 study examined 37.5 million patients of eighteen different types of cancer diagnosed from 2000 to 2014, and America far outperforms Scandinavia in five-year survival rates.[43]

There are eight different types of gastrointestinal cancers surveyed, and the US outperforms all Scandinavian countries in terms of cancer survival rates for six of them. The only exceptions are that:

- Rectum cancer survival rates are 3 percent lower in the US than Norway.
- Melanoma cancer survival rates are 0.22 percent lower in the US than Sweden.

Seven other types of cancer surveyed were breast, cervix, ovary, prostate, brain, myeloid, and lymphoid. The US outperforms Scandinavia in survival on just over half of those cancers—and it's notable that even when Scandinavian countries outperform the US in cancer survival rates, *it's never by more than 10 percent.* In stark contrast, the survival rates for esophagus, stomach, pancreas, and lung cancer are all at least 50 percent higher in the US than in Denmark, and the survival rate for liver cancer is 153 percent higher in the US than Denmark.

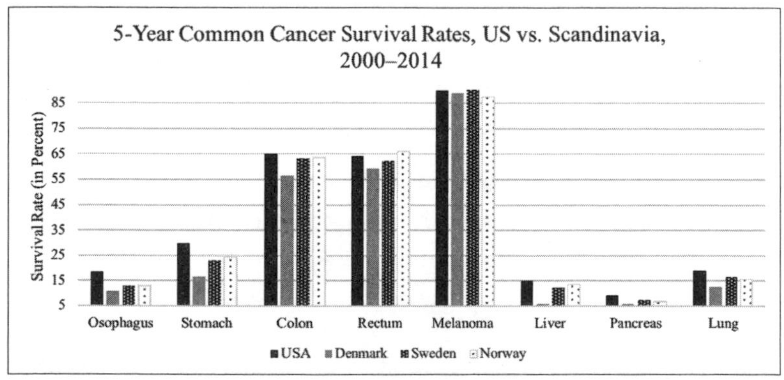

Source: The Lancet

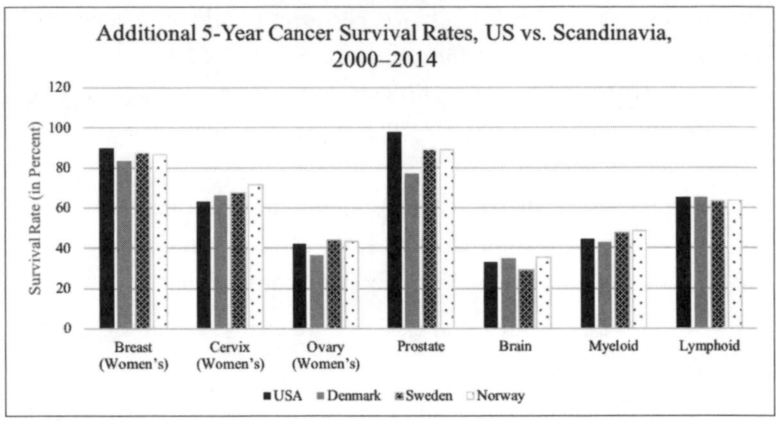

Source: The Lancet

Wait Time Statistics

The wait time to see a doctor and receive care is also significantly longer in Scandinavia than in the States according to data from the 2010 Commonwealth Fund Survey.[44] The survey lacks data on Denmark.

While only 20 percent of Americans waited four weeks or longer to see a specialist, the percentage of citizens who waited that long in Scandinavia were:

- 55 percent in Sweden
- 50 percent in Norway

Likewise, only 7 percent of Americans waited over four weeks for an elective surgery. In Scandinavia, the figures were:

- 22 percent in Sweden
- 21 percent in Norway

In both cases, the percentage of people waiting over a month for a surgery is at least double in Scandinavia than the US.

Is Scandinavia Even Socialist?

Every year, both the conservative Heritage Foundation[45] and conservative/libertarian-leaning Fraser Institute[46] publish studies on the economic freedom of the world. Both rankings are biased in that the more economically free a nation is (i.e., the more capitalistic), the more favorably they rank. However, because of that, if the Scandinavian countries rank favorably, it casts substantial doubt on whether they can be characterized as "socialist." With these rankings we can compare the Scandinavian countries' levels of economic freedom to capitalist countries (such as the United States) or (mostly) socialist countries such as Venezuela and Cuba, among many others.

Contrary to what we would expect if Scandinavia were socialist, both studies find that Sweden, Denmark, and Norway all enjoy levels of economic freedom among the highest in the world.

To prove this point, I benchmarked Scandinavia against the most economically free nations, the United States, countries with references to socialism in their constitutions, multiparty states with governing socialist parties, and explicitly socialist countries. What I'm calling "explicitly socialist" states are those governed by a single socialist or communist party government (which includes China, Cuba, Laos, North Korea, and Vietnam).

Heritage Foundation 2018 Study

The Heritage Foundation's methodology is based on four factors encompassing how well protected property rights are, the size of government spending and taxes, business/labor/monetary freedom, and trade/investment/financial freedom. From that criteria, nations are ranked on a scale of one to one hundred, with one being the least free and one hundred the freest.

The quintile with the freest economies averaged a score of eighty-four, while the second quintile of free nations (what Heritage calls "mostly free") is seventy-five. Sweden has a score of seventy-six, Norway of seventy-four, and Denmark of seventy-seven, putting them on par with the mostly free nations. Most notably, the United States is ranked as less free than Sweden and Denmark, with a score of just under seventy-six. In other words, if Scandinavia is socialist, so is the United States.

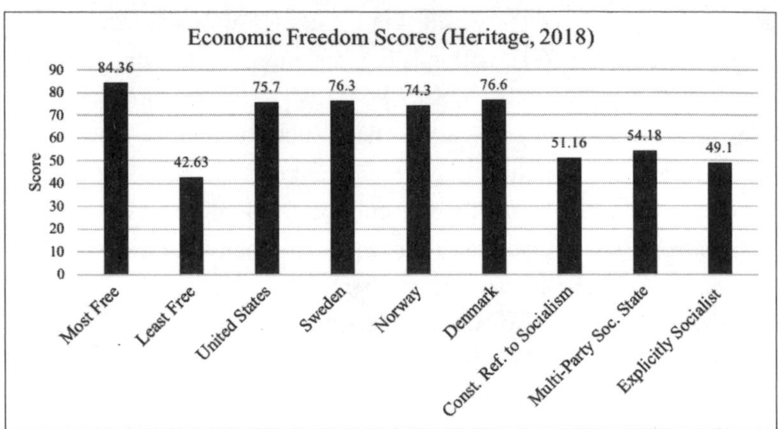

Source: The Heritage Foundation

Countries that have references to socialism in their constitutions average a score of fifty-eight, while multiparty states with governing socialist parties average a score of fifty-four. Explicitly socialist nations average forty. Two of the poster children for socialism in the twenty-first century, Venezuela, and Cuba, have scores of twenty-five and thirty-two, respectively.

Fraser Institute 2018 Study

The Fraser Institute's scores are computed based on five factors—including the size of government, protection of property rights, monetary policy, trade freedom, and levels of business regulation.

Unlike Heritage, Fraser scores on a scale of one through ten, with one being least free and ten being the freest. Fraser also ranks nations in four quartiles, while Heritage uses quintiles. Of note, Fraser appears to offer more generous rankings to less free nations relative to Heritage's study, but the same overall trends hold.

The freest nations averaged a score of 7.8, while the second quintile of free nations (mostly free) averaged 7.2. Sweden has a score of 7.4, Norway of 7.6, and Denmark of 7.8, for an average of 7.6. That puts them at par with the freest nations. The United States does rank higher than

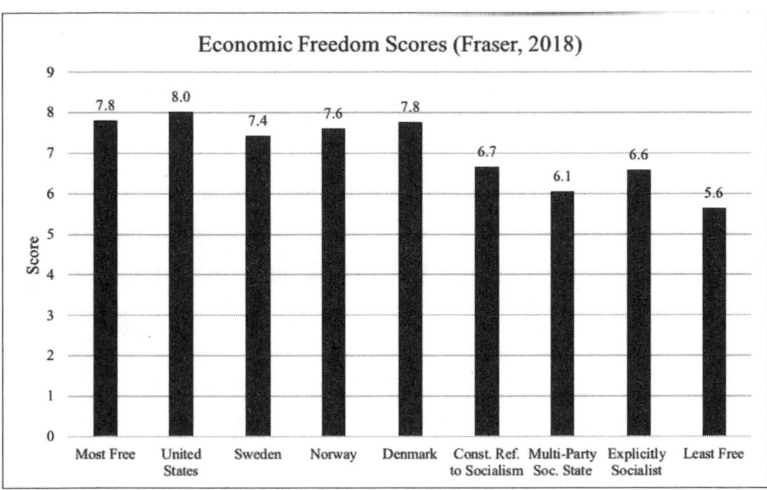

Source: Fraser Institute

the Scandinavian nations in Fraser's rankings with a score of eight, but is still relatively close.

Countries that have references to socialism in their constitutions average a score of 5.6. Multiparty states with governing socialist parties average a score of 6.1. Explicitly socialist nations average 6.6 (but Cuba doesn't have a ranking in Fraser's study, while it does in Heritage's). Cuba is the third least-free nation in Heritage's study (after North Korea and Venezuela), so its inclusion would drive down the average.

Venezuela has a score of 2.9, making it the least free nation in Fraser's study. Clearly, Scandinavia is worlds away from ranking on par with Venezuela or similar socialistic countries.

Scandinavian Leaders Deny "Socialist Slurs"

Scandinavian politicians, even those who support their nation's generous welfare states, dispute the notion that their nations are in any way socialist.

Danish prime minister Lars Løkke Rasmussen, speaking before the Kennedy School Institute of Politics at Harvard University on October 30, 2015, responded to the "slur" (in his words) that his country is socialist. He said:

> *I know that some people in the US associate the Nordic model with some sort of socialism. Therefore, I would like to make one thing clear. Denmark is far from a socialist planned economy. Denmark is a market economy. The Nordic model is an expanded welfare state which provides a high level of security for its citizens, but is also a successful market economy with much freedom to pursue your dreams and live your life as you wish.*[47]

Similarly, former Sweden PM Carl Bildt tweeted out footage of Bernie Sanders praising the USSR on his Twitter account in February 2019, adding the mocking commentary "Bernie Sanders was lucky to be able to get to the Soviet Union in 1988 and praise all its stunning socialist achievements before the entire system and empire collapsed under the weight of its own spectacular failures."[48]

Whether the likes of Bernie Sanders want to describe Scandinavia as "socialist" or "democratic socialist," the term is an oxymoron if it requires this much capitalist freedom to enable it. The Scandinavian economies are free capitalist economies with high levels of taxation and public spending, and a body of evidence showing that they've performed better economically when scaling back the taxing and spending.

Socialist Damage Control on Venezuela

In just a single year, 2016, nearly 75 percent of Venezuelans lost weight, averaging nineteen pounds each in total.[1]

They weren't on a diet by choice.

Food shortages have become common in Venezuela as the country's economy spirals into nothingness. Electricity and water are rationed, unemployment tops levels higher than the peak during America's Great Depression, and inflation exceeds a million percent per year.

In response to Venezuela descending into hell on Earth, Telesur, a Latin American socialist propaganda network funded by the governments of Cuba and Venezuela (among others), is playing the blame (and denial) game. Admittedly, the justifications for their denial would be hilarious if it weren't for the grim reality of what they're denying. "The facts are clear—Venezuela does have a food crisis," reported Telesur, after acknowledging the "nineteen pounds lost" statistic.[2] According to them, it's "right-wing US-backed opposition forces" that are intentionally sabotaging the economy by encouraging supermarket owners to hoard food, all as an attempt to make Venezuela's socialist government look bad.

That's certainly one theory.

The only remotely sensible argument I've seen from a socialist is that Venezuela's problems have more to do with declines in the price of oil than socialism, because oil exports account for 25 percent of Venezuela's GDP.[3] One can only then wonder why the citizens of Saudi Arabia aren't starving in the streets too, given that a larger percentage of the Saudi economy is dependent on its petroleum sector.[4] Oil exports as a percentage of total exports is also higher in Saudi Arabia. Similarly, while oil revenues account for upward of 70 percent of Venezuela's government revenue (when prices are high),[5] they account for 85 percent of government revenues in Saudi Arabia.[6] None of this is to say that the price of oil doesn't have a massive effect on Venezuela's economy, but rather that the collapse was inevitable independent of Venezuela's oil sector's performance.

Furthermore, Venezuela's problems predate a crash in oil prices. Food shortages began in 2011 when Hugo Chávez was still alive and oil prices were at their peak, near $110 a barrel.[7] Inflation also soared to nearly 30 percent that year, though that's nothing compared to the incredible 1 million percent inflation seen in 2018.[8]

Instead, for Venezuela's decline, we can blame socialism and the incompetence of Hugo Chávez. Venezuela's oil industry actually makes for a good case study of the destructive effects of socialism on an industry.

Venezuela's oil industry has been nationalized since 1976, and the industry has since been dominated almost exclusively by the nation's largest firm, Petróleos de Venezuela, S.A. (PDVSA). While some capitalist countries have nationalized oil industries too (such as Mexico, Norway, and Saudi Arabia), that kind of pot of gold in socialist hands has proven disastrous. Hugo Chávez took power in 1999 and quickly began milking PDVSA to fund his socialist vision.

In protest of Chávez during 2002–2003, PDVSA workers went on strike with the goal of forcing a new election. In response, Chávez fired half of PDVSA's workforce, twenty thousand workers in total. Opposition was strongest among top management, 80 percent of whom were fired (which also included engineers and the firm's research arm).

Replacing those employees with others equally knowledgeable about the oil industry proved impossible, and they were instead replaced by political allies of Chávez. In fact, it became company policy during Chávez's reign that only his supporters would be hired—regardless of competency. While PDVSA produced 3 million barrels of oil a day before Chávez, they only averaged 2 million per day by 2017,[9] and 1.6 million per day at the beginning of 2019.[10]

This is where socialist economics become truly incredible. The one million barrel per day decline in production came even though PDVSA has since seen its workforce explode from the pre-Chávez forty thousand employees to an unjustifiable one hundred fifty thousand employees today. Even with that massive increase in employment, the decline in barrel-per-day production has declined in percentage terms by what the nation saw during the 2002–2003 worker strikes. In other words, twenty thousand striking (competent) workers caused as much damage to PDVSA's production as the hiring of an additional one hundred thirty thousand socialist workers. The workforce is up almost fourfold, yet production is down a third.

Socialism also naturally discourages capital investments needed to simply maintain infrastructure. Every dollar spent maintaining Venezuela's oil infrastructure was seen as a dollar taken away from spending on social programs, so the nation's oil infrastructure began to rapidly depreciate, lessening production ability year after year. Though an estimated $8 billion in annual spending was needed to simply maintain Venezuela's oil infrastructure, the government only spent half of that.[11]

Perhaps Venezuelans wouldn't have to worry about low oil prices if it weren't for their socialist government mismanaging the industry into oblivion.

Venezuela Was "Real Socialism" Until It Wasn't

When Hugo Chávez came to power, there were noticeable improvements for the Venezuelan people that socialists highlighted, such as the poverty rate being cut in half (from 54 percent to 27.5 percent from 2004 to 2007).[12] Of course, to brand that an example of socialist success would be like branding Bernie Madoff a success by only analyzing his hedge fund's results up until the day before it was exposed as a Ponzi scheme. By 2014, the poverty rate had nearly caught up to where it was in 2004, and in 2018 the poverty rate skyrocketed to 90 percent.[13]

The Reagan Deficits

There's no denying that in economic terms, the Reagan years were nothing short of spectacular—a modern Roaring '20s—thanks in large part to tax reform. But even most conservatives praising Reagan for his economic record acknowledge a fault during his two terms: an explosion in deficits and the national debt.

And indeed, there was plenty of debt. While Jimmy Carter's deficits averaged $57 billion a year (2.4 percent of GDP), Reagan's averaged $167 billion, or 4.2 percent of GDP.

By the end of his administration, Reagan had added $1.86 trillion to the national debt, and you don't need to take a guess at what liberals blame for the soaring deficits: tax cuts.

After accounting for other variables, practically none of the Reagan deficits can be attributed to tax cuts, however.

Defense Spending and the Deficit

Democrats can blame their newfound foe for a healthy chunk of the Reagan deficits: those damned Russians. Since Reagan beefed up America's military during the Cold War, spending was well above the baseline.

While $2.2 trillion would've been spent on defense during the Reagan administration had he let the budget increase according to its baseline, Reagan spent $800 billion on top of that, or $3 trillion total.[1]

Thus, the increase in defense spending alone explains away 43 percent, or nearly half of the Reagan deficit.

Inflation and the Deficit

Unfortunately for the American taxpayer in the 1970s and '80s, tax brackets were not indexed to inflation. Someone who sees their income rise only proportional to inflation is losing money, because they're paying more taxes on increasing nominal income, but the same real income. The government benefits from this, of course, as it means it collects more than it otherwise would.

During the hyperinflation of the Carter years, "bracket creep"—taxpayers being pushed into higher tax brackets due to inflation, not because they were really earning more—was a real problem.

The opposite happens when inflation comes crashing down. When inflation fell sharply during the Reagan years, so did tax revenue.

Because inflation plunged from 13 percent in 1980 to 4 percent by 1982, far faster than anyone had expected, nominal incomes and revenues came in lower as well. According to the American Enterprise Institute:

> *The Carter administration's last budget predicted 12.6% inflation in 1981 and 9.6% inflation in 1982. It also predicted each percentage point decline in inflation below its forecasts would reduce tax revenue by $11 billion. Inflation actually came in at 8.9% in 1981 and 3.8% in 1982, suggesting the inflation drop increased the deficits those years by 50 percent* [emphasis added].[2]

An early recession provided further fiscal challenges.

The Recession of 1980–1982

Although Paul Volcker's Federal Reserve succeeded in reducing inflation, that isn't to say it wasn't harsh medicine.[3] While hikes in interest rates reduce inflation, they're also contractionary in the short term for the economy. Volcker's aggressive Federal Reserve succeeded in squelching inflation—but caused a recession in the early '80s as a result.

From the beginning of 1980 to the end of 1982, the unemployment rate increased from 6 percent to 11 percent. A near doubling in the number of people unemployed means less tax revenue and more people receiving unemployment and other government benefits. It was during this period that the federal deficit as a percent of the economy ballooned from 2 percent (in the beginning of the '80s) to 7 percent by mid-1983.[4]

In total, the 1980–1982 recession *reduced federal revenue twice as much as the Joint Committee on Taxation estimated the entire Reagan tax cuts would in 1982.*[5]

Conclusion

Despite the initial adverse effects that the reduction in inflation had on tax revenues, they increased greatly under Reagan in the face of massive reductions in rates.[6]

Growth in Federal Tax Revenue, 1980–1990

Year	Total Revenues ($Billions)	Annual Change	Growth Above 1980	Growth Above 1980 ($Billions)
1980	956	—	—	—
1981	1,005	5.08%	5.08%	48.6
1982	967	-3.7%	1.19%	11.4
1983	899	-7.11%	-6.00%	-57.4
1984	950	5.76%	-0.59%	-5.6
1985	1,012	6.48%	5.86%	56
1986	1,034	2.26%	8.25%	78.9
1987	1,119	8.1%	17.02%	162.7
1988	1,154	3.16%	20.72%	198.1
1989	1,213	5.11%	26.89%	257.1
1990	1,222	0.71%	27.79%	265.7

Source: Department of the Treasury

The entirety of the debt accrued under Reagan can be attributed to an increase in defense spending, reverse bracket creep, and an early recession caused by the Federal Reserve. Without those factors, the Reagan tax cuts would've been implemented with no meaningful increase in the deficit.

Red State Welfare

In one of life's ironies, I've seen a few liberals temporarily retire the narrative that Republicans are a bunch of old rich white men—to try to argue the opposite, that we're actually the *real* moochers.

- "Red States Are Welfare Queens" reads one headline over at *Business Insider*. The article noted that of twenty states that receive more funding from the federal government than they pay in, sixteen are red states.[1]
- "Residents of the 10 states Gallup ranks as 'most conservative' received 21.2 percent of their income in government transfers, while the number for the 10 most liberal states was only 17.1 percent" wrote Paul Krugman in the *New York Times*.[2]

Certainly an economist like Krugman would realize that a state is not a person. For example, most of the violence in red states occurs in blue counties and cities within those states.[3] Do "red states" bear the responsibility for their blue counties and cities? Obviously not, and a similar statistical contortion is happening here. Red states are taking more in government handouts—but Republicans aren't, as a Maxwell Poll on the political affiliation of those in public assistance has proven:[4]

Similarly, an NPR study of the long-term unemployed found that 72 percent favor Democrats, who are all likely to be receiving benefits.[5]

If it's mostly Democrats receiving public assistance, why the heck is it red states receiving most of the benefits? A few possible explanations include the facts that:

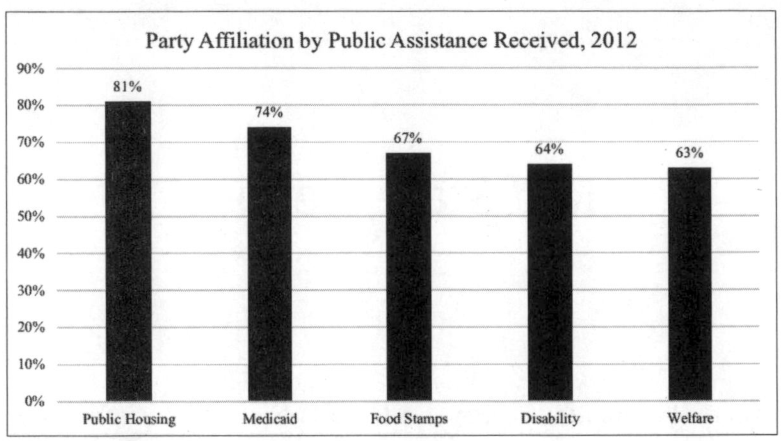

Source: Maxwell Poll

- Red states are naturally more eligible for public assistance because they have lower costs of living—and the federal poverty line (and eligibility for benefits) don't take that into account. As elaborated on in a later essay in this book, Texas has a higher poverty rate than California in the official statistics, but California has a higher poverty rate once adjusting for cost of living differences. Despite this, Texas would still be eligible for more federal assistance.[6]
- Many of these types of analyses are including Social Security and Medicare as "welfare"—as if recipients have the choice of foregoing them. Given that seniors tend to lean Republican, this could tilt the stats.

People aside, what about the claim that red states as a whole are moochers (as the *Business Insider* article implied)? It is true that red states tend to have a larger percentage of their budgets subsidized by the federal government than blue states—but only because their budgets are relatively smaller. According to *The Federalist*'s Kyle Sammin:

> *Against a national average of 32.62% [of a state's budget] being federally subsidized, the blue states received 30.80%. Purple states were almost exactly at the national level with 32.92% coming from Washington. Red state budgets averaged 35.75% federal money.*

A problem with this metric is that although federal funds make up a larger percentage of red states' state budgets, the budgets in those states are generally lower overall than those of the free-spending blue states [emphasis mine]. If, instead of comparing federal funds to state budgets, we look at how much the federal government spends in intergovernmental grants per resident of a state, the results are turned on their heads.

Against a national average of $1,935 in intergovernmental spending per American, red states receive just $1,879. Blue states get considerably more, at $2,124 per resident. Purple states see the least of their money returned to them per capita at just $1,770.[7]

States	Population	Intergovernmental Spending	Intergovernmental Spending Per Capita
Total Red State	96,086,631	$180,551,551,000	$1,879
Total Purple State	77,676,459	$137,532,631,000	$1,771
Total Blue State	134,982,448	$286,776,111,000	$2,125
Grand Total	312,471,695	$604,860,293,000	$1,936

As common sense would dictate, those most opposed to welfare aren't receiving the bulk of it.

Do We Need a $15 Minimum Wage to Prevent Full-Time Workers From Living in Poverty?

Senator Bernie Sanders has repeated an emotionally convincing quip several times in defense of a $15 an hour minimum wage; that "nobody who works forty hours a week should be living in poverty."

It's not even a particularly left-wing statement, and people of all ideological stripes can probably resonate with it a bit. After all, we're against moochers, but someone that's poor despite working forty hours a week can hardly be considered one. Nor would anyone see a working poor person as "deserving" of their situation.

While we can all sympathize with the working poor, the problem with turning Bernie's statement into an argument for hiking the minimum wage is that poverty is not a wage problem, it's a work problem. After all, the poverty threshold is low enough where a single person working forty hours a week, fifty weeks a year would be over the poverty line (as they'd earn $14,500).[1]

So how would one find themselves in poverty? Having a child, and thus an extra person in the household (who isn't generating income while consuming it), is one obvious answer. But there's an even bigger reason why: not working full-time.

In 2015, only 11 percent of working-age people in poverty worked full-time. By contrast, 63 percent of those in poverty don't work at all.[2]

2018 Poverty Guidelines for the 48 Contiguous States and the District of Columbia	
Persons in Family/Household	Poverty Guidelines
1	$12,140
2	$16,460
3	$20,780
4	$25,100
5	$29,420
6	$33,740
7	$38,000
8	$42,380

Source: Department of Health and Human Services

Of full-time workers, only 2 percent live in poverty (compared to 32 percent of the unemployed). If we look at those with families, the numbers become even more stark. For instance, in 2011 only 0.3 percent of families in poverty worked an hourly job earning the minimum wage.[3]

The minimum wage can't help people who don't work—and every conservative and their mother are aware that hikes in the minimum wage increase unemployment among the most vulnerable, but those aren't the only consequences. Minimum wage hikes also reduce hours worked and decrease the labor force participation rate.

A study published in 2001 at North Carolina State University by Dr. Walter J. Wessels looked at past minimum wage hikes, finding that hikes from 1978 to 1981 reduced teen labor force participation by 3.62 percentage points, 1990–1991 hikes by 2.07 percentage points, and 1996–1997 hikes by 1.31 percentage points.[4] I'm using the youth as a proxy for the low skilled.[5]

In the case of reduced hours, that reduction can offset the benefits of a minimum wage hike entirely. Take Seattle as an example, which was one of the first cities to pass a $15 an hour minimum wage ordinance in 2014 (that took full effect on January 1, 2018). That's the exact wage Bernie would like to see to lift all our full-time workers out of poverty,

defined poverty by Oxfam's criteria, the poverty line would be increased to $28,808 for a family of three, which would obviously increase the number of people in poverty on paper. While America's childhood poverty rate in the census statistics (15.6 percent in 2016) is slightly higher than the overall poverty rate (12.7 percent in 2016), it's drastically lower than the 23.1 percent UNICEF arrived at.

To illustrate just how ridiculous UNICEF's methodology is, they rank countries where the average income is below the US poverty line as having less child poverty than the US! UNICEF lists Bulgaria as having 18.8 percent child poverty, Lithuania with 15.4 percent, and Slovakia with 11.2 percent. The average monthly income in Bulgaria is $416, $655 in Lithuania, and $853 in Slovakia.[4]

By 2014, UNICEF began changing the definition of poverty further in updated versions of the study, to anyone in a household earning below 60 percent of the median national income. America is a country where a full-time minimum wage worker earns more than 91.3 percent of the world, so it's no surprise that UNICEF literally has to redefine poverty to portray America in a negative light.[5]

The Cost of Illegal Immigration

The same individuals happy to extoll the alleged economic benefits of illegal immigration are seldom willing to acknowledge the exceeding costs.

The great libertarian economist Milton Friedman famously argued decades ago that illegal immigration was preferable to low-skilled legal immigration because illegals at least can't apply for welfare benefits. It's basically true in that illegals cannot apply for federal assistance (with exceptions for the case of welfare fraud), but that's irrelevant because the real major cost of illegal immigration is secondary—through their American-born, and thus legal-citizen, children.

Birthright Citizenship Is the Biggest Cost of Illegal Immigration

Education is the biggest cost. According to the Pew Research Center, from 1995 to 2012, the percentage of K–12 students with at least one undocumented immigrant parent rose from 3.2 percent to 6.9 percent.[6] The cost to taxpayers to educate the children of illegals comes out to $59 billion according to a 2016 study from the Federation for American Immigration Reform (FAIR).[7] The Pacific Institute's Lance Izumi estimated the cost at $44.5 billion in 2010, which is in line with FAIR's estimate when you take into account inflation and increases in population. Both estimates were calculated by simply multiplying the number of students with illegal immigrant parents by the average cost of educating a child K–12, and the cost trend is rising.

Just as these legal children of illegal immigrants are entitled to a taxpayer-funded education, they're entitled to a whole host of welfare benefits because illegal immigrant families mostly earn incomes low enough to qualify a legal family for federal aid. Though the parents don't qualify for the aid themselves, their legal children do open some doors.

Unfortunately, the last time the Government Accountability Office (GAO) studied the cost of benefits to the children of illegals was in 1997, and it only provided estimates for food stamps, so it's hardly comprehensive. Since a lack of comparable unbiased literature exists, it is worth noting, however, that they placed the cost of food stamps to children of illegal immigrants at $1.75 billion (in 2018 inflation adjusted dollars) per year, and obviously that's an understatement as illegal immigration has increased since 1997.[8]

There was not enough data for the GAO to provide total cost estimates for housing assistance but estimated an illegal household with a child would be eligible for $612 a month in benefits, compared to an average $112 food stamp benefit per child (both figures adjusted for 2018 dollars). In other words, the cost of housing assistance to taxpayers likely significantly eclipses that of food stamps.

The Overlooked Cost of Health Care for Illegals

The emergency room loophole guarantees that illegal immigrants will benefit from free health care on the taxpayer's dime. Despite federal regulations preventing taxpayer funding of Medicaid to illegals, *Forbes* health care analyst Chris Conover estimates that roughly 3.9 million illegal (uninsured) immigrants receive health care each year,[9] costing the following in uncompensated care:

- $4.6 billion in health services paid for by federal tax dollars
- $2.8 billion in health services paid for by state and local tax dollars
- $3 billion in cost-shifting (charging legal citizens more to compensate for illegals)
- $1.5 billion in pro-bono care from physicians

Adding in the implicit federal subsidies that nonprofit hospitals receive,[10] among other indirect costs, brings us to a total cost of $18.5 billion a year to taxpayers. None of this includes the cost of the legal children of illegals, who likely qualify for Medicaid.

Similarly, Conover estimates that health care costs for illegal immigrants alone total nearly $20 billion.[11]

All factors considered:

- FAIR finds the net cost of illegal immigration (i.e., net of taxes paid by illegals) to be $116 billion.[12] This is particularly notable because they assume that illegals pay $19 billion annually in taxes—far more than our liberal friends typically claim.
- The conservative Heritage Foundation's 2013 study on the same subject finds a comparatively lower $55 billion net cost to American taxpayers.[13]

What could be funded by the massive cost of illegal immigration? At least one (big beautiful) border wall—many times over.

Do Illegal Immigrants Pay Taxes?

A7re illegal immigrant laborers putting money into the pot just like the rest of us? That's what a number of pundits on the left have claimed, always with a figure in the range of $10+ billion a year.

- *PolitiFact* rated the statement "undocumented immigrants pay $12 billion of taxes every single year" from María Teresa Kumar of Voto Latino true—even though the "$12 billion" figure was based off payroll taxes, half of which are paid by the employer. On the other hand, her estimate didn't include state and local taxes.[14]

- A 2016 study by the nonpartisan Institute on Taxation and Economic Policy found that illegal immigrants paid $11.64 billion in state and local taxes in 2013.[15]

Combining the former estimate of payroll taxes paid and latter of state and local taxes, that implies illegals are paying about $18 billion in taxes each year. So there is some truth to the claim, but it's first worth answering the lingering question of how the heck illegal immigrants are paying taxes in the first place.

The IRS issues individual taxpayer identification numbers (ITINs) to individuals who must file taxes but either don't have or are ineligible for a Social Security number. ITINs are issued regardless of immigration status. Of an estimated illegal immigrant workforce of 8 million, 3.4 million, or less than half, are registered with ITINs and are paying taxes.[16] In other words, the majority are not.

For some perspective, in 2017 the federal government spent $4 trillion, or *$10.95 billion per day.* The entirety of the nation's taxpaying illegals barely pays enough in taxes to cover what the federal government spends in half a day (of all the taxes illegals pay, only $6 billion is going to the federal government).

And remember, this is tax revenue from eight million illegal workers. The American labor force had roughly one hundred sixty million workers in 2017.[17] Just for the sake of a thought experiment, if we were to replace the entire labor force with illegal immigrants and have them pay all their state and local taxes to the feds, the federal government would've collected approximately $360 billion in tax revenue in 2017, as opposed to the $3.3 trillion that the federal government actually collected.[18]

And seldom do those pointing out that illegals pay taxes mention how much they take from the pot. In addition to all the aforementioned costs in this essay:

- Because illegals displace legal American employment (100 percent of which would be paying taxes—and at higher wages), illegal immigrants impose a $30 billion annual cost in lost tax revenue.[19]
- Because of pressure on wages, illegal immigrants are costing American workers $118 billion annually in lost wages.[20]

So yes, we are getting about $18 billion a year in tax revenue from illegals. The problem is, it costs a lot more than $18 billion to collect it.

How Bill Clinton Faked the Clinton Surplus

The so-called "Clinton surplus" is often cited by liberals who wish to show that the "tax and spend" philosophy isn't as fiscally reckless as it sounds. If we look at the government's budget statistics, there does appear to be a budget surplus during the last four years of Bill Clinton's presidency, bolstering this talking point. However, as anyone who looked at the national debt would also notice, that figure rose every year under Clinton. So how did both these things happen simultaneously?

To recap Clinton's tax policies, in 1993 two new top income brackets of 36 percent and 39.6 percent were added, as was a hike in the corporate tax to 35 percent, an extension of the Medicare payroll tax to all levels of income, and a small increase in the gas tax. Overall, these taxes were expected to boost revenues by 0.36 percent of GDP during their first year and an additional 0.83 percent by 1997. Clinton did manage to see an annualized 19.3 percent increase in tax revenues from 1993 to 1996, though it should be noted that Reagan managed an even more impressive 24.1 percent during his presidency.[1]

In 1997, the Republican-controlled Congress reversed some of the Clinton tax increases by lowering the capital gains tax, creating a child tax credit, increasing the estate tax exemption, and increasing the income levels that could claim tax-deductible IRA contributions. In all, these cuts reduced the burden of federal taxation by about 0.22 percent of GDP (or in other words, the tax cuts reduced taxes by $30 billion—26 percent of the 1993 increase). Economic performance under Clinton fared better from 1997 to 2000 compared to the 1993–1996 period in terms of job creation, wage increases, and GDP growth.[2]

To talk back in time just a bit—two years following the Clinton tax hikes in 1993, in April of 1995 the Congressional Budget Office (CBO) released deficit projections for the following years of the Clinton presidency. Below they are tabled against the actual realized deficits. All figures are in billions of dollars.

Predicted vs. Realized Deficits, FY 1994–1999			
Year	Predicted	Actual	Difference
1994	-$203 billion	-$203 billion	0
1995	-$175 billion	-$164 billion	$11 billion
1996	-$205 billion	-$107 billion	$98 billion
1997	-$210 billion	-$22 billion	$188 billion
1998	-$210 billion	+$69 billion (surplus)	$279 billion
1999	-$200 billion	+$126 billion (surplus)	$326 billion
Total	-$1,203 billion	-$301 billion	$902 billion

Source: Arthur Laffer, Stephen Moore, and Peter Tanous, *The End of Prosperity*, p. 129. Based on data from the CBO forecast, April 1995. Note: "Surpluses" continued into 2000 and 2001.

Keep in mind here, this *was after the Clinton tax increases* and *before the Republican tax cuts*, and yet the *CBO still projected deficits in years to come*. So, what actually happened?

Clinton was more fiscally conservative than most conservatives. Federal spending as a percentage of GDP has been lowest under Clinton out of the past seven presidents, so liberals would have to thank small government for the surplus had it existed anywhere else than on paper. Unfortunately, paper is the only place the Clinton surplus existed. Tax revenues under Clinton still never managed to eclipse government spending, and if you look at the following table, you'll see that the national debt increased every year under Clinton.

Increases in the National Debt, FY 1993–2001			
Fiscal Year	Year Ending	National Debt	Debt Increase vs. Year Prior
1993	9/30/1993	$4.41 trillion	
1994	9/30/1994	$4.69 trillion	$281.26 billion
1995	9/29/1995	$4.97 trillion	$281.23 billion
1996	9/30/1996	$5.22 trillion	$250.83 billion
1997	9/30/1997	$5.41 trillion	$188.34 billion
1998	9/30/1998	$5.52 trillion	$113.05 billion
1999	9/30/1999	$5.65 trillion	$130.08 billion
2000	9/29/2000	$5.67 trillion	$17.91 billion
2001	9/28/2001	$5.8 trillion	$133.29 billion

Source: Department of the Treasury

So how is this possible? How did Clinton produce a surplus when he never collected enough tax revenues to fund government entirely, and why did the national debt increase in the face of an alleged surplus?

That's where a piggy bank other than the American taxpayer comes into play: the Social Security trust fund. Tabled below are the components of the national debt—public debt plus intragovernmental holdings. Public debt is the discrepancy between taxes and spending (accumulated deficits), and intragovernmental holdings is money borrowed from and now owed to government trust funds. An increase in intragovernmental holdings would signify that more money is owed to the Social Security/ Medicare trust funds.

Note that *every single year there was a claimed surplus, the money owed to intergovernmental holdings increased by a larger amount than the claimed surplus*, meaning that borrowing from other areas of government filled both the gap between tax revenues and government spending and produced the "surplus." This is the governmental equivalent of paying off the Amex card with a Visa.

This Clinton surplus cannot be used to discredit conservative fiscal policy because the "surplus" itself was a phenomenon of creative accounting, not policy.

Change in Public Debt vs. Intergovernmental Holdings, FY 1997–2001					
Fiscal Year	End Date	Claimed Surplus	Public Debt	Intergovern-mental Holdings	Total National Debt
1997	9/30/1997		$3.79 trillion	$1.62 trillion	$5.41 trillion
1998	9/30/1998	$69.2 billion	$3.73 trillion ($-55.8B)	$1.79 trillion (+$113B)	$5.53 trillion (+$113B)
1999	9/30/1999	$112.7 billion	$3.64 trillion (-$97.8B)	$2.02 trillion (+$227.8B)	$5.66 trillion (+$130.1B)
2000	9/29/2000	$230 billion	$3.4 trillion (-$230.8B)	$2.27 trillion (+$248.7B)	$5.67 trillion (+17.9B)
2001	9/28/2001	$127 billion	$3.33 trillion (-$66B)	$2.47 trillion (+$199.3B)	$5.81 trillion (+$133.3B)

Source: Townhall Finance[3]

And we're still paying off the Visa today.

Did We Used to Tax the Rich at 90 Percent?

There's one regard in which some fiscal liberals want us to return to the "good ol' days"—insanely high tax rates on the wealthy.

While the top tax rate is 37 percent today (previously 39.6 percent), debating raising or lowering the rate a few percentage points pales in comparison to the rates of 70–92 percent we had in the past, we're told.

- "When radical socialist Dwight D. Eisenhower was president, I think the highest marginal tax rate was something like 90 percent," Bernie Sanders informed us, speaking tongue in cheek regarding that "socialist" quip.[1]
- "That 90% top rate in the 60s wasn't as crazy as modern context might make it seem. And remember, economy thrived" tweeted *New York Times* columnist Paul Krugman, who somehow has a Nobel Prize in economics.[2]
- "The income tax rate, through the early '60s…is I think 91 percent on incomes over $200,000," said author Malcolm Gladwell. "The thing is, if you bring this up now, people don't even believe you that was in place fifty years ago."

Gladwell is famous for stating that it takes ten thousand hours of practice to master a skill, but as comedian David Angelo once joked, it doesn't take more than ten minutes of research into historical tax rates to prove his argument wrong.

As everyone who has filed taxes knows, the *marginal* tax bracket you fall into isn't the *effective* tax rate you pay—because of deductions and other factors. In the past, the tax code was ridden with loopholes (many of which were closed when rates were lowered).

When the Revenue Act of 1935 was passed, raising the top income tax bracket to 75 percent, literally only one person paid it: John D. Rockefeller. Only eight taxpayers paid the 91 percent rate present in 1960.[3]

It is true that we did use to have massively high marginal tax rates, but it was never the case that we had high effective tax rates. Nor are the top rates of the past comparable in the levels of income they affect. The new top income tax rate for households of 37 percent kicks in at $500,001 of income. The 91 percent rate in 1955 kicked in at an inflation-adjusted $3.5 million in today's income.[4]

As you can see in this chart from the Congressional Research Service, the top effective income tax rate in America has never exceeded 30 percent.[5]

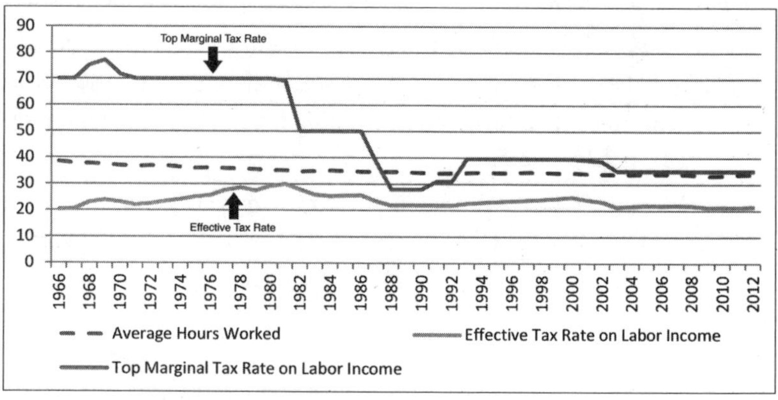

Source: Congressional Research Service

If we isolate just the often-maligned top 1 percent of income earners, their tax rate is less than 6 percentage points lower today than what it averaged in the 1950s. A decline for sure, but hardly the 60-or-so percentage point decline claimed. Historically, the effective tax rate of the top 1 percent has averaged in the 30s, according to the Tax Foundation.

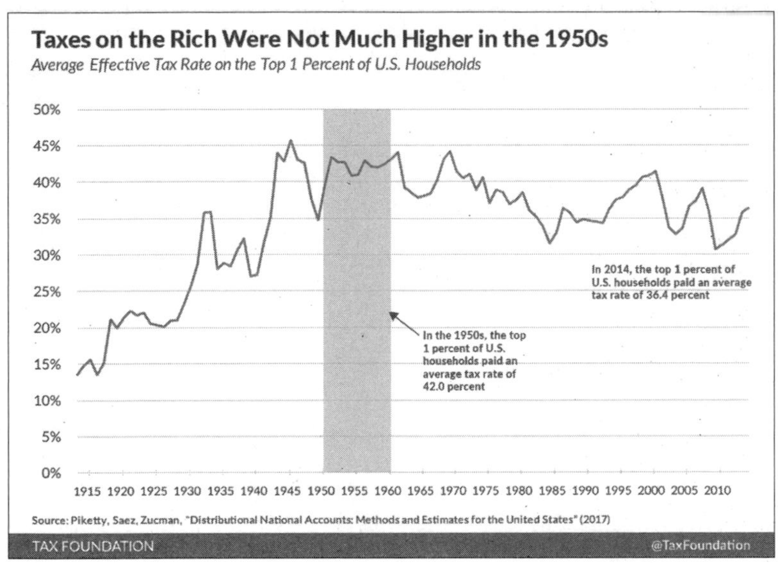

Source: Tax Foundation[6]

The government hasn't been starved of revenue in light of the decline of marginal tax rates—because it's the effective rate that matters.[7]

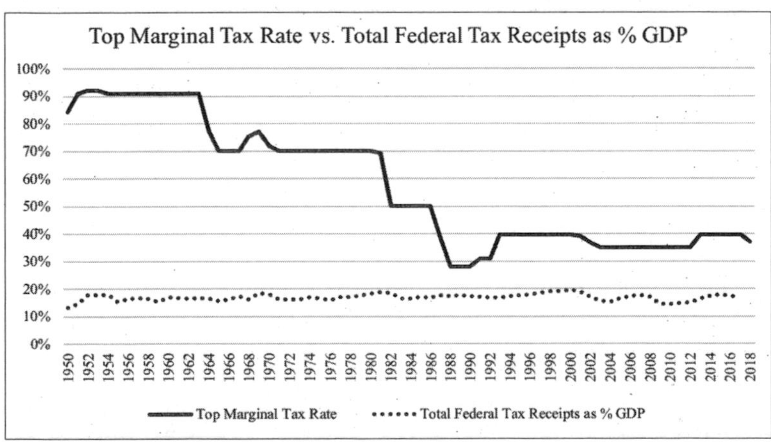

Source: St. Louis Federal Reserve

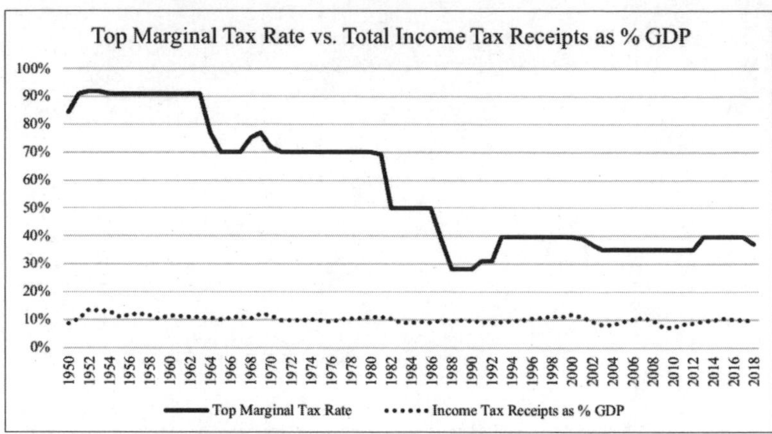

Source: St. Louis Federal Reserve

Krugman and company are right in that tax rates on the rich used to be much higher.

But the tax rates that the rich actually paid? Not so much.

Debunking Four Crazy Cortez Ideas

The new democratic socialist darling Alexandria Ocasio-Cortez called out CRTV's Allie Stuckey for a satirical video Stuckey released poking fun at a then-recent gaffe of hers. The video featured Stuckey "interviewing" Cortez, with Cortez's "replies" being clips taken from a disastrous PBS interview she gave with Margaret Hoover. Under the impression that the obviously satirical video was somehow a "hit piece," Cortez responded, "Republicans are so scared of me that they're faking videos and presenting them as real on Facebook because they can't deal with reality anymore."

That's certainly an ironic statement if I've ever heard one, though it's understandable why Cortez thinks a casual observer could've mistaken Stuckey's satirical video as legitimate—because Cortez's views truly are indistinguishable from parody.

What's an Unemployment Rate?

Despite boasting an economics degree, it's no wonder she was never employed in the field. In the aforementioned PBS interview that Stuckey excerpted from, Cortez told host Margaret Hoover that the only reason the unemployment rate is so low in the Trump economy is because everyone is working too hard. "Well, I think the numbers you just talked about is part of the problem, right?" Cortez said. "We look at these figures and we say, 'Oh, unemployment is low, everything is fine, right?' Unemployment is low because everyone has two jobs," she continued.

"Unemployment is low because people are working sixty, seventy, eighty hours a week and can barely feed their family."

That's not how any of this works.

A person's employment status is binary—they're either employed or they aren't. Having multiple jobs doesn't have any effect on the unemployment rate, because the employed person's status remains "employed" when they take another job. I'm unsure how Cortez thinks the unemployment rate is calculated, but she must think it has to do with the ratio of unfilled jobs to the percentage of total jobs, while in reality it's the number of unemployed divided by the total size of the labor force.

And speaking of people working two jobs, the percentage of Americans in that situation are among the lowest it has ever been since the St. Louis Federal Reserve began tracking data on it.

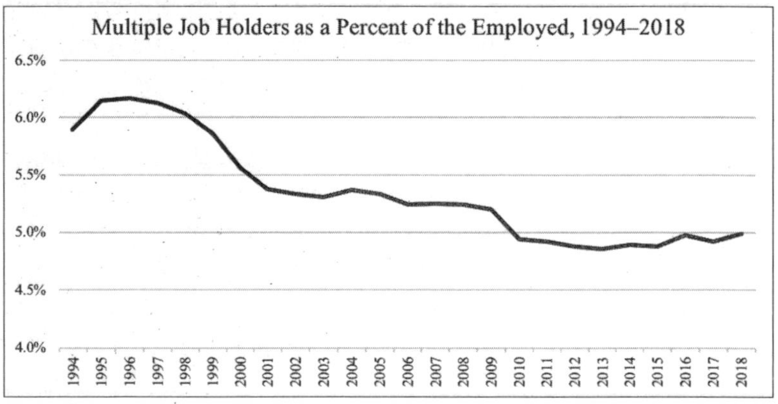

Source: St. Louis Federal Reserve

Whites (5 percent) and blacks (5.3 percent) were the most likely to hold two-plus jobs, while Asians (3.2 percent) and Hispanics (3.4 percent) were the least likely. Half of multiple jobholders work one full-time job and a second part-time job, while 35 percent had two part-time jobs. The latter appear to be trying to piece together a full-time job. Another 13 percent were described as having their hours vary on the primary or secondary job, according to the Bureau of Labor Statistics.[1]

The Federal Jobs Guarantee

To combat the current nonexistent unemployment problem, Cortez proposed a federal job guarantee as part of her platform. The concept is relatively straightforward—if anyone is out of a job in the private (i.e., real) economy, the government will find a government job for them. What could possibly go wrong?

A lot.

For one, while liberals may view a federal job guarantee as a safety net for when private sector employees become unemployed, it would contribute to an ever-expanding federal workforce. Given that federal employees rarely quit and almost never get fired, we'd be employing everyone at the Hotel California before we know it.[2]

This would further contribute to the program's own sustainability. Who in their right mind would work in the private sector when they can work in the public sector, work less, and have almost no risk of being fired? As a result, we'd see a smaller private labor force, which means less tax revenue for the government, while a larger government workforce means more revenue will be needed. Deficits would naturally explode.

The biggest problem, however, is that such a policy would put the government in charge of allocating labor. What kind of jobs will the government create for people? Will they require training? Will there be any safeguards against workers who don't do anything? Spoiler alert to that last question: there won't be.

As insane as such an idea is, House Democrats did introduce a federal jobs guarantee bill in July 2018.[3]

The Assault Weapons Ban

This too is part of Cortez's platform, and it's relatively easy to debunk because Bill Clinton put an unsuccessful assault weapons ban into effect. Since roughly three hundred people are killed each year by all rifles (regular and "assault" rifles), it seems like an odd way to combat gun violence (but then again, liberals only really try to campaign against "scary" guns).[4]

The Department of Justice (DOJ) studied the 1994 Assault Weapons Ban and concluded that "we cannot clearly credit the ban with any of the nation's recent drop in gun violence."[5] Although there was an overall drop in gun violence during the 1990s, all crime was declining (and gun ownership was increasing). Plus, assault weapons are a small fraction of all firearms, so it would be silly to attribute their ban to a decline in all gun violence.

Or, as the DOJ puts it, "Should it [the Assault Weapons Ban] be renewed, the ban's effects on gun violence are likely to be small at best and perhaps too small for reliable measurement." It's ironic that it's liberals who often call for the government to fund more research on gun violence and gun control, and yet when they do, the results seldom confirm their bias.[6]

Housing (or Any Service) as a Human Right

Cortez's platform calls for "housing (not sheltering) the homeless," with zero actual solution for how to achieve that. I mention that because liberals love to talk about things that people have a "right" to, but they really mean a "right to something for free." And for that, you need some sort of enforcement mechanism that guarantees the production and distribution of these "rights," which is easier said than done.

To give just one example, a right to housing is written into Section 26 of South Africa's constitution, and yet the nation faces chronic housing shortages. Nearly a fifth of their entire population (twelve million people) lacks adequate housing. Is it really a surprise that calling housing a right didn't lead to everyone magically having a house?[7]

Think about it—isn't housing already a human right? Isn't health care a human right? Isn't education? Of course they are—just as everyone has a "right" to own a gun too. The difference is that conservatives don't think that means the government should purchase everyone a firearm.

California–Model for America?

California continues to hemorrhage residents every year, and the most popular destination for arrivals is Texas (which is interesting, given the immense ideological divide between the populations of those states).

If California is the future, you'd think so many people wouldn't be running from it.

Disputing reality is the famous liberal economist Robert Reich, who doesn't actually have a real economics degree and has never published a single economics paper. According to him, "California just became the world's fifth largest economy, surpassing the United Kingdom." And why? Because their "success has depended on bottom-up economics—putting tax revenues into public investments, and regulations that protect the environment and public health, not trickle-down economics."[1]

To prove his point, Reich cites Texas and Kansas as states with the "lowest taxes, least regulations, and lowest wages." By contrast, we're told that California has high taxes on the wealthy, strong regulations, and high wages. Only near the end of his argument does Reich acknowledge that low oil prices have damaged the economies of Kansas and Texas, but then chastises them for not doing enough to diversify their economies.

It's truly incredible that someone who whines about income inequality as much as Reich thinks the fact that California has the "biggest" economy means anything (because for once he's ignoring inequality). And it's even more incredible that an economist like Reich can't grasp concepts like the "cost of living" when talking about wages.

Consider the following.

The Cost of Living Brings California's Incomes Below the National Average—and Puts Them #1 in Poverty and #3 in Homelessness

Californians earn 11 percent more than the national average—so Reich is correct on the surface that Californians are out-earning their peers, but only on a nominal basis.[2] What Reich excludes is the fact that the average mortgage costs 44 percent more in California, while rents cost 37 percent more on average. Unless one wants to go homeless, those cost of living differences more than erase any nominal wage gains that Californians can boast.

Ironically, it's regulation that's responsible for those high home and rent prices, as it has thwarted the ability of developers to build at a pace to keep up with demand. To give just one example, nearly half of all housing in San Francisco was built prior to 1940.[3] Five times as many housing units were built from 1940 to 1949 than from 2010 to 2014. To little surprise, California ranks third nationwide in the number of homeless per capita.

And regarding poverty, while California appears to have a poverty rate of roughly 15 percent (measured by the Census Bureau's official poverty measure), that only defines poverty for a family of four as $24,036 (in 2015), without any considering for the cost of living. If the cost of living were adjusted for, California's poverty rate would instead be 20.6 percent (as measured by the Census Bureau's Supplemental Poverty Measure), compared with a national average of 15.1 percent. Texas ranked just below average, with a cost-of-living adjusted poverty rate of 14.9 percent.[4]

So for all the emphasis Reich made on how California's economy is the "biggest" (who is he, Trump?) with the "highest wages," it also boasts a real poverty rate 38 percent higher than Texas, which Reich claimed had among the "lowest wages."

California's Public Investments Are Underperforming

Reich touted all kinds of "public investments" that Californians' tax dollars have gone toward. How is that working out?

- Even though 43 percent of California's general-fund budget is earmarked for K–14 education (kindergarten through the first two years of university),[5] California students underperform the national average on reading and math scores.[6]

- The percentage of Californians attending a four-year college hasn't changed in fifty years, despite the trend nationally being upward.
- During a time period when California's prison population declined 12 percent, spending on prison guards increased by $500 million.[7]
- California only builds 44 percent of the housing it needs annually, costing the state $140 billion a year in economic output due to people who can't afford to live and work in California.[8]
- Electricity prices in California rose five times faster than the national average between 2011 and 2017, and Californians pay 60 percent higher than the national average for electricity. This is despite California having the highest output of hydroelectricity, which is the state's cheapest source of electricity.[9]
- According to the American Society of Civil Engineers "report card," California earns a D+.[10] Texas wasn't much better with a C-,[11] but you'd expect them to have an F- if you listened to Reich.
- And for all Reich said about environmental regulations, CO_2 emissions rose in California from 2011 to 2015, while they fell in the rest of the country during the same period.[12]

If this is what a healthy society looks like to progressives like Reich, it's no wonder Venezuela could seem like nirvana.

Blue State vs. Red State Economic Performance

I've long wanted to do a debunking of the claim that red states are economically inferior to blue states, and little did I expect that Hillary Clinton would include that very claim in her portfolio of excuses for her loss to Trump. "I won the places that are optimistic, diverse, dynamic, moving forward," Hillary said, citing Illinois as an example of a progressive state. In other words, the "non-deplorable" parts of the country.

Contrary to her rhetoric, it's red states that are the dynamic ones. Just like the American public voted against Hillary Clinton, they are voting with their feet too, as one thousand people move from blue to red states every day, on net.[1] Three liberal bastions, California, New York, and Hillary's favorite, Illinois, are hemorrhaging the most citizens.

Meanwhile, it's conservative states reaping the benefits. According to a study from the American Legislative Exchange Council, from 1998 to 2008, the nine states with no personal income tax saw their economies grow 86 percent, their populations grow 16 percent, and employment grow 18 percent. In stark contrast, the nine states with the highest personal income tax rates (averaging 10 percent) saw their economies grow 60 percent over the same period, while population grew 6.3 percent and employment grew 8.5 percent. The figures for the US as a whole were 66 percent, 10 percent, and 10.4 percent, respectively.[2]

The same held true in the most recent ten-year time frame the Exchange Council studied, from 2007 to 2017. States lacking a personal income tax outperformed in terms of employment growth and population growth, only lagging slightly in gross state product growth.[3]

Economic Performance of the Nine States with the Highest and Lowest Personal Income Tax (PIT) Rates, 2007–2017

State	Top PIT Rate	Gross State Product Growth	Population Growth	Non-Farm Employment Growth
Alaska	0%	7.3%	8.7%	3.8%
Florida	0%	25.7%	14.2%	7.5%
Nevada	0%	18.3%	15.3%	3.8%
South Dakota	0%	42%	9.9%	7.4%
Texas	0%	43.8%	18.8%	18%
Washington	0%	46.4%	14.6%	12%
Wyoming	0%	10.9%	8.3%	-4.1%
New Hampshire	0%	31.2%	2.3%	4.9%
Tennessee	0%	42.1%	8.7%	7.8%
9 States with no PIT	**0%**	**29.7%**	**11.2%**	**6.8%**
US Average	**5.6%**	**32%**	**7.5%**	**5.3%**
9 States with highest PIT	**10.31%**	**33.6%**	**5.7%**	**5.2%**
Hawaii	8.25%	32.5%	8.5%	4.8%
Maryland	8.95%	37.3%	7.1%	5.6%
Vermont	8.95%	29.6%	0%	2.5%
Minnesota	9.85%	35.6%	7.1%	6.3%
New Jersey	9.97%	23%	3.8%	1.1%
Maine	10.15%	24.2%	0.7%	0.6%
Oregon	10.64%	38.2%	11.3%	8.4%
New York	12.7%	38.8%	3.7%	9.2%
California	13.3%	40.4%	13.3%	8.5%

Source: American Legislative Exchange Council

It's those low-tax (and low-spending) states attracting the most people, and it's not just their economies outperforming.

When it comes to fiscal solvency, comparing red and blue is black and white. An analysis from Truth in Accounting examined the budgets of every state and discovered that in states with a Democratic governor and state legislature, there is an average of $22,214 in unfunded debt. By contrast, in states with a Republican governor and state legislature, the figure is only $1,473. In states where power is split, the average is $14,963, with the trend showing the bluer a state is, the most debt it racked up.[4]

In other words, the Democrat-run states have fifteen times more debt than GOP-run states.

Among the worst states are nearly all blue—New Jersey with $67.2k in debt per citizen, Illinois with $50.4k in debt per citizen, Connecticut with $49.5k, and Massachusetts, with $32.9k. The only red state exception is Kentucky, which has $39k in debt per citizen. All three states with greater than a $10k surplus per citizen have a Republican governor and majority in their state legislatures. Among them are Alaska ($38.2k), North Dakota ($24k), and Wyoming ($20.5k).

What sounds more dynamic to you, Illinois with over $50,000 in debt per citizen, or your typical deplorable-run state with an average debt burden that could be paid off if each citizen worked a minimum wage job for five weeks?

Blue State Inequality

Do conservative fiscal policies drive economic inequality? Every liberal and their mother will tell you as much.

"The GOP tax bills look like attempts to entrench a hereditary plutocracy…it's class warfare aimed at perpetuating inequality into the next generation" wrote the nauseatingly partisan Paul Krugman ahead of the passage of the wildly successful Trump tax cuts.[1]

Others known for sounding the alarm bells on income inequality, such as Robert Reich (who isn't an actual economist, he just plays one on TV), commonly cite Ronald Reagan's supply-side policies in the 1980s for the relatively high levels of income inequality we see today.

While tax and spending policies obviously do affect levels of income inequality (how could they not?), other structural changes to the nation's economy over the past half century have played a much larger role.

- To give just one such example: according to a handful of studies, 41 percent of the economic inequality created between 1976 and 2000 was the result of the increase in single-parent households.[2]
- The poverty rate would be 25 percent lower if today's family structure resembled that of 1970.[3]

I bring that up only to point out that there are more causes of income inequality other than how the government dictates the level of taxes and transfers.

At the state level it's blue, not red states with the most inequality.

Measuring inequality between the much-maligned "top 1 percent" and the bottom 99 percent, based on *Gallup*'s definition[4] of red and blue states:

- Of the top ten most unequal states (the District of Columbia is being included for the purpose of this exercise), there are eight states that are "solid Democratic," one that "leans Democratic," and one purple state.
- Of the ten equal states, two are "solid Republican," three "lean Republican," one is "solid Democratic," one "leans Democratic," and three are purple states.[5]

Of course, these are just states, and countless variables could be tainting the data. That objection considered, the correlation between liberalism and inequality remains at the "congressional district" level. According to *Axios*, "Blue districts are more likely to have high levels of income variation than red districts. Red districts have more people with similar incomes."[6]

When it comes to measuring the top 1 percent against the bottom 99 percent, an analysis from the left-wing Economic Policy Institute found that:[7]

- In states that voted for Clinton, the top 1 percent earned 23.6 times more than the average person in the 99 percent.
- In states that voted for Trump, that ratio was 19.7 to 1, or 17 percent lower.

It's no wonder liberals are the ones talking about inequality the most—they apparently can't stop causing it. Just take a liberal bastion such as San Francisco as a glowing example where one can literally only afford to live there if they're extremely wealthy (and can thus afford it) or extremely poor (and be subsidized).

Are 97 Percent of the Poorest Counties Really Republican?

It's common to hear conservatives point to impoverished cities that have long been under Democratic control as a testament to the failure of liberal policies. Likewise, liberals can just as easily point to impoverished southern states under Republican leadership as evidence of the failure of conservative policies.

The smallest level we can analyze a population and their political leanings in the US is at the county-by-county level. The claim I'd like to explore here is that 97 percent of the poorest one hundred counties are in Republican states, a claim which apparently originated from the negative-IQ political group Occupy Democrats.[1]

Before diving into the claim, it's worth reviewing a few ways that statistics can mislead and how seemingly contradictory statistics can be reconciled based on what type of analysis is used. The statements "60 percent of our *schools* had lower test scores this year than last year" and "80 percent of our *students* had higher test scores than last year" can both be true if most schools are failing—but the successful schools have a disproportionate number of students. Or to give a more relatable example, think of the marketing strategies of Verizon and AT&T. Most readers have probably seen Verizon's advertisements showing the vast geographic regions they cover against AT&T's coverage, which look skimpy in comparison. But at the same time, AT&T advertises that they cover 97 percent of Americans, and they're not lying either. Although they cover less geographic surface area, they're focused in areas with high population density.

The Verizon and AT&T example is probably more applicable in explaining why so many of the poorest counties are in Republican states. The reason why is quite simply that most counties are Republican counties, and red states tend to have more counties than blue states.

Look at any electoral map by county and every election looks like a red tsunami hit the country—even in elections where Democratic presidents won. How could this be the case? Simply refer to the two examples above—there are more Republican counties, but the fewer Democratic ones have all the population.

As *PolitiFact* acknowledged, of the one hundred poorest counties in question, forty of them are from Texas, Georgia, and Kentucky. Not coincidentally, Texas, Georgia, and Kentucky rank first, second, and third in the list of states with the greatest number of counties. Of the nation's 3,144 counties and county equivalents, nearly 17 percent of them are located in those three states. Blue states tend to be sliced into smaller numbers of counties than red states, so they're going to be overrepresented in any list of the top "x" poorest or richest counties. Liberal Massachusetts only has 14 counties, and New Jersey has 21.

According to my own calculations, blue states made up 52.9 percent of all states but had 39.1 percent of the counties, while red states made up 47.1 percent of states but 60.9 percent of the counties.[2] The District of Colombia is counted as a "state" for the sake of the calculations, and states are designated as "red" and "blue" depending on how they voted in the 2012 presidential election. This isn't to say that only 60.9 percent of counties lean Republican, just that 60.9 percent of all counties are located in Republican states. You can glean from the previously mentioned electoral maps that the number is likely much greater than 60.9 percent.

This essay was initially published as an article prior to the 2016 election, so it must be noted that the numbers are even more in my favor if we were to define "red states" by how they voted in 2016, because we could add another six states to the sample.

Also worth mentioning is that in this claim of red-county poverty, poverty is being measured in nominal terms, not adjusting for cost of living differences. As mentioned elsewhere in this book, Texas has more poverty than a blue state like California, but after adjusting for differences in the cost of living, Texas actually has less poverty than California. Areas with higher population density have higher costs of living, and areas with high population density tend to be the most liberal.

When comparing cost of living differences among red and blue states, only one of the twenty-four red states had a cost of living above the national average (Alaska), while fourteen of the twenty-six red states and the District of Columbia had costs of living above the national average. On average among red and blue states, compared with the national average cost of living, the relative value of $100 in a red state is $109 but only $98.08 in a blue state. In other words, a dollar can purchase slightly over 11 percent more in a red state than in a blue state.[3]

As for the verdict on the claim that most poor counties are in red states, it's a claim that's "technically" true but greatly misleading. Even if politics has no effect on whether a state is rich or poor, we should expect a disproportionate number of poor counties to be Republican for the sole purpose that most counties are Republican counties.

Corporate Myths–Tax, Wages, and CEO Pay

While seldom advertised as such, President Donald Trump's 2017 tax reform largely took the form of business tax reform by reducing the corporate tax rate from 35 percent to 21 percent.

For the average person (who still benefited from the individual tax cuts), though, it's not immediately clear how cuts in corporate taxes could possibly benefit them, even though the White House argued they could boost wages by as much as $4,000. After all, aren't corporate tax cuts just yet another form of "tax cuts for the rich"?

No shortage of myths surrounding corporations exists, including the extent to which they should be taxed, whether corporate profits are at the expense of worker wages, rising CEO pay, and the effect of corporate taxes on the economy as a whole.

Was the US Corporate Tax High or Low?

Prior to President Donald Trump's sweeping tax reform, the United States had a 35 percent top marginal tax rate, which critics often referred to as the "highest in the world" to emphasize how uncompetitive such a rate was.

In response, supporters of high corporate taxes usually seized upon a single 2010 Government Accountability Office (GAO) study that estimated the effective US corporate tax rate at 12.6 percent for that year. It is noteworthy that this is the only study that puts the figure this low. A year later, another government agency, the Congressional Research Service, put the figure at 27.1 percent, more than double that GAO estimate but lower than the average among OECD nations of 27.7 percent at the time.[1]

Before surveying the literature to approximate a better estimate of what the US effective tax rate truly was pre-reform, it's worth showing the flaws in the infamous GAO report.

First, the GAO report didn't include any taxes on foreign earnings that corporations pay when determining the 12.6 percent estimate, so what's being measured is what American corporations allegedly pay on domestic earnings.[2] According to their data, the effective rate would rise to 16.9 percent with taxes on foreign earnings reported. But the biggest flaw in the 12.6 percent figure isn't the lack of inclusion of taxable foreign earnings, it's that 2010 began just as the 2008–2009 recession ended. Since many corporations had suffered losses as a result of the recession, there was a spike in the number of write-offs they could take that year, thus lowering their effective tax rate, and many didn't generate any taxable income in the first place.

Using the GAO's own data, if we measure from 2008 to 2010 instead of just 2010, the average effective tax rate for US corporations (with foreign taxes included) was 30.3 percent. If the time frame was stretched from 2004 to 2010, that figure increases to 37.1 percent.[3]

Thus, the oft-cited GAO number only holds true in telling us the US corporate tax rate for a single year, and under poor economic conditions that reduced taxable income.

Tabled below is a series of more recent and comprehensive studies on the US effective corporate tax rate and whether it was above or below the average of OECD nations prior to tax reform. Because different studies differ not only on what the US effective corporate tax is but what the corporate tax of other nations is as well, there are some cases where studies find a similar effective corporate tax rate in the US but different relative to other nations. When I refer to the US corporate tax rate as being the "highest" or "second highest" in the world in the chart, I'm solely speaking of OECD nations.

Studies on US Effective and Relative Corporate Tax Rate			
Study	**Organization**	**Effective US Corporate Tax Rate**	**Above/Below OECD Average**
"Paying Taxes 2013: The Global Picture"(2014)[4]	World Bank	27.9% (in 2014)	Above, second highest in world
"U.S. Corporations Suffer High Effective Tax Rates by International Standards" (Dittmer, 2011)[5]	Tax Foundation	27% (average from 2005–2011)	Above, second highest in world
"International Corporate Tax Rate Comparisons and Policy Implications" (Gravelle, 2011)[6]	Congres-sional Research Service	27.1% (in 2011)	Below by 0.6 percentage points
"Report Card on Effective Corporate Tax Rates" (Hassett, Mathur, 2011)[7]	American Enterprise Institute	29% (in 2010)	Above by 8.4 percentage points
"Another Look at Corporate Effective Tax Rates 2004–2010" (Lyon, 2013)[8]	Alliance for Competitive Taxation	37.1% (2004–2010)	Above
"Corporate Inversions" (Clausing, 2014)[9]	Tax Policy Center (Urban Institute, Brookings)	N/A	"…similar to that firms from many other countries pay."
"The Budget and Economic Outlook: 2014 to 2024"[10]	CBO	16% (in 2013)	Below
"Cross-Country Comparisons of Corporate Income Taxes"[11]	National Bureau of Economic Research	N/A	Above. "U.S. multinationals are among the highest taxed."

Of the eight studies above, five found the US corporate tax to be above the OECD average, two found it to be below, and one "similar."

Noteworthy, however, is that of the studies above that found the US corporate tax to be below average, one (from the Tax Policy Center) was referencing a GAO report for the claim. Another, the Congressional

Budget Office included S corporations in their sample, but S corps don't pay the corporate income tax; they pass their profits or losses onto shareholders, who then pay tax on them. In other words, S corporations have the tax advantage of avoiding double taxation that C corporations face.

The CBO's methodology was to take revenues from the corporate income tax and divide it by the combined profits of C and S corporations. Roughly 30 percent of the profits divided came from S corps. With S corporation profits removed from the data, the CBO's effective corporate tax estimate would be roughly 50 percent higher.[12]

The picture is clear: there's no question that without Trump's tax reform, the US would still have among the highest corporate taxes in the developed world.

Corporate Profits: History, Wages, Workers

Are corporate profits at the expense of the American worker?

According to Pat Garofalo of ThinkProgress, corporate profits hit record highs in 2012 as wages hit record lows, and we're made to believe those events are correlated. "In the third quarter of this year, 'corporate earnings were $1.75 trillion, up 18.6% from a year ago.' Corporations are currently making more as a percentage of the economy than they ever have since such records were kept. But at the same time, wages as a percentage of the economy are at an all-time low," he wrote.[13]

While corporate profits hit a record $824 billion, total wages fell to a record low 43.5 percent of GDP, down from 49 percent in 2011, Garofalo concluded.

Notice that what's being compared is corporate profits to the wages of all workers, not corporate employees. Excess corporate profits would be at the expense of the employees of those corporations, not the entire labor force. Likewise, fringe benefits, which make up 19 percent of the average worker's income, aren't measured by wages.[14]

When we measure total employee compensation against pretax corporate profits as a share of the economy, we find that historically, corporate profits have averaged 12 percent of national income while employee compensation has averaged 63 percent.

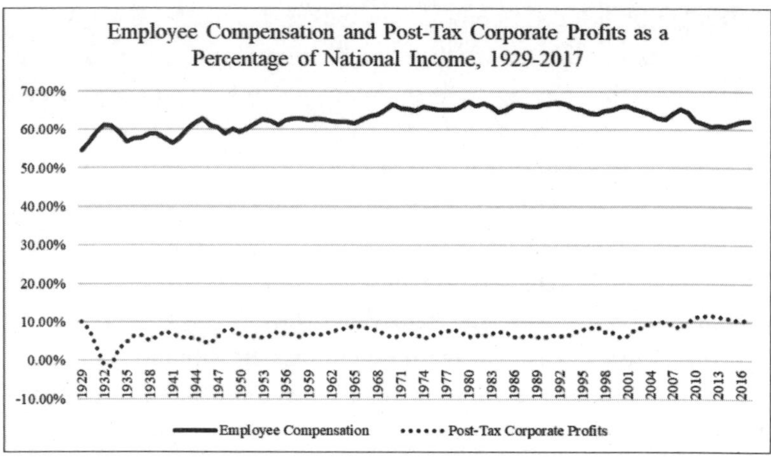

Source: St. Louis Federal Reserve[15]

Corporate Tax's Effects on Wages and Growth

In the United States—specifically, a review of eighty-two studies published since 1990 that have analyzed the effects of state and local corporate taxes on economic growth—67 percent found they have statistically significant negative effects growth, whereas only 9 percent found they have a statistically significant positive effect on growth.[16] Speaking of the federal corporate tax (as opposed to state corporate taxes), the Federal Reserve Bank of St. Louis estimated that a corporate tax rate of 12 percent would maximize the economic welfare of the United States.[17]

Another body of literature suggests that corporate taxes negatively impact worker's wages quite dramatically. Any tax that reduces domestic investment naturally reduces investment in capital, and slow growth in the capital stock slows growth in worker's wages because wages are based on worker productivity. According to a noteworthy study published by the CBO, "domestic labor bears slightly more than 70 percent of the burden of the corporate income tax."[18]

Numerous other studies challenge the belief that the burden of the corporate tax falls solely on the shoulders of the owners of capital:

- A review of the empirical literature on corporate tax incidence conducted by the US Department of the Treasury found that "labor may bear a substantial portion of the burden from the corporate income tax."[19]
- Economist Arnold C. Harberger found that labor bears over 80 percent of the corporate tax.[20]
- Kevin Hassett and Aparna Mathur of the American Enterprise Institute found that for every 1 percent increase in corporate tax rates, wages decrease by nearly 1 percent.[21]
- Wiji Arulampalam, Michael P. Devereux, and Giorgia Maffini of Oxford University found that each dollar in additional corporate tax paid reduces wages by 92 cents in the long run.[22]
- According to economist Alison Fenix, "a one percentage point [or $1] increase in the marginal corporate tax rate decreases annual wages by 0.7 percent [or $0.7]."[23]

While many people may be under the impression that investors are the ones shouldering the burden of the corporate tax, and that a tax on corporations is a tax on the rich, the evidence suggests this may not be the case. In fact, it appears as though workers bear most of the tax burden according to the aforementioned findings.

Facing a large corporate tax burden, investors can send their money overseas and companies can move production offshore. Their workers have no such luck. They are now deprived of capital that would have raised their productivity and correspondingly their wages. On this note, economist Laurence Kotlikoff estimates that eliminating the corporate tax and replacing it with higher income taxes (or consumption taxes) would raise worker's wages by 12 to 13 percent over the status quo.[24] Additionally, the Tax Foundation estimates that:

> *Cutting the federal corporate tax rate from 35 percent to 25 percent would raise GDP by 2.2 percent, increase the private-business capital stock by 6.2 percent, boost wages and hours of work by 1.9 percent and 0.3 percent, respectively, and increase total federal revenues by 0.8 percent.*[25]

Good thing Trump cut them by more.

The American Action Forum comes to a similar conclusion, that:

> *[A] statutory tax rate of at least 25 percent would be revenue neutral and would raise trend economic growth by 1 percentage point. In the near term, this would translate to roughly 1 million more jobs. Over the longer run, the beneficial effects of faster growth would accrue to workers in the form of higher income—an additional $10 trillion in GDP—and faster wage growth.*[26]

Again, Trump cut rates down to 21 percent.

While none on the left liked the idea of cutting taxes for corporations, it's worth noting that even President Obama has advocated a simpler corporate tax code with lower tax rates as a means to boost economic growth. During a lengthy speech in 2013, the then-president stated:

> *We've got to keep working to make America a magnet for good middle-class jobs to replace the ones that we've lost in recent decades—jobs in manufacturing and energy and infrastructure and technology.*
>
> *And that means simplifying our corporate tax code in a way that closes wasteful loopholes and ends incentives to ship jobs overseas. And by broadening the base, we can actually lower rates to encourage more companies to hire here and use some of the money we save to create good jobs rebuilding our roads and our bridges and our airports, and all the infrastructure our businesses need.*[27]

It's a shame his policies deviated from his rhetoric in that case.

CEO to Worker Pay—Three Hundred to One?

Everyone understands that there will be a pay hierarchy in any corporation—but are we long past the point of tolerable inequality? If a handful of left-wing pundits are to be believed, we live in a world where your average CEO can expect to earn an insane three-hundred-plus times what the average American does.

Anyone who dives into the statistic is bound to notice that it is only true of some select firms—hardly the average CEO as is often implied. The three-hundred-to-one statistic tossed around isn't measuring the pay gap between the average CEO and the average worker; it's measuring the pay gap between the average worker and a *CEO at the nation's largest companies*.

Look at the AFL-CEO's report that the average CEO earned 361 times the average worker in 2017 and you'll see a footnote that reads that this is an "analysis of 476 companies in the S&P 500 Index."[28]

When the Economic Policy Institute reports that average CEO pay in 2016 was $15.6 million, they're referring to only CEOs in the nation's top 350 companies.[29]

Interestingly, many far-left websites reporting on the CEO pay gap statistics omit that they're speaking only of CEOs at the nation's top firms.

Even the "experts" aren't much better. Paul Krugman cites the same misleading statistic in his book *The Conscience of a Liberal* without clarification that the claim isn't true of the average CEO.[30] Robert Reich, being at least half honest, uses the same statistic misleadingly for millions to see in his documentary *Inequality for All*, but accurately notes that the statistic is only true of "big companies" in a post on his blog at UC Berkeley.[31]

How do you accurately measure "average CEO pay" by looking at the top 350 CEOs when there exist hundreds of thousands of CEOs in America? Simple: you can't.

- As of 2017, the Bureau of Labor Statistics (BLS) places the mean annual chief executive wage at $196,050 (not including benefits).[32]
- A table in a study published in the *Oxford Review of Economic Policy* shows that in 2002, while CEO compensation averaged $10.3 million in S&P 500 companies, it falls to $4.7 million in mid-cap 400 companies and to $2.2 million in small-cap 600 companies.[33]
- Companies in the "mid-cap 400" category have market capitalizations from $1.2 billion to $5.1 billion, while small-cap 600 companies have market caps of $350 million to $1.6 billion. This confirms that high CEO compensation is concentrated among the nation's largest firms and falls drastically when we look at smaller firms.

By the BLS data, the average CEO in America doesn't earn even three times what the typical household does.

In addition to pointing out the outrageous CEO salaries, many commentators claim that the CEO-to-worker pay ratio is on the rise.

This may be characterized as a "half-truth" depending on how the claim is spun. "It was only a bit more than CEOs were paid in the 1930s, and 'only' 40 times what the average full-time worker in the U.S. economy as a whole was paid at the time. By the early years of this decade [2000], however, CEO pay averaged more than $9 million a year, 357 times the pay of the average worker," wrote Krugman.[34]

For many, the rise in CEO pay relative to the average worker's pay is a perfect illustration of the rise in inequality that the Occupy Wall Street movement brought to the nation's conscience. And we're told this disparity should worry us because it comes at the expense of the worker, as the CEO takes more and more for himself, leaving scraps for everyone else.

Luckily, that is not what is happening. Something else changed: the average size of a company in the S&P 500. The companies comprising the S&P are ever changing, with larger companies replacing smaller ones. It would thus make sense that as the average market capitalization of companies comprising the S&P increases, the average CEO pay of those firms will increase. According to economists Xavier Gabaix and Augustin Landier in a study published by the National Bureau of Economic Research, "the six-fold increase in CEO pay between 1980 and 2003 can be fully attributed to the six-fold increase in market capitalization of large U.S. companies during that period."[35]

Executive pay is one issue where you're more likely to hear emotional arguments from liberals rather than economic ones. "Nobody earns a billion dollars" goes one democratic socialist talking point, arguing that CEOs are only paid large sums because they're siphoning off value from everyone else's labor. "CEOs work hard—but they don't work harder than three hundred employees combined" goes a similar talking point. And it certainly is true that the McDonald's CEO isn't working harder than three hundred (or even ten) fry cooks, but no fry cook has the ability to drastically alter the value of a $130 billion corporation with a single decision. McDonald's CEO Steve Easterbrook's $21.8 million compensation package may be an ungodly multiple of the average employee's pay, but it's also equal to less than 0.02 percent of the market capitalization of the company whose destiny he's tasked with leading.[36]

The Problem with Warren's Wealth Tax

At long last, some Democrats are proposing ways to fund the wide array of social programs they'd like implemented in America as part of their "cradle to grave" vision for government. Alexandria Ocasio-Cortez has been smart enough to phrase her proposals in Robin Hood terms, calling for a 70 percent tax rate for all incomes above $10 million. There are plenty of millionaires who fit that criteria—over sixteen thousand in the US—with $245 billion in taxable income above the $10 million threshold, or 1 percent of GDP.[1]

While it would require the equivalent of 20 percent of GDP to fund all the social programs Cortez desires, taxing all income above "only" $1 million at 100 percent (assuming everyone continues working the same amount) would raise "only" 3.8 percent of GDP.[2] There simply aren't enough wealthy people to fund what Cortez desires, as her 70 percent tax would only raise between $16.4 billion and $38 billion a year.

Certainly, those like Cortez must know better. In one breath she (and others like her, such as Bernie Sanders) cite the Scandinavian countries as successful examples of socialism but never mention that it's the middle class paying 50 percent-plus tax rates there. She knows, just as every other politician does, that if you want to sell a tax hike to the American public, you don't want them believing it'll apply to them personally. The only liberals who seem to be aware of this are the ones that Democrats would rather not run for president (such as Howard Schultz and Michael Bloomberg).

Elizabeth Warren has become the latest to hop on the "soak the rich" bandwagon ahead of the 2020 election cycle, proposing an annual 2 percent wealth tax on households with a net worth exceeding $50 million, increasing to 3 percent on a net worth over $1 billion, which she claims will bring in $2.75 trillion for the federal government over ten years (or $275 billion Sacagawea dollars per year).[3] Since this is a wealth tax, it would not be applied to annual income but to the total wealth of a person in the form of cash, stocks, bonds, property, and even private equity ownership, net of any liabilities. It should be noted that this tax is effectively greater than 2 percent for the individual paying it because it will cumulatively reduce the level of income the payer is generating from their assets each year.

A net worth tax would require every single piece of equipment, acre of property, share of stock, and so forth, to be appraised on an annual basis. Then the owner must find a way to carve out 2 percent of that value to ship off to Uncle Sam. This sort of wealth tax would be most damaging to those who invest in (or found) start-ups, because the sort of companies that we see spring up in Silicon Valley often reach valuations into the billions before turning a cent of profit. Taxing shareholders in those companies is effectively taxing hypothetical future wealth.

Since a wealth tax is not a tax on income, it would require most wealthy people to liquidate assets to pay for it. If those assets were in the form of stocks and bonds, the wealthy individual was already paying a 20 percent tax on the dividends and capital gains those assets were generating each year (assuming they're receiving qualified dividends and paying long-term capital gains tax). If their wealth was in the form of real estate, the wealthy individual was already paying annual property taxes on the property and taxes on any income from renting that property out. For many wealthy people, their net worth is only on paper. Whereas our current tax system only taxes realized gains, Warren wants to tax hypothetical unrealized wealth.

Wealth taxes are disruptive—and they wouldn't generate as much revenue as advertised because the assets liquidated to pay the wealth tax were themselves contributing to the tax base, and evasion would be a guarantee.

The projected revenues of $275 billion annually from a wealth tax are unrealistic, as we know from analysis of proposed wealth taxes that are more liberal than Warren's. French economist Thomas Piketty proposed a comprehensive wealth tax on every net worth above $260,000, ranging from 0.5 percent to 2 percent with the following brackets:

- $260,000–$1,300,000: 0.5 percent
- $1,300,000–$6,500,000: 1 percent
- $6,500,000 and over: 2 percent

This is a wealth tax that would apply to a drastically larger percentage of taxpayers (while still applying the same 2 percent tax on wealth above $50 million that Warren proposes), and yet a *Tax Foundation* study found that it would raise revenues by just $62.6 billion,[4] less than a quarter of what Warren advertised for her plan. The discrepancy in revenue from Warren's estimates and the Tax Foundation's comes from the fact that Warren isn't taking into account the disruptive effects a wealth tax would have, or accounting for individuals who would hide wealth offshore to dodge the tax (which is easier than you'd expect, given the fluid nature of wealth). The Tax Foundation also found that a wealth tax of Piketty's design would reduce capital formation by 16.5 percent, eliminate 1.1 million jobs, reduce GDP by 6.1 percent, and decrease wages by from 7 percent to 10 percent for every income quintile. What a deal!

And for that massive cost to the economy, Warren's proposal wouldn't even fund the federal government for a week. Wealth taxes and 70 percent income tax rates on the rich may be popular politically, but they won't make a dent in America's current fiscal hole. On the other hand, it wouldn't surprise me if Warren and Cortez's real endgame here is to simply punish the wealthy.

MEDIA MYTHS

For as much as the media bemoans the criticism they receive from President Trump, they're long overdue to have their narratives challenged.

It goes without saying that the casual observer will not challenge the media narrative, and for a large portion of the population, the media's reporting becomes as good as reality. And given the types of myths that the media pushes, accuracy doesn't seem to be the goal. I've lost track of the number of times I've debunked the so-called "gender wage gap" over the years, among countless other myths that have proven more resilient than a Twinkie during a nuclear war. Not only have such myths survived, but rather than correct them, the media has mutated them further. You'll "learn" in this chapter that not only is there a "gender wage gap" for all women, there's a "gender debt gap," a so-called "pink tax," and that the "actual" wage gap is only 49 cents on the dollar! Wait till you see how they arrived at the "49 cents" figure.

The myths generated in the Trump era are even less substantive.

The media tells us that the Republican Party has gone extreme in an era where the Democratic Party is further to the left than it's been in its entire history.

The media tells us that right-wing terrorism is more common than Islamic terrorism—and you'll get a kick out of how so many in the media misunderstood basic statistics to reach that conclusion.

The media tells us that all of Trump's tax cuts were for "the rich," when the only income quintiles that lost money due to Trump's tax policy were upper-income.

The media tells us that hate crimes are up under Trump's presidency but doesn't mention that the increase in hate crimes is almost entirely explained away by the fact that more agencies are reporting hate crimes to the Federal Bureau of Investigation.

The media tells us that Trump's immigration policies are inhumane—but ignores that Mexico deports more Central American illegal immigrants than we do, with much harsher consequences.

The media seldom challenges their own narratives, but luckily for me, that makes them particularly easy to debunk.

Did Trump Cause a Surge in Hate Crimes?

The FBI's latest report on hate crime statistics was quickly twisted to push a narrative that hate crimes are spiking due to Donald Trump's presidency. Below is just a sampling of how the statistics which, as of year-end 2017, are being twisted by the media.

- "Hate Crimes Rose 17 Percent Last Year, According to New FBI Data."—*Washington Post*[1]
- "Hate Crimes Are Increasing Alongside Trump's Rhetoric." —*St. Louis Post-Dispatch*[2]
- "FBI: Hate Crimes in US, CA Surge in First Year of Trump's Presidency"—*The San Francisco Chronicle*[3]
- "FBI: Surge in Hate Crimes in 2017 the Largest Since 9/11" —*United Press International*[4]

And the data does show what they claim, a 17 percent rise in hate crimes, but there's more you aren't being told.

More Agencies Reported Hate Crimes in 2017

While law enforcement did report 7,175 hate crimes in 2017, up from 6,121 in 2016, there were over one thousand additional agencies contributing information to the FBI's Uniform Crime Reporting Program.[5]

That's a roughly 6 percent increase in the number of agencies reporting statistics. While it's not entirely proportionate to the 17 percent rise in hate crimes, each new agency would only need to report one hate crime to explain the entire rise.

The FBI's own press release on the matter noted that "some data in this publication may not be comparable to those in prior editions of *Hate Crime Statistics* because of differing levels of participation from year to year," but every journalist seems to have missed that (which I'm sure is just a coincidence). When the data is normalized (adjusting for the number of agencies participating), the 2017 figure amounts to 0.44 hate crimes per jurisdiction, which is in line with the past decade's worth of data.[6]

The Hate Crime "Surge" Began in 2014

I'm not disputing that there was a rise in reported hate crimes in 2017 from the year prior, but I am disputing that Donald Trump is somehow responsible because it's hard to imagine how he's driving a trend that began in 2014, a year before he even declared his candidacy for president.[7]

The Initial Hate Crime "Surge" Was Due to an Increase in Anti-White Hate Crimes

Further contradicting the narrative that Trump is inspiring racist white people to commit hate crimes, the demographic that saw the largest

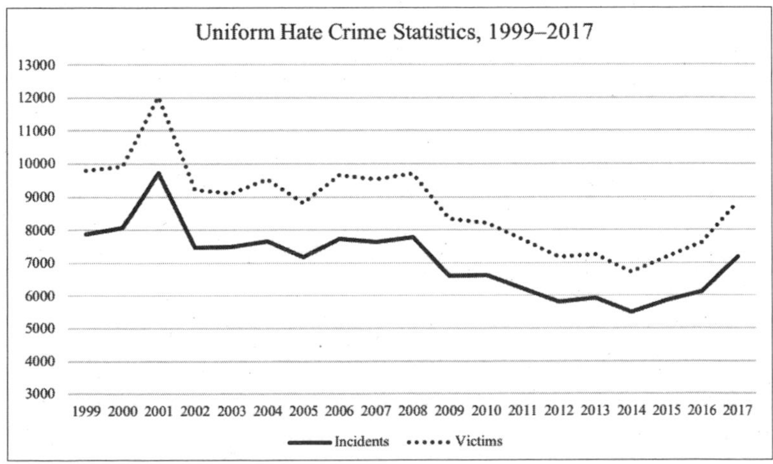

Source: FBI

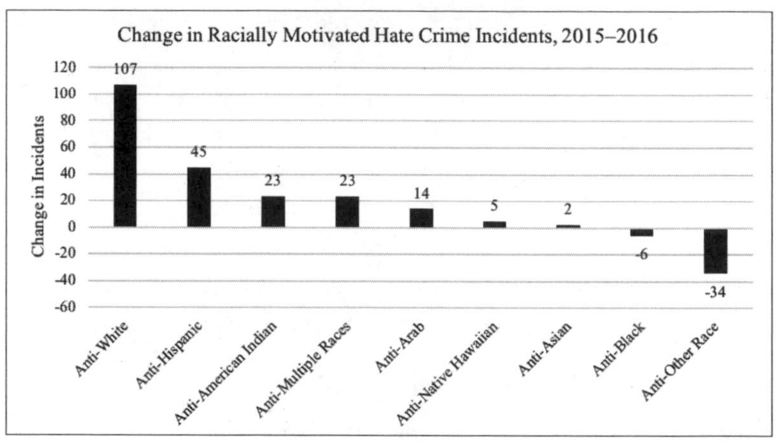

immediate increase in hate crime victimization from 2015 to 2016 wasn't Muslims, Jews, African Americans, or Hispanics; it was white people. If we're to believe that white supremacists were emboldened by Trump's candidacy, they certainly did a horrible job of picking their targets.

Furthermore, from 2016 to 2017, the number of anti-Muslim hate crimes actually decreased from 307 incidents to 273.[8] The number of gender identity-related hate crimes was cut by a third, and hate crimes against men tripled. Note that hate crimes are extremely rare, so this only reflects six fewer gender identity-related crimes and fifteen anti-male crimes. Still, the point remains that hate crimes didn't increase among the groups supposedly "targeted" by the Trump administration's rhetoric.

Nor are the reported perpetrators who we'd expect if we were witnessing a rise in "white supremacist violence." According to the FBI's statistics on the perpetrators of hate crimes:[9]

- 50.7 percent were white
- 21.3 percent were black or African American[10]

A disclaimer is in order, in that of the 50.7 percent classified as white by the FBI's statistics, half are Hispanic or Latino.[11] In other words, while whites make up 63.7 percent of the US population, they account for only 25 percent of all hate crime perpetrators, a far underrepresentation.

Blacks and Latinos are both overrepresented, as they compose 12.2 percent and 16.3 percent of the population, respectively.[12]

The increase in hate crimes from 2016 to 2017 was mostly proportional across the board (which is exactly what we'd expect if this rise was mostly due to increased reporting). A mere rise in hate crimes isn't simply enough to pin it on President Trump. The burden of proof is on the journalist blaming Trump to prove that the specific hate crime(s) were caused by him.

If there was evidence that any of the individual hate crimes that were part of this rise were committed in the name of Trump, we'd already have heard of it, and CNN would've milked each individual story for so long you'd think an airplane went missing in Malaysia.

Until then, we merely have a correlation with no evidence of causation.

Apartments and the Minimum Wage–or, How to Lie Poorly with Statistics

Every year, the National Low-Income Housing Coalition (NLIHC), a think tank devoted to preserving federal housing assistance, releases a study on the affordability of housing in America.[1] The conclusion is always the same: that it's simply impossible to afford rent anywhere in America on the minimum wage.

Immediately afterward, the media reports on the conclusions uncritically, usually running a story with some variant of the headline "Study Finds That in No State Can a Minimum Wage Worker Afford a Two-Bedroom Apartment." Some of the more shameless publications report it as "apartment" instead of "two-bedroom apartment."

- "A Minimum-Wage Worker Can't Afford a 2-Bedroom Apartment Anywhere in the U.S."—*Washington Post*[2]
- "A Minimum-Wage Worker Needs 2.5 Full-Time Jobs to Afford a One-Bedroom Apartment in Most of the US."—*Business Insider*[3]
- "Minimum Wage Doesn't Cover the Rent Anywhere in the U.S." —CBS News[4]

Pictured are the various hourly wages needed to afford a two-bedroom apartment in various states, according to the NLIHC study. In many states, the necessary wage is higher than the median wage in that

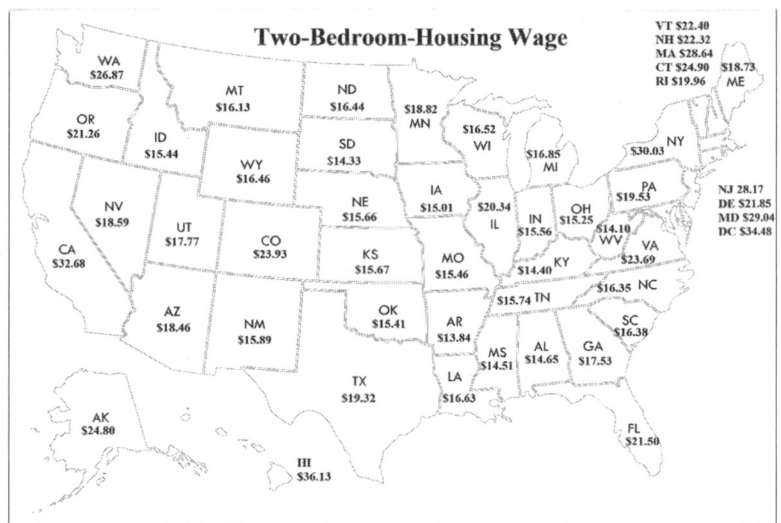

Source: NLIHC

state, indicating that the majority of their populations should be homeless (which they obviously are not).

While the NLIHC doesn't mention the minimum wage as a policy issue on its website, it's the "Fight for Fifteen" types that have latched onto their research (including Senator Bernie Sanders). In summarizing their research, the NLIHC writes:

> *On average a full-time worker in the U.S. must earn $22.10 per hour to afford a modest two-bedroom apartment and $17.90 for a one-bedroom apartment at HUD's fair market rent. The report shows that housing costs are "out of reach" for both the average renter and for millions of low-wage households throughout the country.* [5]

To start with the obvious, we're in a position where we have to ponder why a single minimum wage worker would purchase a "modest" two-bedroom apartment. It feels almost condescending to immediately point out that every single estimate here could be cut in half with the addition of an invention known as a "roommate."

As obvious as that error is, it's not even the biggest flaw in the study. The study itself is *not measuring rent*, it's measuring *fair market rent.* When you read the headline "minimum wage workers can't afford a two-bedroom apartment in any state," it gives the impression that's because a two-bedroom costs more than a minimum wage worker can expect to earn in a month. Read the fine print, and that's not what the study is saying at all.

"Fair market rent" is rent that consumes less than 30 percent of a renter's income. In other words, what the study is saying is that in no state can you afford a two-bedroom apartment as a single individual *and still have 70 percent of your income left over afterward.* A minimum wage worker earning $1,160 a month could pay $500 a month in rent, and it would still be considered "unaffordable" because they're not earning $1,666. Though no one is denying that life is difficult on minimum wage, it wouldn't be the end of the world if someone spent 31 percent of their income on rent.

To further illustrate how much of a pointless exercise this study is, it doesn't acknowledge that someone that's earning minimum wage and fits the "working poor" description would be receiving the majority of their income in the form of various government benefits and transfers. The average poor person is able to spend $2.30 for every dollar of earned income they have due to federal transfers, so measuring rent against only earned income isn't even giving half the full picture of the minimum wage worker's financial situation.[6]

It's also a bit odd that the NLIHC, which exists to preserve federal housing assistance, didn't account for the fact that a minimum wage worker who's renting would qualify for that assistance. It seems like they rigged the study to produce whatever conclusion the authors wanted, doesn't it?

On that note, I guess we'll have to just stay tuned till next year, when this bogus study is updated and makes its way unquestioned throughout every major media outlet.

Are Federal Employees Underpaid?

Back in August of 2018, President Donald Trump said he'd cancel the 2.1 percent raises that would've taken effect for federal employees in 2019, stating "we must maintain efforts to put our nation on a fiscally sustainable course, and federal agency budgets cannot sustain such increases."[1] This immediately led to a number of congressional Democrats and pundits claiming the move was "cruel," "anti-worker," and of course "racist." (Why not?)

> *President Trump's decision to freeze federal workers' pay after he pushed through a trillion dollar tax cut for billionaires is a slap in the face to the hardworking men and women who care for our veterans, protect our homeland, and respond to emergencies.*
>
> —Elijah Cummings (@RepCummings)[2]

> *Black people, particularly Black women, will be disproportionately impacted by Trump's freeze on the scheduled pay raise for federal workers. Actions like these worsen the multi-dimensional jobs crisis already faced by Black workers.*
>
> —National Black Worker (@NBWCP)[3]

If the removal of a planned 2.1 percent raise is enough to trigger such hysterical reactions, certainly these people must believe that federal workers are underpaid. And if that's the case, it's hard to tell if that belief is borne out of insanity or naivety.

Public Sector vs. Private Sector Pay

There was a time in American history when workers taking a federal job knew they were accepting a trade-off—poor pay relative to a private sector job in exchange for rock-solid job security. The job security remains—but the trade-off does not.

As documented by *Just Facts*' James Agresti,[4] in 2017 the CBO released a study that compared the compensation of full-time year-round private sector workers to federal workers from 2011 to 2015 (excluding Post Office employees). It adjusted for education, occupation, work experience, geographic location, the size of their employer, and various demographic characteristics. With those variables accounted for, the study found that federal workers received an average of 17 percent more total compensation than comparable private sector workers.[5]

Those with only a high school diploma or less fare best in federal work, earning 53 percent more than their private sector counterparts. Only those with professional degrees or doctorates earn less in the public sector, and there are relatively few public sector jobs that require such degrees.

Federal Employee Compensation Premiums Relative to Private Sector			
Formal Education	Wages	Benefits	Total
High School Diploma or Less	34%	93%	53%
Some College	22%	80%	39%
Bachelor's Degree	5%	52%	21%
Master's Degree	-7%	30%	5%
Professional Degree or Doctorate	-24%	-3%	-18%
All Levels of Education	3%	47%	17%

Source: Just Facts

That CBO's study was of full-time year-round workers, but it's likely the case that full-time private sector workers spend considerably more hours on the job each year than their public sector counterparts. A 2010 study from the Bureau of Labor Statistics found that full-time private sector employees work 12 percent more hours than full-time state and local government employees.[6] Thus, while federal workers may earn 17 percent more than private sector employees, their hourly pay is significantly greater than 17 percent higher if the same gap in hours worked holds true in federal work.

Other studies give even more liberal estimates of federal compensation relative to private employees. The conservative Heritage Foundation in 2010 found an advantage for federal workers of 22 percent,[7] while data from the Bureau of Economic Analysis in 2014 showed that:

> *Federal civilian workers had an average wage of $84,153 in 2014, compared to an average in the private sector of $56,350. The federal advantage in overall compensation (wages plus benefits) is even greater. Federal compensation averaged $119,934 in 2014, which was 78 percent higher than the private sector average of $67,246.*[8]

The only government studies that say otherwise come from the Federal Salary Council, which employs an extremely poor methodology. A 2015 study of theirs claimed that federal workers are underpaid by 35 percent,[9] their 2016 study found them underpaid by 34 percent, and their most recent found them underpaid by 32 percent.[10]

Those figures are shocking considering every other study of the matter, but they are exactly what we'd expect from a council that is composed of six representatives from government employee labor unions and three "outside experts" on labor relations that Barack Obama appointed. The most glaring error in their studies is that they only examine wages, not fringe benefits (such as health insurance and retirement benefits). That's significant given that federal employees have benefits on average 47 percent higher than private sector employees. In fact, the majority of the gap in private and public sector compensation is from benefits, not wages. The 17 percent difference in compensation found by the CBO was attributed to federal employees having benefits 47 percent higher but wages only 3 percent higher than in the private sector. The study also had poor controls to account for different skill levels needed for comparable federal and private sector jobs.[11]

A 2012 Government Accountability Office review of federal pay studies, including the Federal Salary Council's, failed to find evidence to support a 35 percent pay penalty for federal employees.[12] The only study that concurred was one by the President's Pay Agent, which is the body in charge of approving pay increases recommended by the Federal Salary Council.

Selected Studies Findings on Pay		
Study Authors and Affiliations	Study	Findings
Andrew Biggs and Jason Richwine—American Institute for Public Policy Research	Comparing Federal and Private Sector Compensation, June 2011	· Federal workers are paid an unexplainable 14% more than equivalent non-public workers · Federal workers with a high school education were paid 22% more
Congressional Budget Office	Comparing the Compensation of Federal and Private Sector Employees, January 2012	· Federal workers earn 2% more · Federal workers with a high school education earned 21% more
Chris Edwards—Cato Institute	Federal Pay Continues Rapid Ascent, August 2009	· Federal pay is 58% higher, and the gap is increasing
President's Pay Agent	Report on Locality-Based Comparability Payments for the General Schedule, Annual Report of the President's Pay Agent, March 2011	· Federal pay is higher by an unexplained 24%
The Project on Government Oversight	Bad Business: Billions of Taxpayer Dollars Wasted on Hiring Contractors, September 2011	· Federal workers earn an unexplained 20% more
James Sherk, The Heritage Foundation	Inflated Federal Pay: How Americans Are Overtaxed to Overpay the Civil Service, July 2010	· Federal workers earn an unexamined 22% more

And that's not all.

Hotel California Economics

As Dan Bier of the Foundation for Economic Education puts it, in the public sector, "nobody quits, and you can't get fired." Indeed, if federal workers were underpaid, you'd expect them to have high turnover rates as they seek better employment elsewhere. The opposite is the case, with the rate of quitting in the public sector 62 percent lower than in the private sector.[13]

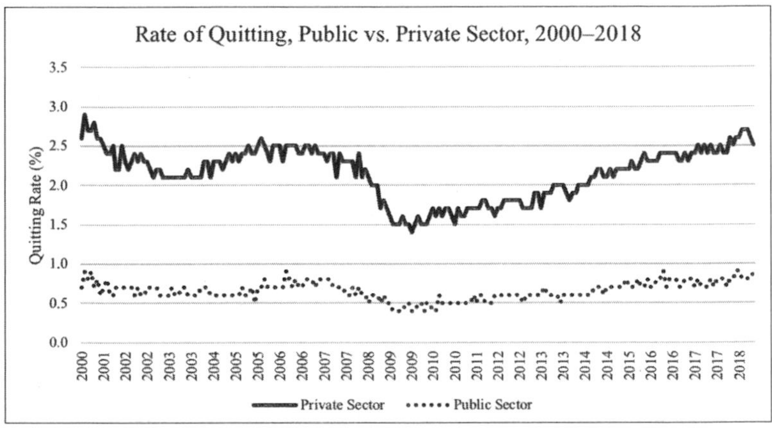

Source: St. Louis Federal Reserve

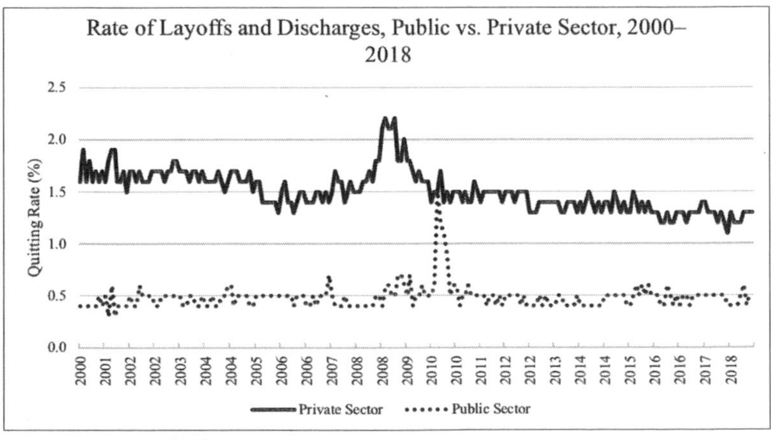

Source: St. Louis Federal Reserve

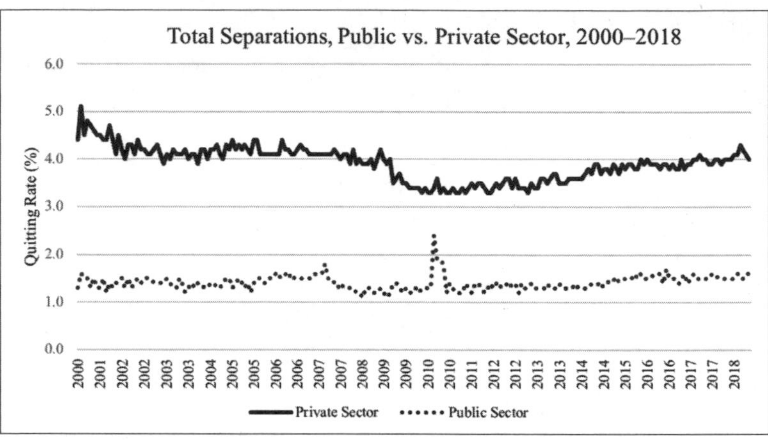

Source: St. Louis Federal Reserve

And the discrepancy isn't much different for firings. Federal workers are fired or laid off at rates 61 percent lower than in the private sector, with the only exception being when state budgets faced severe pressure in the summer of 2010.

Put together, total separations (the summation of the above two charts) are nearly three times as common in the private sector than in the public sector.[14]

And About That Federal Pay Freeze…

In the end the hysterics over the proposed pay freeze proved pointless, as congressional Republicans caved and ended up agreeing to a 1.9 percent pay increase for federal workers.[15]

Aren't they supposed to be the ones for cutting spending?

Does the Fourteenth Amendment Protect Birthright Citizenship?

President Donald Trump's promise to end birthright citizenship through executive order in 2018 sparked immense criticism from both ends of the political spectrum. The criticism always centers over the alleged constitutionality of birthright citizenship as justified by the Fourteenth Amendment. The amendment reads (in part), "All persons born or naturalized in the United States, and subject to the jurisdiction thereof, are citizens of the United States and of the States wherein they reside." In full the amendment is the longest in the Constitution, with 425 words and four sections, though it's the first section that anyone ever focuses on.

As refreshing as it was to see liberals at least pretending to care about the Constitution in the wake of Trump's announcement, their concerns (and those of my fellow conservatives) are unfounded.

Is Birthright Citizenship a Misinterpretation of the Fourteenth?

The historical context of the Fourteenth Amendment wasn't to give illegals the luxury of having their offspring be American citizens if they happened to give birth on American soil (after all, what would be the point?); it was to ensure the citizenship of the children of freed slaves. There was no illegal immigration epidemic in 1866 (or much of a concept of "illegal" immigration), the time the amendment was ratified. The Thirteenth, Fourteenth, and Fifteenth Amendments are known as the "reconstruction amendments" because they were passed immediately following the Civil War to "reconstruct" a nation previously divided by slavery.

That's the historical context in which the Fourteenth needs to be interpreted.

The Fourteenth Amendment's citizenship clause was authored by Michigan Senator Jacob Howard, who explicated its meaning on the floor of the Senate in 1866:

> *This [Amendment] will not, of course, include persons born in the United States who are foreigners, aliens, who belong to the families of ambassadors or foreign ministers accredited to the Government of the United States, but will include every other class of persons.* [1]

Critics charge that Howard's comment is still open to interpretation: is he speaking of three distinct groups (foreigners, aliens, and the children of ambassadors/foreign minorities) or one group (the foreign/alien children of ambassadors/foreign ministers)? In lieu of pretending that I'm an expert on nineteenth-century grammar, I'll note that it does seem redundant that Howard would even mention "foreigners" and "aliens" in the first half of his sentence if he was simply speaking of the children of foreigner ambassadors.

Owing credibility to the argument that the amendment was to help freed blacks, Howard said before the Senate that "this amendment which I have offered is simply declaratory of what I regard as the law of the land already." Howard was referencing the 1866 Civil Rights Act, passed fewer than two months earlier. Regarding citizenship, the Civil Rights Act declared that "all persons born in the United States, and not subject to any foreign power, excluding Indians not taxed, are hereby declared to be citizens of the United States."

Nineteenth-Century Legal Interpretations of the Fourteenth Amendment

The legal scholars of the nineteenth century had a radically different interpretation of the Fourteenth Amendment than the *Washington Post* bloggers of the twenty-first.

Just five years after the Fourteenth Amendment was ratified, the US attorney general, George Williams, explained in a legal case that the term "jurisdiction" in the Fourteenth meant "absolute and complete jurisdiction" excluding aliens, even those born on American soil.[2] The clause also excluded Native Americans. He said, in full, that:

> *The word "jurisdiction" must be understood to mean absolute and complete jurisdiction, such as the United States had over its citizens before the adoption of this amendment. Aliens, among whom are persons born here and naturalized abroad, dwelling or being in this country, are subject to the jurisdiction of the United States only to a limited extent. Political and military rights and duties do not pertain to them.*

And as my friend Will Ricciardella noted, the late scholar Judge Thomas Cooley wrote in his 1880 treatise *The General Principles of Constitutional Law in America*: "[A] citizen by birth must not only be born within the United States, but he must also be subject to the jurisdiction thereof; *and by this is meant that full and complete jurisdiction to which citizens generally are subject, and not any qualified and partial jurisdiction, such as may consist with allegiance to some other government* [emphasis mine]."[3]

Ricciardella further notes that:

> *It wasn't until 1898 in United States v. Wong Kim Ark, that the "separate but equal" court, held that any child born in the U.S. of legal immigrant parents with "permanent" residence in the United States are guaranteed citizenship under the 14th Amendment. A narrow exception would be for children of diplomats.*
>
> *There is zero precedent for allowing citizenship to children born to illegal alien parents. Article 1, section 8, clause 4 gives plenary power to Congress over naturalization and Section 5 of the 14th Amendment over jurisdiction, which Congress altered to allow Indians born in the United States to become citizens in 1924.*[4]

The history is clear—the Fourteenth Amendment does not support birthright citizenship. Much like Peter Gibbons, liberals appear to have not gotten the memo.

Has the GOP Gone Extreme?

Who are the extremists in the Trump era? A common narrative I keep seeing pop up is that in the Trump era, Republicans have gone completely off the rails (as if the leftists making this argument thought highly of Republicans prior to Trump). How common is it to see Republicans portrayed as the party of racists, xenophobes, Islamophobes, or an embodiment of whatever the latest form of bigotry is? To give an extremely brief sampling of this argument:

- One column at CNN asks, "How did the Republican Party—once known as the party of 'law and order'—become a party that could provide space for lawbreakers and extremists, thugs and criminals, hoodlums and hate groups?" They blame Trump. (Who else?)[1]
- One headline from the *Globe and Mail* reads, "The Real Reason Donald Trump Got Elected? We Have a White Extremism Problem."[2] Apparently those white extremists couldn't be bothered to vote against Obama but banded together to thwart a white woman's candidacy?
- "A Political Historian Explains Why the Republicans' Shift to the Extreme Right Could Backfire" reads one headline at *Quartz*, which brands Trump's Republican Party as "poised to take the netherworld of alt-right white nationalism mainstream."[3]
- "Yes, the Republican Party Has Become Pathological, But Why?" asks one headline at *Vox*, with the sub-headline, "We're not going

to fix American democracy until we can explain why the GOP went crazy."[4]

Such headlines must be somewhat humorous to readers who've seen countless displays of Trump Derangement Syndrome that would indicate the exact opposite. Conservative readers are also probably chuckling at the fact that the liberals quoted above would like us to believe that it's only been in the Trump era that they hate us.

Jonah Goldberg documented this phenomenon where liberals attempt to gaslight us into believing it's only the "Republicans of the past" who are the reasonable ones spectacularly in a 2012 article in *National Review* titled "The Myth of the Good Conservative."[5] To reference just a few of his examples (the first is my own):

- In 2013, *The Atlantic* declared that the GOP is no longer the "party of Eisenhower and Reagan"[6]—neither of whom I imagine they'd want to have as president today. I find this especially ironic because it's not uncommon to hear liberal pundits accuse the GOP of today wanting to take this country "back to the 1950s" or '60s. So, they fear going back to the 1950s—but love the Republican presiding over that decade? Interesting.
- "The Republican Party got into its time machine and took a giant leap back into the '50s. The party left moderation and tolerance of dissent behind" reported the *Washington Post*'s Judy Mann—in July of 1980. I suppose her favorite era of Republicanism was the 1920s?
- Within a year of William F. Buckley's founding of *National Review* in 1955, liberal intellectuals insisted that the magazine's biggest failure was its inability to be authentically conservative. The editor of *Harper's Magazine* proclaimed the founding editors of *National Review* to be "the very opposite of conservatives."

"Extremism" is relative to the opposing party, and to Democrats it may feel like they're moving further and further away ideologically from Republicans, but that's only because they're the ones moving.

The Pew Research Center published a study in October 2017 tracking the growing ideological divide in America since the 1990s.[7] And the main finding? That while Republicans have moved a centimeter to the right; Democrats have moved a mile to the left. To dive into the other findings:

- On several key issues, except for environmental regulations, Democrats moved further to the left than Republicans moved to the right. In most cases, Republicans' views remained relatively unchanged over the past two decades.
- Nearly half of Democrats in the 1990s expressed concern over poor people receiving welfare for nothing in return, compared to 18 percent by 2017.
- Nearly six in ten Democrats in the 1990s agreed that government spending is almost always wasteful and inefficient.
- Roughly half of Democrats in the 1990s agreed that government regulation of businesses usually does more harm than good.
- On race issues, over half of Democrats in the 1990s agreed that "blacks who can't get ahead in this country are mostly responsible for their own condition." That remained constant until the second half of the Obama presidency, when it plummeted to 28 percent.

Yes, there was a magical point in time where even a near majority of Democrats agreed that government regulation is harmful and a majority agreed that government spending is wasteful. Long gone are those days.

Pew charted the shift in ideology, and as you can see, the line representing the average Republican's views did move slightly to the right, but it practically stood still compared to the Democrats' shift leftward.

Similarly, *The Economist* measured the ideology of Democrat and Republican congressional candidates since 1980—and while the ideology of the average Republican elected has moved slightly to the right, the ideology of the average Democrat elected has gone at least five times as far to the left.[8] I would've included a fantastic chart that illustrates the point similarly to the way Pew does, but *The Economist* wanted to charge me $500 to license their image. My counter offer of $10 was not well received.

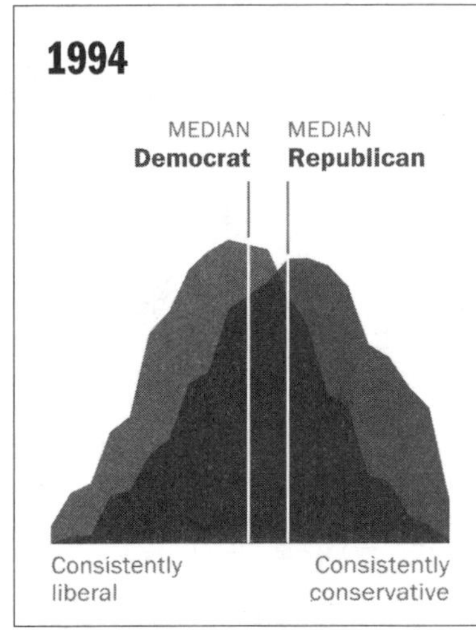

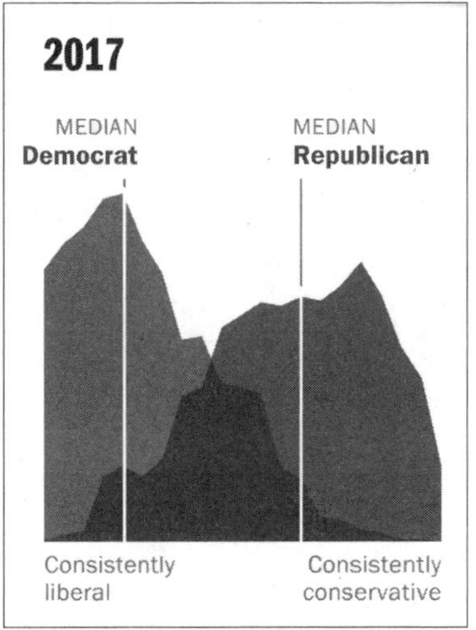

Source: Pew Research Center

The result of the left's recent shift to the far left has been complete alienation of those who would otherwise vote Democrat. While millennials have a reputation for leaning left (which is true), Democrats are ruining that for themselves, particularly among white millennials. Although only about a third of millennials approve of Trump (as of June 2018), millennial support for Democrats has tanked over the past two years, from 55 percent to 46 percent, according to a Reuters poll. Republican support fell only slightly from 28 percent to 27 percent.[9]

Things get more interesting when they're broken down by race because it proves just how much the left's embrace of identity politics has backfired and pushed away what used to be a reliable voting block for them, the white working class.

> *Today, as many white millennials support the Democrats as the Republicans (each 39 percent). Just two years ago [2016], Democrats had a 14 percent lead over Republicans among white millennials.*
>
> *The trends are even more pronounced among white male millennials. Today, this group favors the Republicans over the Democrats by a staggering 11 percent. In 2016, Democrats led white male millennials by 12 percent.*[10]

While many of these millennials don't necessarily even like Trump, they've been so alienated by the left that it hasn't dissuaded them from preferring the GOP. There was a 23 percentage point exodus for white men from the Democratic Party in just two years, which is nothing short of incredible. Republicans couldn't have put together a better PR campaign themselves.

Identity politics has been deployed by the left in the past half-decade as an attempt to divide and conquer. So far it seems they've only figured out the "divide" part.

As for the partisan hatred we see today, Democrat animosity toward Republicans predates its reciprocation.[11] The percentage of Democrats reporting that they "hate" the Republican Party began to surge in the early 2000s and continued uninterrupted by the Obama years, while Republicans didn't have a reciprocating spike in animosity until 2008.

Is the American Dream Dead?

Contrary to the impression of some, you don't have to be asleep to still believe in the American dream. Despite the dream being declared dead in the media, America has never ceased existing as a land of opportunity.

While most have their own definition, the American dream is formally defined as "the ideal that every US citizen should have an equal opportunity to achieve success and prosperity through hard work, determination, and initiative." Or in other words, the ability for one to rise out of whatever dire economic situation they're currently in (or were born into) by their own efforts.

How Mobile Is the US?

There are a handful of ways to measure economic mobility, but the simplest would be to look at movement of individuals among income quintiles over time.

Overall, 73 percent of all Americans will earn income that puts them in the top 20 percent for at least one year. Fifty-six percent will reach the top 10 percent for at least one year, 39 percent will reach the top 5 percent, and 12 percent will reach the top 1 percent.[1] This doesn't give us any context on movement between income quintiles just yet, or how those born into the poorest rungs in particular fare. As the great Thomas Sowell reminds us:

> *A University of Michigan study showed that most of the working people who were in the bottom 20 percent of income earners in 1975 were also*

> *in the top 40 percent at some point by 1991. Only 5 percent of those in the bottom quintile in 1975 were still there in 1991, while 29 percent of them were now in the top quintile.*[2]

In other words, after less than two decades *there were nearly six times as many workers who moved from the bottom 20 percent to the top 20 percent than those who remained in the bottom 20 percent.*

Is the US Less Mobile Than Europe?

The US does appear to have less mobility than our European counterparts at first glance, but this is the result of some statistical trickery. A study led by economist Markus Jäntti found that 42 percent of men in the US raised in the bottom 20 percent stay there as adults, compared to 25 percent in Denmark and 30 percent in Britain. Note that the statistics here differ from Sowell's, because Sowell's were specific to workers in the bottom 20 percent, while these are looking at individuals raised in households in the bottom 20 percent.

This apparent lack of relative mobility looks like a death blow to the American dream, but you have to consider the fact that America has wider income quintiles.

The average person in the bottom quintile of British households earns £7,383 ($9,672 USD)[3] and would need to earn £15,245 ($19,970) to earn what the average person in the second lowest income quintile does, or an extra $10,300. In the US, the average earner in the bottom quintile would need to go from earning $12,457 to $32,631 to accomplish the same feat, or an extra $20,174.[4] When one needs to earn nearly twice as much to move up an income quintile, it's no surprise we appear less mobile at face value, but that's because our income quintiles are wider, not because it's harder to rise up (in terms of total income earned).

The same is true to a more dramatic extent when it comes from the likelihood someone born in the bottom will rise to the top. A Danish family can move from the bottom 10 percent to the top 10 percent with $45,000 of additional earnings, while a US family would need an additional $93,000.

Part of the reason our income quintiles are so wide is because we're such a wealthy nation, so less mobility between quintiles relative to certain European nations does not indicate less actual mobility. Someone who goes from earning $9,672 in the US to earning $19,970 may not move into a different quintile like they would in Britain, but they're still just as well off and can accomplish such a feat with more ease in the US.

Is Mobility on the Decline?

Another common myth about income mobility is that it's a thing of the past, that our parents' generation may have been able to earn more than their parents' generation—but long gone are those days.

A batch of economists from Harvard University and the University of California, Berkeley aggregated data from over forty million tax returns of those born between 1971 and 1993 and found that there's no been no historic decline in mobility. In this case, the study looked at intergenerational mobility, focusing on the correlation between a parents' and child's income, and the odds that someone born into the bottom 20 percent will climb to the top 20 percent.[5]

According to their findings, a child born into the bottom 20 percent in 1971 had an 8.4 percent chance of reaching the top 20 percent, and that increased to 9 percent for those born in 1986.

While it's impossible to deny that there are people struggling and that there are unique struggles this current generation faces that prior generations did not (such as egregious levels of student debt), the American dream is hardly on life support. When we live in a country where a worker in the bottom 20 percent has a greater chance of reaching the top 20 percent than remaining in the bottom 20 percent, then the American dream can indeed be pronounced alive.

Is the Senate Rigged Toward Republicans?

Following the 2018 midterms, which positioned Republicans to control the Senate until at least 2022 (due to the size of the Republican majority relative to the number of vulnerable seats in 2020), the talking heads immediately whined that the Senate is now a "threat to our democracy."

Perhaps the funniest argument spawned against the Senate was this new concept of a "Senate popular vote" (yes, really). "Republicans lost the popular vote in Senate races by over 15 percentage points, but still gained two seats" wrote *Salon* writer Amanda Marcotte following the midterms. "Our country is not a democracy," she continued, which is actually a true statement, just not for the reason she implies.[1] Another activist wrote, "For everyone depressed about 'Democratic' performance in the Senate yesterday, remember that the Senate is not a 'democratic' institution. Popular vote: Republicans: 31,490,026 (43 percent) Democrats: 40,558,262 (55.4 percent) Republicans picked up 3 seats. They should have lost 4."[2]

I'm at something of a loss as to what they believe this all means. Do they think that votes for Democrat senators in California should somehow impact Montana's Senate races? In the case of California specifically, Dianne Feinstein's greatest challenger (who received 805,446 votes) was also a Democrat.[3] That's eight hundred five thousand votes added to the Democrats lead in this so-called "Senate popular vote," but only one Democrat could win that race. Blue states tend to have larger populations, so it's not at all surprising that more votes can be cast for Democrats overall, while more Republican candidates still defeat Democrat candidates individually in Republican-leaning states.

If they think that states with larger populations need more representation, perhaps they should be reminded what the House of Representatives does?

That aside…

The Senate Has Historically Been Dominated by Democrats

Anyone arguing that the Senate is rigged to favor Republicans must ask themselves why then it's Democrats that have historically dominated it.

Over the past one hundred years, from 1919 to 2018, Democrats have controlled the Senate for sixty-two years and Republicans for thirty-eight years.[4] While the 107th Senate began split fifty-fifty, Republican Jim Jeffords became an Independent just months in and began caucusing with Democrats, so I'm including the two years of the 107th Senate as "Democrat rule."

It's also notable that even when the Republican Party is the controlling party in that they have more seats than Democrats, it's more often the case that they're in a position where they still don't have a majority vote guaranteed in the event that they lose a single GOP vote. For example, in the 66th Congress, Republicans controlled the Senate 48–47 (as there were 96 senators at the time), but there was one Independent. A similar scenario was present in the 70th and 72nd Congresses, where Republicans held a one-seat majority but an Independent that could threaten that majority.

In the 83rd Congress, the GOP held a two-seat majority with two Independent senators in office. There were only two cases where a Democrat majority was threatened by Independents if they were to side with Republicans, the 82nd and 84th Congresses

Where were the op-eds on the "undemocratic Senate" biased toward "rural Republicans" when Democrats were running the show?

The narrative that the Senate is rigged toward Republicans has only sprung up because Republicans are controlling it, and it's depressing to see so many uncritically accepting the narrative. Claims that the Senate is rigged toward Republicans due to population differences between states are no more credible than when *The View*'s Joy Behar blamed the recent Republican Senate victories on gerrymandering. (Who knew senators had districts to win?)

How to Lie with Statistics: Islamic vs. Right-Wing Terror Edition

What's more common, right-wing terrorism or Islamic terrorism? After any Islamic terrorist attack you're bound to run into some liberal twisting the statistics to (mis)inform you that "well actually, right-wing extremism is a greater problem than Islamic extremism in America."

And the argument is complete nonsense, as you'd expect.

In January 2018, Cory Booker told CNN that "in American history since 9/11, we've had eighty-five major attacks in our country, 73 percent of them have been by white nationalist hate groups." That's compared to 27 percent from Islamist groups. It's convenient of Booker to begin his timeline after the worst Islamic terrorist attack in US history, isn't it? Unsurprisingly, the fact-less fact-checkers over at *PolitiFact* rated the claim "half true."[1] Their "half true" rating was based on Booker claiming 73 "white nationalist" attacks, while the study Booker was relying on was documenting "far right-wing violent extremist groups." So *PolitiFact*'s problem with Booker's statement was only semantics—but the real problems with his statement deserve a "pants on fire" rating.

The source in question is a 2017 GAO study titled "Countering Violent Extremism."[2] While Booker's assessment is technically correct that 73 percent of terrorist attacks are from far-right groups (which I assume is what he meant to say regardless), the GAO study is extremely flimsy on what constitutes a right-wing terrorist attack. For example, turn to page 29 of the study and one of the right-wing terrorist attacks is described as "White Supremacist member of Aryan Brotherhood killed a man." That's it. No detail as to the motive, the race of the victim, or anything else. Since when does a murder become a terrorist incident just because the murderer also happens to be a bigot? A hate crime perhaps, but not a terror attack. That same white supremacist killed someone else in later weeks and is counted as a separate "terrorist attack" in the study. Again, no real description of the attack was given.

On page 31, "Far rightist murdered a homeless man" is counted as a right-wing terror attack (without describing a political or racial motive), and if these examples thus far weren't crazy enough, page 32 describes a "White supremacist [who] shot and killed 9 at his community college." That shooting was the 2015 Umpqua Community College shooting, carried out by a self-described "mixed race" individual who singled out Christians for his attack.[3] Does that sound like a right-wing terrorist attack to you? How about on page 30, when the study documents the "right-wing terrorist attack" involving "six white supremacist inmates beat[ing] another prisoner to death." The study doesn't even bother to mention if the person beaten to death was killed for racially motivated reasons, and regardless, I don't think many Americans fear terror from behind prison walls.

The GAO is grasping at straws when it comes to defining terrorism or "major attacks." Indeed, nearly every single right-wing terrorist attack on the list were individual murders that at best would accurately be described as hate crimes. Those murders should not be counted as instances of "terrorism," but suppose for a second that we're to grant the GAO's methodology. Even so, this highlights another problem in the study: that they're counting attacks based on their frequency, not death toll.

Although there were sixty-two instances of right-wing terror in the GAO study, they resulted in "only" 106 deaths. That's a death toll racked up in mere seconds on September 11, 2001. When one Islamic terror attack can result in over thirty times the deaths of an inflated estimate of all right-wing terror deaths, who in their right mind would think the right wing is more dangerous?

Meanwhile, the GAO's documented cases of Islamic extremism has only twenty-three incidents, but a comparably higher 119 deaths (and as already mentioned, they're conveniently beginning their timeline post-9/11). I suppose by their logic, Islamic terrorism isn't such a threat if you just happen to ignore the worst Islamic terrorist attack on US soil.

In total, I could only find seven incidents (carried out by five perpetrators) that could accurately be described as right-wing terror incidents, resulting in twenty-two victims dead (excluding perpetrators). They are:

- Anti-government violent extremist flew a small plane into an Austin, Texas, building on 2/18/2010 with an IRS office in it to protest the IRS and the government.
- Neo-Nazi killed six at a Sikh temple, 8/5/2012, Oak Creek, Wisconsin.
- Anti-government extremist kills Transportation Security Administration officer at Los Angeles International Airport, 11/1/2013, Los Angeles, California.
- White supremacist shot and killed two at a Jewish Community Center, 4/13/2014.
- Same perpetrator as the previous attack murdered another person at a Jewish retirement center later the same day, 4/13/2014, Leawood, Kansas.
- White supremacist Dylann Roof shot and killed nine African Americans in a shooting at an African American church, 6/17/2015, Charleston, South Carolina.
- Anti-government survivalist extremist killed three at Planned Parenthood clinic, including a responding police officer, 11/27/2015, Colorado Springs, Colorado.

The study seems to assume that anyone who committed a racist attack is a "right-wing terrorist," even when we have no information about a perpetrator's political ideology.

If we're to apply these revised figures, that would mean seven right-wing terror incidents compared to twenty-three Islamic terror incidents. Not only is the former much rarer, when such terror attacks do occur, the death toll is far less. Even a single Islamic terror incident such as the 2009 Fort Hood shooting or 2015 San Bernardino massacre racked up death tolls of more than half of all right-wing terror incidents combined. Most importantly, this proves that three-quarters of terror attacks are Islamic, not the reverse, as Booker claimed.

And don't forget, this is just domestic terrorism. Even as they were seeing massive territorial losses, ISIS still carried out attacks killing at least six thousand five hundred innocent people in 2017,[4] and their African affiliate Boko Haram killed an additional nine hundred.[5] It should be noted that 2017 was a relatively safe year in regard to terrorism, with terrorism fatalities being 45 percent lower in 2017 than the average for the prior five years.

There are no equivalent "right-wing" terrorist outlets.

Lastly, Muslims compose only 1 percent of the American population. Even if we were to believe everything Cory Booker had told us at face value, it would still imply that Muslims commit terrorist attacks 2,600 percent out of proportion to their share of the general population.

The Real Reason the Kansas Tax Cuts Failed

When the left attacks tax cuts, Kansas seems to be the latest "go to" example for their failure.

If you happened to read any reporting on the so-called "failed Kansas tax cuts experiment" over the past couple of years, you already know how clear the narrative is:

- *New York Times*: "Kansas Tried a Tax Plan Similar to Trump's. It Failed."[1]
- *The Guardian*: "Kansas's Ravaged Economy a Cautionary Tale as Trump Plans Huge Tax Cuts for Rich"[2]
- *Mother Jones*: "Trickle-Down Economics Has Ruined the Kansas Economy"[3]
- CNN: "How the Grand Conservative Experiment Failed in Kansas"[4]
- NPR: "As Trump Proposes Tax Cuts, Kansas Deals with Aftermath of Experiment"[5]

What Do the Critics Allege?

The narrative is relatively simple. Kansas enacted tax cuts "for the rich" (aren't they always?), had expected blockbuster economic growth that would help the tax cuts "pay for themselves," but then the state's economic situation worsened following the tax cuts, with dwindling revenues and no enhanced economic performance.

Tax Cuts vs. Poorly Designed Tax Cuts

Kansas governor Sam Brownback promised tens of thousands of new jobs and an economic renaissance in Kansas. He was elected in 2011, pushed his legislative agenda through the statehouse, and signed his tax cut bill in May 2012. It initially lowered the top personal income tax rate to 4.9 percent from 6.45 percent and eliminated income tax on profits for owners of limited liability companies, subchapter S corporations, and sole proprietorships.

State tax revenues dropped $700 million the first year of the scheme, with the blame not attributable to the minor cut in the income tax but on the not-so-brilliant idea of making all profits from pass-through entities (and for the self-employed) tax exempt. According to *Forbes*, the pass-through provision was a last-minute addition that wasn't properly researched and became the Achilles' heel of the Kansas tax cuts.[6]

Even the generally anti-tax *Tax Foundation* testified against the exemption, noting that it incentivizes corporations to restructure as LLCs without making any actual economic improvements. The foundation cites this change alone as contributing $200–$300 million toward Kansas's state budget deficit. When the exemption was passed in 2012, it was projected that 191,000 entities would take advantage of the provision. By 2015, that number had grown to 393,814—twice as many as expected.[7]

The foundation's researchers further argued that "it's important to note here that while decreasing taxes is generally associated with greater economic growth, the pass-through carve-out is primarily incentivizing tax avoidance, not job creation." As predicted, the policy change incentivized tens of thousands of Kansans to claim their wages as business income rather than from employment to avoid paying income tax.

Kansas's Economy Mainly Suffered Because of Oil Prices, Not Tax Changes

The Kansas economy grew 0.2 percent in 2015, which represented a decline from 1.2 percent in 2014. Kansas ended 2015 with two quarters of economic growth, meaning it entered 2016 in a recession. By the end of 2016, Kansas ranked forty-fifth in private sector job growth for the prior twelve months. Neighboring Colorado led the region with the tenth highest rate of private sector job growth, while Missouri and Nebraska ranked thirty-first and thirty-ninth respectively. This is the basis for the claims the tax cuts failed to stimulate growth.[8]

However, Kansas was in recession in 2016 for the same reason Canada also briefly fell into recession the same year: a collapse in oil prices. Kansas ranks tenth in crude oil production,[9] and the price of a barrel of crude fell from around $100 in 2014 to an average of around half that in 2015 and 2016.[10]

As *Investor's Business Daily* reported, "When these hard-hit sectors [oil and natural gas] are taken out of the equation, the remainder of the private sector workforce in Kansas outperformed its neighboring states of Missouri, Nebraska and Oklahoma."[11]

The Republican-controlled Kansas legislature recently pulled the plug on these tax cuts, but it's foolish to infer any national implications from them.

Poorly designed tax cuts don't prove that tax cuts are bad, nor are the Kansas tax cuts even remotely comparable to the Trump tax cuts.

Who Has Stricter Immigration Laws–the US or Mexico?

Although combating illegal immigration has long been a bipartisan issue, that changed with the rise of Trump. The plight of the illegal immigrant has become a cause for the modern left, and with it comes the usual guilt-tripping we receive on any other issue. We've all heard the arguments: that those opposing illegal immigration are hurting people "just looking for a better life" or are in favor of "separating families" or "putting children in cages." And of course, there's the most clichéd insult that enforcing immigration laws is "racist."

But are America's immigration laws or our treatment of illegal immigrants uniquely awful? Certainly not compared to Mexico, that's for sure.

Mexico Rejects More Asylum Requests Than the US

Speaking of the rise in asylum request rejections under Trump, a writer at the *Austin American-Statesman* noted a "dramatic" change. "Immigration judges, who are employed by the Justice Department and not the judicial branch like other federal judges, rejected 61.8 percent of asylum cases decided in 2017, the highest denial rate since 2005."[1]

Meanwhile in Mexico, nearly 90 percent of asylum requests are denied (and the figures are similarly high for other Latin American countries, including El Salvador, Honduras, and Guatemala).[2]

Mexico Regulates Immigration Based on Nationality

I only bring this up because for all the rhetoric about Trump's supposed racism or disdain for certain immigrants, there is one country that does regulate its immigration flows by nationality, and ironically it's the country Trump is most accused of being racist against.

In Article 37 of Mexico's General Law of Population, we learn that its Department of the Interior shall be able to deny foreigners entry into Mexico if, among other reasons, they may disrupt the "domestic demographic equilibrium." Additionally, Article 37 also states that immigrants can be removed if they're detrimental to "economic or national interests."[3]

Mexico Deports More Central American Illegal Immigrants Than the US

In July 2014, former Mexican president Enrique Peña Nieto and former president of Guatemala, Otto Pérez Molina, announced the start of a migration security project called Plan Frontera Sur (Southern Border Plan). The US has committed at least $100 million toward this plan to help aid Mexican border security because the project is mutually beneficial. Mexico wants to keep out Central American illegals, and the US benefits from Mexico having strong border security because some percentage of their Central American illegals has the goal of reaching the US.

Since Plan Frontera Sur, Mexico has deported more Central American illegal immigrants than we have in the US. Even CNN had to acknowledge this fact:

> *According to statistics from the US and Mexican governments compiled by the nonpartisan Migration Policy Institute, Mexico in 2015 apprehended tens of thousands more Central Americans in its country than the US did at its border, and in 2015 and 2016 it deported roughly twice as many Central Americans as the US did.*[4]

Since migrant children are the hot-button topic in the American immigration debate currently, in 2014 there were 18,169 migrant children deported from Mexico and 8,350 deported to Central America the year before.[5] From January 2015 to July 2016, 39,751 unaccompanied minors were put in the custody of Mexican authorities.[6]

A 2018 report from Amnesty International concluded that "Mexican migration authorities are routinely turning back thousands of people from Honduras, El Salvador and Guatemala to their countries without considering the risk to their life and security upon return, in many cases violating international and domestic law by doing so."[7]

Mexico Has Its Own Southern Border—and Invisible Wall

For as much as Donald Trump is criticized by the political class in Mexico for wanting to beef up security on the US-Mexico border, as previously mentioned, Mexico has accepted our help in enforcing its immigration laws on its own southern border with Guatemala. Although they don't have a literal border fence, they do have checkpoints, patrols, raids, and the like. According to NPR:

> *Rather than amassing troops on its border with Guatemala, Mexico stations migration agents, local and federal police, soldiers and marines to create a kind of containment zone in Chiapas state. With roving checkpoints and raids, Mexican migration agents have formed a formidable deportation force.*[8]

Is there any criticism of American immigration laws that can't be made of Mexico's?

No, Trump Did Not Kick Immigrants Out of the Army

"Some immigrant U.S. Army Reservists and recruits who enlisted in the military with a promised path to citizenship are being abruptly discharged," opened a bombshell report from the Associated Press.[1]

You can guess the angle of the article; that it's the Trump administration's rhetoric on illegal immigration or policies that are somehow responsible for immigrant recruits being silently discharged to avoid giving them citizenship. "MAVNI" (Military Accessions Vital to the National Interest) is the program that grants expedited citizenship to noncitizens.

The Associated Press wasn't able to quantify how many people who enlisted through MAVNI were kicked out of the army, but they write "immigration attorneys say they know of more than forty who have been discharged or whose status has become questionable, jeopardizing their futures."

Here's a sampling of the liberal hysteria in response to the report:

> *The United States of America had a strong history of proudly having immigrants serve in the US Army. Then Trump was sworn in. Since then, his administration has quietly been discharging immigrants from the Army. Putin's puppet is harming our military.*
>
> —Scott Dworkin (@funder)[2]

The Trump (mis)Administration is discharging and breaking promises to immigrants willing to do what the Draft-Dodger-in-Chief was not willing to do, risk their lives serving in our Armed Forces. Shameful.

—Ana Navarro (@ananavarro)[3]

There were so many tears in my eyes that my hands couldn't move fast enough to wipe them away...I was devastated, because I love the U.S. and was so honored to be able to serve this great country. This is disgraceful. Shame on us.

—Gavin Newsom (@GavinNewsom)[4]

Not surprisingly, the Associated Press had the story all wrong. While many somehow got the impression that the immigrants in question are active duty, the AP article is about immigrants who have enlisted in the army—but have not gone to basic training yet. Such a mistaken impression can be forgiven, as few liberals read past the headline in the Trump era anyway.

There are numerous reasons one could enlist but then be discharged before basic training (such as health reasons, gaining too much weight, failing to pass a background check, and the like). The overwhelming number of people discharged are not immigrants.

The AP has failed to do two things: prove that these forty discharges are due to immigration status, and prove that there's a change in policy under the Trump administration that's causing the problem they can't prove exists. According to national security commenter John Noonan, the problem here has more to do with how US Army background checks work than any anti-immigrant policies.

*So here's where I think the @AP reporter got a little confused. When you raise your hand and take an oath, you belong to the military. But you're not technically *in* the military. It's common to get the oath out of the way while initial background checks are on-going.*

—John Noonan (@noonanjo)[5]

If you separate within 180 days of service, you are given an entry-level separation. It's not an honorable discharge. It's not a dishonorable discharge. It's just "hey, this isn't going to work." This 180 days requirement reiterated in Section 3A of the memo (above)

—John Noonan (@noonanjo)[6]

Sorry, but DoD [Department of Defense] is going to separate you. Does it happen often? Not really...which is why AP is talking about 40 or so people out of 70,000 immigrants in service. But is it indicative of a wider policy to expunge non-citizens from active service (as AP story suggested)? No.[7]

—John Noonan (@noonanjo)

At the time of the AP's story, there were still eleven hundred people accepted into the MAVNI program that had not started basic training pending completion of a background check, and many had been in limbo for years, according to the Pentagon.[8] It's the background checks that have added to delays in approving applicants, and when did the army further strengthen background checks for the MAVNI program? Under the Obama administration.

According to the military publication *Stars and Stripes*:

Since 2009, more than 10,000 MAVNI soldiers were recruited because their backgrounds and talents, particularly their language or medical skills and their cultural knowledge, filled a critical need for the Army. In exchange, they were offered a promise of professional advancement and a fast track to citizenship. But growing national security concerns led the Defense Department in fall 2016 to institute enhanced security screenings for these foreigners, casting a shadow of suspicion on the group and creating a backlog. MAVNI soldiers who were recruited in the months leading up to that time were stuck waiting for the completion of security checks at whatever stage of entry they'd reached.[9]

The root cause of the problem stems from Obama opening up MAVNI to those protected by Deferred Action for Childhood Arrivals (DACA). According to retired US Army Lieutenant Colonel Margaret Stock, who created the MAVNI program, "DACA sounded the death knell for the program because MAVNI was never intended as a way to address the political hot potato of citizenship for undocumented long-term residents."[10] Rather, MAVNI was created to attract recruits who speak languages that are of strategic use to the armed forces, such as Mandarin, Dari, Farsi, and Russian (with a path to citizenship as a reward).

MAVNI was never intended to be a loophole to obtain citizenship. The program was expanded far beyond its original scope and eventually collapsed under its own bureaucracy in 2016 thanks to Obama and is currently closed to new applicants.

And for all that, the media blamed Donald Trump.

Do Illegal Aliens Really Commit Fewer Crimes?

The Cato Institute's Alex Nowrasteh appeared on Tucker Carlson's show in 2018, leading to a fiery debate in the aftermath of the then-recent death of Mollie Tibbetts at the hands of an illegal alien. Nowrasteh's research into illegal immigration argues that contrary to popular belief, illegal aliens are more law abiding than the rest of us.

In the segment, most of Tucker's argument centered on how illegal immigrants are disproportionately represented in federal prisons, while Nowrasteh pointed out that federal prisoners are a small percentage of total prisoners and argued that most illegals in federal prison are there for immigration-related offenses. Nowrasteh also pointed to his own research, which has found that illegals are imprisoned at rates lower than the general population in Texas (which he extrapolated from to argue that illegals are more law abiding overall).

It should be noted off the bat that all estimates of illegal immigration crime are underestimates for a simple reason. In America the average convict released has 3.9 prior convictions (excluding convictions that didn't result in jail time). Because illegal immigrants will simply be deported at the end of their sentence (or be deported in lieu of other punishment), the chance of them re-offending is essentially zero (unless they're able to reenter the US). Furthermore, illegal immigrant victims of crimes committed by other illegals go unreported nearly 100 percent of the time for an obvious reason (except in the case of more egregious crimes). Given that most white crime victims are victimized by other white people and most black crime victims victimized by other black people, would it be a stretch to suggest that the majority of illegal immigrant crimes are going unreported since they're against other illegals?

Right off the bat, we're comparing a native population that can re-offend against one that will experience difficulty in doing so, as it'll require them to again illegally immigrate. Despite that, US Census data from 2011 to 2015 shows that noncitizens are 7 percent more likely than the US population to be incarcerated in adult correctional facilities.[1]

For some perspective on how deportations may have understated those figures, note that 1.5 million illegals who committed crimes were deported from 2005 to 2015, which is ten times higher than the number of adult illegals imprisoned in 2015.[2] In other words, annual deportations of criminal illegals were approximately equal to the total illegal alien prison population (and yes, I realize how redundant the phrase "criminal illegals" is).

Additionally, illegals tend to congregate in cities where law enforcement solves crimes at a rate lower than the national average. Over 61 percent of illegal aliens live in just twenty sanctuary cities (compared to 36 percent of the overall population that lives in those same cities).[3] In 2015, 46 percent of the violent crimes and 19 percent of the property crimes reported to police in the US were cleared, according to FBI data.[4] In San Francisco and Los Angeles, only about a third of violent crimes were cleared.[5]

With all those variables that would naturally help in underestimating any attempt at measuring illegal alien crime in mind, there are studies contradicting Nowrasteh worth reviewing.

Illegals in Arizona

According to one study of illegal immigrants in Arizona by John R. Lott Jr.:

> *Undocumented immigrants are at least 142% more likely to be convicted of a crime than other Arizonans. They also tend to commit more serious crimes and serve 10.5% longer sentences, more likely to be classified as dangerous, and 45% more likely to be gang members than U.S. citizens.*[6]

If those figures were extrapolated nationally, illegals in 2016 "would have been responsible for over 1,000 murders, 5,200 rapes, 8,900 robberies, 25,300 aggravated assaults, and 26,900 burglaries."

Nowrasteh's Criticism of Arizona Study

Nowrasteh's main criticism is that Lott overstated the number of illegal immigrants by looking at the incarceration rates of "noncitizens," which includes people besides illegal aliens (such as green card holders, who Nowrasteh points out account for 10 percent of those deported). Fair enough.

To narrow down which "noncitizens" are illegal aliens, Nowrasteh isolates which have ICE detainers outstanding (which require an inmate be deported at the end of their sentence). About 38 percent of illegals in his sample had ICE detainers.

There were 1,823 Arizona prisoners with ICE detainers in 2017, which out of a prison population of 42,200 amounts to an incarceration rate to be "a maximum of only 4.3 percent of all prisoners," compared to the 4.9 percent of Arizona's population illegals compose. In that light, illegals appear underrepresented relative to their share of the population.

Where Nowrasteh and I disagree is in our interpretation of those ICE detainer figures. Nowrasteh sees them as the maximum number of noncitizens that are illegals, whereas I see that as the absolute minimum. Politics has played a large role in the number of ICE detainers outstanding, with fewer than half in existence by 2017 than their peak in 2010.[7] Unless illegal aliens suddenly began committing crimes at half the rate they did a half-decade prior, we can assume that politics determines which percent of illegals properly have an ICE detainer attached to their name.

Furthermore, to believe that 62 percent of the noncitizen prison population in Arizona is not illegal immigrants would betray everything we know about legal immigrant crime statistics (that legal immigrants commit fewer crimes than the general public, which is to be expected given the extensive process to legally immigrate). There are about thirteen million legal permanent residents in the US, which is similar to the illegal alien population of ten to fifteen million.[8] Are we to believe that

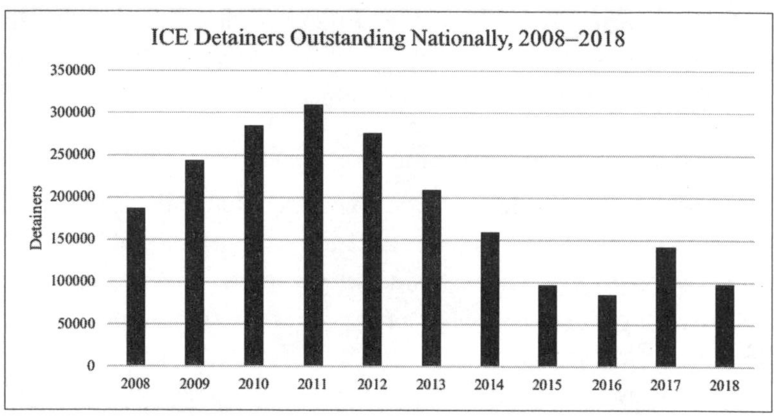

Source: TRAC Immigration

legal immigrants, who have gone through background checks (among all the other hurdles to immigrate), are committing crimes at double the rate of illegal immigrants?

That's impossible—but also it is exactly what Nowrasteh's argument would imply, and as Lott himself noted, "if we adjust the 2017 rate of detainers during the Trump administration to equal the Fiscal Year 2011 rate, then Nowrasteh's range of [illegal alien] incarceration rates would actually be from 6.79 percent to 7.89 percent," which is greater than their share of Arizona's population.[9]

Government Studies on Illegal Alien Murder Rates

A 2011 Government Accountability Office study of the illegal alien populations in Arizona, California, Florida, New York, and Texas found much of the same as Lott.[10]

Looking at murder rates, the study found:

- Arizona: 68.57 illegals imprisoned for homicide per one hundred thousand illegal aliens, compared with 54.06 per one hundred thousand for legal citizens in Arizona (21.16 percent higher).
- California: 92.7 illegals imprisoned for homicide per one hundred thousand, compared with 74.1 per one hundred thousand for legal California residents (25.1 percent higher).

- New York: 168.75 per one hundred thousand illegals imprisoned for homicide, compared with 48.12 in the legal New York population (250.69 percent higher).
- Texas: 54.54 illegal aliens per one hundred thousand imprisoned for homicide, compared with 63.43 in the legal Texas population (14.02 percent lower).
- Florida: 54.85 per one hundred thousand illegals imprisoned for homicide, compared with 67.8 for legal Florida residents. (19.1 percent lower).

Note that these are *rates of imprisonment per one hundred thousand*, not annual homicide rates.

By the GAO's figures, illegals actually are safer than the general population in Texas (and Florida), in line with Nowrasteh's study on the matter, but casting doubt on whether its conclusions can be extrapolated nationally.

However, the statistically lower rates at which illegals commit homicides in Florida and Texas are far overshadowed by the states where they commit far more crimes. If we average together the average murder rates from the five states, we find that there are 87.882 illegal aliens imprisoned for homicide for every one hundred thousand illegal aliens, compared to a rate of 61.5 per one hundred thousand for the legal population. In other words, illegal aliens commit murders at a rate 43 percent higher than the general population.

Nowrasteh's Criticism of GAO Study

The GAO study provided state-level illegal immigrant crime statistics based on the State Criminal Alien Assistance Program (SCAAP), which reimburses states for the costs of illegal immigrant prisoners. That report found that in 2009, there were 295,959 criminal aliens in state, local, and federal prisons, which Nowrasteh says suffers from double counting because the 296k figure is based on total incarcerations, not incarcerated individuals.

As an alternative figure, Nowrasteh uses the American Community Survey (ACS), a census-like survey that (among many other things) gathers data on prisoners, including whether they're American citizens and their country of origin. Nowrasteh cites 156,329 noncitizens incarcerated at the federal, state, and local level in 2008, about half the SCAAP figure. The ACS is self-reported data, and some noncitizens could slip through the cracks when it comes to reporting their citizenship status.

In my view the SCAAP survey is an absolute maximum figure for illegals incarcerated (because of the double counting issue). Though it does suffer from double counting, it's hard to imagine it's by a large extent, unless we're to believe that the illegals are only being incarcerated for months at a time—then immediately re-offending—and all without risking deportation. Meanwhile, I'd view the ACS figure as a minimum because it's self-reported data (and one's illegal status isn't something that one would exactly be eager to disclose).

The truth is likely somewhere in the middle, and it's not possible to know. I will note, however, that there is another way to look at the data: based on the percentage of overall prison time illegals serve instead of the percentage of prisoners they compose. According to the 2009 SCAAP data, illegal aliens accounted for 5 percent and 6 percent of the *total days of prison time served* in state and local jails, respectively. If we're to assume 12.5 million illegal aliens in America and an overall population of three hundred twenty-five million, illegals account for 3.8 percent of the population, making them upwards of 50 percent overrepresented.

And Let's Suppose I'm Wrong

Hypothetically speaking, let's say I'm wrong that illegal aliens commit crimes at rates higher than native-born Americans. That still doesn't change the fact that there are crimes being committed that otherwise wouldn't have happened. Suppose for the sake of a thought experiment that there was a city of one million people and an additional one million illegals began living in the city. For the sake of this thought experiment, natives are victimized at a rate 85 percent higher than they were before the influx of illegals, due to increased crime from the illegal share of the population.

But at the same time, the population of the city doubled, meaning there would be simultaneously more native victims of crime and yet the crime statistics would decrease on a per capita basis. Would any of those victimized notice (or find comfort in knowing) that they were technically being victimized at a lower statistical rate? I have my doubts.

Trump's Tax Cuts Didn't All Go "to the Rich"

It's inevitable in any debate over tax cuts that you'll run into the cliché that they're only "for the rich," and that's certainly been the case when it comes to Donald Trump's recent tax reform package.

Such an argument can be made against any across-the-board tax cut, even when lower income brackets are cut more than top income brackets. After all, a 1 percent tax cut is going to save a millionaire more money than a 50 percent tax cut is going to save for a poor person, even though the poor person benefits more relative to their current wealth.

The Trump tax cuts composed of both corporate tax reform (cutting the corporate tax rate from 35 percent to 21 percent) and across-the-board cuts to individual income tax brackets. Below is tabled the percentage point decline for each bracket (for a single taxpayer). Also note the $5,650 increase in the standard deduction.

Claims that the Trump tax cuts go mostly to the "top 1 percent" are commonplace. Democratic Policy and Communications Committee Co-Chair David Cicilline claims that "80 percent" of the Trump tax cuts go to "corporations and the top 1 percent."[1] Nancy Pelosi has claimed that 83 percent of the Trump tax cuts went to the top 1 percent.

A more useful way to analyze the Trump tax cuts is to look at how they benefit each income quintile relative to how much of the tax burden they shouldered before the cuts. Before the Trump tax cuts, the bottom 80

Tax Rates on Income 2018 ($12,000 Standard Deduction)		2017 Tax Rates ($6,350 Standard Deduction)	
10%	0–$9,525	10%	0–$9,325
12%	$9,525–$38,700	15%	$9,325–$37,950
22%	$38,700–$82,500	25%	$37,950–$91,900
24%	$82,500–$157,500	28%	$91,900–$191,650
32%	$157,500–$200,000	33%	$191,650–$416,700
35%	$200,000–$500,000	35%	$416,700–$418,400
37%	$500,000+	39.6%	$418,400

Source: KDP[1]

percent of income earners paid roughly 33 percent of all federal income taxes but received 35 percent of the benefits from the Trump tax cuts. The top 1 percent paid 27 percent of all federal taxes and received only 21 percent of the tax cut, according to the center-left Tax Policy Center.[2]

The Tax Policy Center found that more than 80 percent of taxpayers received a tax cut (with an average of $2,200 saved), with less than 5 percent receiving a tax increase. The 5 percent who saw increases were mostly wealthy people in coastal states who had their write-offs for mortgage interest and for state and local taxes capped.

The top 1 percent are not receiving 80 percent or 83 percent of the benefits; they're receiving roughly 21 percent. However, there is some slight truth to Cicilline and Pelosi's claims, but only in one scenario where they're to blame for it. What Cicilline and Pelosi didn't mention is that they're specifically speaking about the year 2027, when the individual income tax cuts expire, and thus most of the remaining benefits shift to corporations (whose reduced tax rates remain unchanged).

No shortage of Democrats have criticized the Trump tax cuts for keeping the corporate tax cuts in effect after ten years while having the individual tax cuts last only a decade. But there's a simple fix, isn't there? Simply pass legislation to make the individual cuts permanent.

Senator Ted Cruz introduced legislation in January 2018 to make the individual cuts permanent, but to little surprise, he didn't find any Democrat takers.[3]

As recently as late September, the House passed a bill to make the Trump tax cuts for individuals permanent. Again, Democrats were hardly enthused by the bill.[4] It seems like they'd rather create a scenario where 80 percent of the Trump tax cuts go to the top 1 percent, just so they can use that as an excuse to justify raising taxes on everyone.

Tax Refund Confusion

Are middle-class taxes going up under President Trump? During the 2019 tax season, there was no shortage of confusion.

The Democratic Coalition wrote on their official Twitter account; "Many people are seeing an increase in taxes due to the bill eliminating many of the deductions that were used by middle-class families in order to lower the amount of taxes they were required to pay" and linked to a *Yahoo! News* article.[1] The article reported on the anecdotes of a few individuals who saw their taxes increase.

Another angle had to do with supposedly declining tax refunds. A widely read CNN article was misinterpreted as claiming that taxes up are in 2018. "The average refund is down about 8% under the first full year of the overhauled tax code, according to data released by the IRS. Refunds averaged $1,865 compared to $2,035 for tax year 2017," reported Victoria Cavaliere.[2]

A large source of the confusion came from the fact that the percentage of income withheld from paychecks has decreased. Suppose for the sake of simplicity that someone earns $50,000 a year, pays 20 percent tax ($10,000 annually), and pays that tax in the form of $200 a week for a 50-week work-year. Since they pay exactly what's owed, they would receive no refund. Now suppose the tax rate decreases to 18 percent (so $180 a week is owed), but because a smaller percentage of taxes are withheld, only $170 is actually paid. Thus, while that person had their taxes decrease by $100 overall, they would still end up owing $500 at the end of the year.

Or put more simply, people are receiving smaller refunds because they paid fewer taxes in the first place.

It's doubtful that the average employee is paying attention to such a thing, so you can hardly fault some people for mistakenly believing their taxes went up (though you'd think they would notice the extra change in their pockets). Regardless, those economically inclined have known that smaller refunds were at least a possibility since July 2018 when the Government Accountability Office released a report stating that thirty million taxpayers would end up owing money in 2019 due to insufficient withholding, a significant increase over the year prior. The percentage of employers that over-withheld employees' taxes *decreased* from 76 percent to 73 percent from 2018-2019, and the percentage that under-withheld tax increased from 18 percent to 21 percent. Both groups are likely to see an increase in their taxes owed.[3] Bear in mind that the US has a labor force of over one hundred sixty million people, so each percentage point change is equal to 1.6 million workers (or 9.6 million overall who experienced a change).

As is documented in more detail elsewhere in this book, all individual tax brackets did decline under Trump, and the standard deduction was doubled. Under such a scenario, most will see their tax burden decrease.

Now we're learning that the left's confusion of how taxes work wasn't even predicated on any (misunderstood) truth. While there was a slight decrease in the percentage of people receiving refunds, according to a newer article from CNN's Donna Borak, it turns out that refunds were up after all! As she wrote:

> *The average refund check was $40 more this year than last year through the week ending February 22, according to data released by the Internal Revenue Service on Thursday. That's just 1.3% more for the roughly 47.4 million Americans whose returns were processed for the most recent week, compared to the same period last year. The Treasury also noted in its latest release that tax refunds on average week-over-week jumped 19% to $3,143 compared to last week's average of $2,640. The increase, they said, is largely due to remaining earned income tax credits and child tax credits that were disbursed this week. The two tax credits couldn't be*

> *paid out until Feb. 15 under the law, resulting in bigger refund checks for Americans in the past two weeks* [emphasis mine].[4]

So, they jumped the gun on that one.

I must note, while the left was wrong about tax returns decreasing, you really ought to have wished they were right. After all, wouldn't you rather have your money when you earn it instead of waiting a year for the government to hold it interest-free before refunding it to you?

There are exceptions, however, and those likely to actually be paying more this year are homeowners on coastal states, which tend to have higher property tax burdens (mainly stemming from higher housing prices in those states), and high state income taxes. The Trump Tax cuts capped state and local tax (SALT) deductions to $10,000 a year, so those who pay more than that sum are losing out on deductions.

Prior to the Trump tax cuts, 77 percent of the benefits of SALT deductions went to those earning above $100,000, while only 6.6 percent went to those earning below $50,000 (who are unlikely to be affected by the SALT cap anyway, unless they're paying over 20 percent of their income in state and local taxes).[5]

While this is inflated by high-income earners, the average SALT deduction claimed nationwide in 2015 was $12,471, meaning the average person claiming is losing a $2,471 write-off. Assuming they fall in the 24 percent income bracket, the value of that write-off is approximately $593, which would be more than offset by declines in individual tax brackets. A 2016 Tax Policy Center study found that a complete elimination of SALT deduction would raise taxes on 88 percent of households earning over $1 million, raising the taxes of the average millionaire by $46,550.[6]

Overall, the average taxpayer saw a $2,200 cut under the Trump tax plan, while 6 percent of households saw an increase of $2,800 (nearly all of which were concentrated in the top 10 percent of income earners).[7]

While it is true that the Trump tax plan did raise taxes on some earners, there were roughly ten people who saw a cut (most of whom were concentrated in the bottom 90 percent of income earners) for everyone who saw an increase (most of whom were in the top 10 percent).

Admittedly, I'd have preferred if all brackets saw cuts, but liberals can hardly mischaracterize the Trump tax cuts as "tax cuts for the rich."

Trickle-Down Talking Points

In addition to the inevitable anti-tax talking point that they're all "for the rich," we're also to believe that any gains from economic growth that tax cuts may spur will all go to the top as well.

Wage stagnation has been one major argument against Trump's tax plan, allowing liberals to make the same tired old arguments against so-called "trickle-down economics" that we've heard for the past five decades. As a few writers at the Center for American Progress put it last year, "On measures that determine whether workers' wages are keeping up with the cost of living, there has been little improvement and even some regression since the start of 2017, when President Donald Trump took office."[8] Chuck Jones of *Forbes* wrote halfway into 2018 that "while GDP hit 4.1 percent for the June quarter...the unemployment rate is hovering at all-time lows, inflation continues to increase, real wages are stagnant."[9]

Before completely tearing apart a claim, it's always worth explaining the basis for why people believe it to be so. At first glance, the talking points appear true. Private sector wage growth in 2018 was about 3.2 percent,[10] respectable at face value, but only a net 0.76 percent increase when you account for inflation of 2.44 percent that year. That came after wages rose 2.5 percent in 2017—which was almost eliminated by the inflation of 2.13 percent that year.

Rather than take isolated statistics at face value, it's important to remember that all the figures we're dealing with are averages and can be affected by external factors, such as:

- An increase in the rate that people are retiring. Since those nearing retirement have decades of work experience, they far out-earn the average American. In fact, 55- to 64-year-olds boast wages 28 percent higher than those age 25 to 34.[11] If my workplace consisted of me earning $10 an hour, Dan earning $15 an hour, and a prospective retiree earning $30 an hour, the average wage would be $18.33. But suppose the prospective retiree retires while Dan and I simultaneously see our pay hiked to $15 an hour (plus 50 percent!) and $20 an hour (plus 33 percent). While every worker saw their wages increase massively, the average wage at this hypothetical firm as decreased to $17.50 an hour.

- The labor force participation rate has finally increased under Trump after a secular decline under Obama. Those who previously had given up looking for work are now reentering the labor force. Those who've been out of the workforce for an extended period of time tend to have fewer skills in the first place—and those skills they do possess have atrophied over time. Though they're not dragging anyone's individual wages down, their addition to the workforce does lower average wages on paper.

As the San Francisco Federal Reserve wrote regarding those two phenomena, "Counterintuitively, this means that strong job growth can pull average wages in the economy down and slow the pace of wage growth."[12] The San Francisco Fed's most recent calculations quantifying the effects of those variables were in the second quarter of 2018 and estimated a drag of about 1.5 percentage points.[13] Assuming that remained constant for the year, it would imply nominal wage growth of 4.7 percent in 2018, or 2.26 percent post-inflation, a respectable figure.

Though I chose to focus on 2018 in particular because it's the first year to be impacted by the Trump tax cuts, wages in 2017 were also higher than advertised. As alluded to earlier, private sector wages rose 2.5 percent in 2017 (about in line with inflation of 2.13 percent)[14] but rose close to 4.5 percent (or over roughly 2.4 percent net of inflation) once accounting for retirees and those rejoining the workforce.

I've been using the consumer price index thus far in making all my inflation adjustments (because it's the most commonly used inflation metric), but it does tend to overstate inflation relative to other inflation measurements. For example, if I instead measured inflation using the personal consumption expenditures index (PCE), inflation is roughly

0.5 percentage points lower than used in my prior calculations. By that measurement, real wage growth was an even higher 2.9 percent in 2017 and 2.8 percent in 2018.

By those figures, a household with an annual purchasing power of $50,000 when Trump took office should have the equivalent of roughly $53,000 today. I can't image they've noticed any wage stagnation.

A New Wage Gap Myth– Are Women "Really" Earning Only 49 Cents to a Man's Dollar?

We've all heard the long-discredited statistic that "for every dollar a man earns, a woman earns only 77 cents," but have you "learned" that it's actually even worse than that? That's what a new study is claiming. Forget 77 cents; the true figure is closer to 49 cents, says the Institute for Women's Policy Research (IWPR). It's a shocking conclusion, and like clockwork, the mainstream media has had no problem uncritically adopting and reporting on the study's findings.

Vox writer Anna North summarizes the IWPR study titled "Still a Man's Labor Market" as follows:[1]

- Measures of the pay gap typically compare the wages of men and women working full-time in a given year. However, women are more likely to drop out of full-time work to take care of children or other family members. To account for this, the report's authors looked at women's earnings across three fifteen-year periods and compared those with men.
- The study found that 77 percent of men worked every year in the last time period sampled (2001–2015), compared to only 57 percent of women.
- For women, a one-year gap in employment reduced earnings by $15,200. For men, the figure was $22,300. *Vox* mistakenly claims

that women suffered a greater income penalty for taking off work, which is only true in other periods the study sampled (1968–1982 and 1983–1997), but not the most recent.

- In conclusion, the study found a pay gap nearly twice as big as what's traditionally reported: averaged out over fifteen years, women made just 49 cents for every dollar men made.

For decades now conservatives have been pointing out that the infamous "77 cents" statistic is only comparing male and female full-time workers, with no adjustments made for the type of jobs worked, or even that "full-time" men still work almost four hours more per week than "full-time" women[2] ("full-time" is defined as 30 hours or more per week or 130 hours per month by IRS guidelines).[3] Like every other wage gap study out there with liberal conclusions, the IWPR study doesn't compare the earnings of men and women in similar jobs, doesn't adjust for differences in hours worked, and doesn't even compare the earnings of men and women of similar ages (and thus at similar stages of their careers).

This latest study suffers from all the usual problems—and then some more, as male workers (mostly working full -time) are being compared to female workers who will have years they earn $0 due to time spent away from the labor force and suffer skill atrophy away from the workforce. Regardless of one's annual earnings, a single year earning $0 will significantly drag down the average.

The only new "revelation" in this study is that we see a larger wage gap when we compare male full-time workers to women who are not always working instead of comparing full-time male workers against full-time female workers. Let he who is completely unsurprised cast the first stone.

What did the IWPR actually prove? That women who work less than men will earn less? No shocker there. Nor should it be, given that earlier in the year Vox's Sarah Kliff published a great piece explaining that childbirth explains away nearly the entirety (80 percent) of the wage gap.[4] I suppose there isn't much intellectual consistency to be found over at Vox, is there?

To borrow a phrase from Al Gore's playbook, on the issue of the wage gap, the science is settled.

Is There a Sports Wage Gap Too?

The United States women's national soccer team has been instrumental in highlighting the gap in pay between them and their male colleagues in an entirely different league. Ranked first in the world with three World Cups and four Olympic gold medals, a number of the team's members went to war with their employer, the US Soccer Federation, in 2016, and five players joined in filing a lawsuit with the Equal Employment Opportunity Commission alleging sex discrimination.[1]

The core of the team's arguments is that they've been more successful than the men's team, and they thus deserve at least equal compensation to them. Not long before their lawsuit, their 2015 World Cup victory against Japan resulted in the most-viewed soccer match in US history.

There's no denying that internationally the US women's soccer team is a better female team than the US men's team is a men's team, but relative ability doesn't translate to eyeballs watching the game (and therefore more revenue). Such logic would be like saying a local team that won a basketball game 50-30 should be compensated better than two professional teams that just closed out a game 40-40. Just because one team did better against an unrelated opponent means absolutely nothing when it comes to pay.

Still, it's easy to see why things seem so unfair. As goalkeeper Hope Solo pointed out, her salary of $366,000 for twenty-three games is less than the $498,494 goalkeeper Tim Howard was paid to play in eight games.

And when it comes to overall pay, things seem even more striking. The women made $2 million for winning the 2015 World Cup, while the men made $9 million in the 2014 World Cup after being knocked out in the sixteenth round. It's these inequalities at the heart of the lawsuit, but they need more context. And that context is that men's soccer is immensely more popular than women's.

FIFA made a profit of over $2 billion on the men's tournament,[2] whereas the women's tournament typically pulls in less than $80 million in total revenue. That's twenty-five times the revenue for men's soccer.

Similarly, while the 2015 Women's World Cup raked in $17 million in sponsorship revenue, the men's tournament brought in an astonishing $529 million.[3]

Due to men's soccer's relative popularity and profitability, American male players simply have more leverage when bargaining for their national team salary because they can make much more money elsewhere. The average salary for a Major League Soccer player is $316,777,[4] and top players can make millions. Male players also have leverage from the fact that they can even earn substantially more in some of the prestigious European leagues.

Meanwhile, the maximum salary in the National Women's Soccer League is $350,000 as of 2018.[5] NWLS games attracted an average of 6,024 audience members per game in 2018 (a 41 percent increase since 2013),[6] while men's games attracted nearly four times as many people: 22,124 per game.

While it's hardly ideal that such talented players are going unwatched, the only visible discrimination against these female soccer players seems to be that the public is uninterested in viewing their games.

Is There a Gender Debt Gap?

The alleged gender wage gap, an economic statistic that's seemingly debunked more often than argued nowadays, has a new spin on it.

The topic of student loan debt has long been a hot-button issue, and a new report revealing that women owe the majority of the nation's student loan debt is pointing the finger at the wage gap. According to the American Association of University Women, women owe approximately $2,700 more than men at graduation, though obviously that can't be attributed to the wage gap because they haven't yet begun their careers.[1]

When it comes to total student debt, women owe $890 billion to men's $490 billion, or 65 percent of outstanding student debt. Naturally, the study's authors think the correct percentage of debt owed by women should be 50 percent. And for that discrepancy, the study blames the gender wage gap for affecting women's abilities to pay back debt (which can make sense in this case because outstanding debt is being quoted, not debt at graduation).

Women owing the majority of student loan debt is exactly what one would expect in country where the majority of college students are women, and one where women apparently spend more on college (as evidenced by their greater debt loads at graduation). Women make up 56 percent of college students, so 40 percent of the "gender debt gap" can be explained by that fact alone.

As for other factors, women also outnumber men in graduate school by a similar margin as they do overall, meaning women (on average)

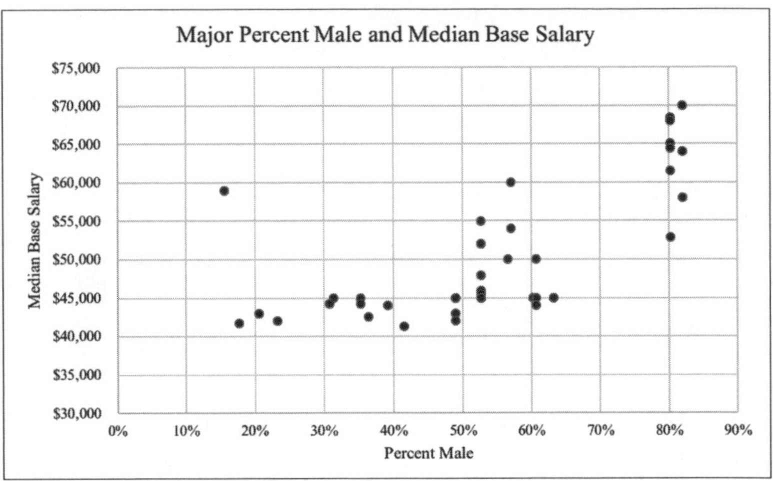

Source: American Enterprise Institute

are remaining in higher education for more years and thus taking on more debt.[2] Even a single extra year in college can mean tens of thousands of dollars extra new debt (plus an extra year of interest accruing on outstanding debt as entrance into the workforce is delayed).

As for why women have less money to pay back their loans, that has more to do with the choice of major than the wage gap. Of the top ten highest-paying majors, only one has a female majority (nursing), and 72 percent of all students in those majors are male.[3] Below is charted fifty college majors by the percent of students that are male, and median pay during the first five years post-graduation.

The wage gap is unlikely to be playing a role in the "gender debt gap" for one reason in particular. Remember, the wage gap is a nominal gap in pay among all men and all women of all levels of education, workplace experience, competence, ages, and so forth in the entire US! The wage gap between recent college grads (in the same major/fields), however, is almost nonexistent. According to the Federal Reserve Bank of New York:

> *Among recent college graduates, women earn roughly 97 cents on the dollar compared with men who have the same college major and perform the same jobs. Moreover, what may be surprising is that at the start of*

> *their careers, women actually out-earn men by a substantial margin for a number of college majors.*
>
> *In fact, according to our estimates, newly minted female college graduates earn as much as, or more than, men in twenty-nine of the seventy-three majors.*[4]

So, there goes that excuse.

Hopefully the gender wage gap remains out of the headlines for at least another year before we need to beat this dead horse again, but I won't hold my breath.

The Pink Tax–Another Feminist Figment

The long-debunked "male female wage gap" (that women earn 77 cents to a man's dollar) has long been the most popular economic statistic from the left in trying to prove gender discrimination in the workforce. As disputed as the reasons for the gender wage gap are, it's still remained a popular talking point among liberals with a feminist tilt, and it's spawned a new cousin, the so-called "pink tax."

The concept of a pink tax is based off the theory that female-branded products cost more than male-branded products, leading to the claim that "women pay more for the exact same products as men." Think: haircuts, razors, shampoo, and similar products and services. According to a 2015 study by the New York City Department of Consumer Affairs:[1]

- On average, products for women or girls cost 7 percent more than comparable products for men and boys.
- Girls' clothing costs 4 percent more than boys, and women's clothing costs 8 percent more than men's.
- Women's personal care products cost 13 percent more than men's.

The 2015 NYC study states that this supposed "pink tax" costs women an extra $1,351 a year, on average.

An obvious question to ask is, if women are paying more for identical products, why wouldn't they just purchase the male equivalent?

And that question alone explains the pink tax—because the pink tax isn't reflecting higher prices for identical female products, it's reflecting prices for *similar* female products. Even the NYC study had to admit that's the main limitation of the study, that "men's and women's products are rarely identical, making exact comparisons difficult."

Just because things are similar does not mean they are identical. In the case of haircuts, women are paying more simply because it tends to take more time and labor to cut women's hair than men's—because women tend to have longer hair. In the case of dry cleaning,[2] women pay more because on average their clothes take more time to dry-clean than men's shirts and require different machinery to complete the job. In the case of razors, women's razors have to be designed to endure more (as men only shave their faces, while women shave up to ten times more surface area).[3] To give just a hint as to how much detail goes into creating something as simple as a razor, the Gillette Mach3 cost an incredible $750 million in research and development to bring to market.[4]

Of course, those are just a few examples—so what of other products?

A recent paper published in the journal *Revista Latina de Comunicación Social* concluded that:

> *Results of analysis performed show three facts: first, that the existence of the pink tax, understood as an extra price in identical/quasi identical products is not significant; second, that price differences in similar products are supported by differences in product features and are potentially generators of value for consumers. And lastly, the enormous offer diversification targeted to women is demonstrated. A wide offer of personal care products is destined to them—without equivalent for men—a consumption that points at them and moves them closer to a social ideal of beauty linked to success.*[5]

Humorously, a table from the study indicates that nearly identical "gendered" products cost slightly less for women. It's only those gendered products with functional differences that cost more (as is to be expected).

Much like the wage gap, the pink tax is a "sexism of the gaps" argument. Those using it as an argument are noticing a disparity—and then assuming the only possible explanation could be sexism.

Product Group	Price € (Men)	Price € (Women)	Price Difference (%)
Quasi-identical product (M-W)	1.9	1.88	-0.9
Similar products with nonfunctional differences (M-W)	1.68	1.73	+3.1
Similar products with functional differences (M-W)	1.44	1.68	+16.4
Total references	1.67	1.76	+5.4%

I'm still not sure what the end goal with pushing this myth even is. If it were true, you'd think those pushing it would just buy the supposedly identical male products and stop complaining.

TRUMP VS. OBAMA MYTHS

It's only natural that a sitting president is compared to their predecessor, and in the case of Donald Trump replacing Barack Obama, we have the media comparing the president they hate the most to one they couldn't stop fawning over for nearly a decade.

And that's why when the media does acknowledge Trump's successes, it's only to immediately credit Barack Obama for them. How often have you seen it claimed that the Trump economy and stock market have only performed the way they did because it was the economy Obama left him?

When the media isn't giving Obama credit, he's taking it for himself. "That was me, people," Obama bragged in 2018 following news that American oil production had again surged to new highs.

And any attempt to attack Trump will do. One of the more bizarre claims debunked in this chapter is that Barack Obama had deported more illegal aliens than Trump, which the media used to mock Trump for being unsuccessful in enforcing policies to reduce illegal immigration. Not only is the claim bogus and misleading, I can't understand the media's motive for it, aside from digging on Trump. These are the same people who will, in the next breath, blast Trump's immigration policies as being cruel and inhumane. Wouldn't that mean Obama's were even crueler, or do even they not believe their talking points?

Those kinds of inconsistencies aside, the media is clearly devoted to protecting Obama's legacy at all costs.

Unfortunately for the American public, it isn't a legacy worth defending.

As one writer for *Investor's Business Daily* noted:

> *Last June (2017), the CBO said GDP growth for 2018 would be just 2%. Now it figures growth will be 3.3%—a significant upward revision. It also boosted its forecast for 2019 from a meager 1.5% to a respectable 2.4%.*
>
> *"Underlying economic conditions have improved in some unexpected ways since June," the CBO says. Unexpected to the CBO, perhaps, but not to those of us who understood that Trump's tax cuts and deregulatory efforts would boosts growth.*[3]

Economists agree too.

The *Wall Street Journal* polled a number of business, financial, and academic economists in January 2018 on who was more responsible for the current economy, most of which "suggested Mr. Trump's election deserves at least some credit" for the upturn. Additionally, a majority said the president had been "somewhat" or "strongly" positive for job creation, GDP growth, and the rising stock market.[4]

To further debunk the myth that Obama is responsible for Trump's economy, Kevin Hassett, the chairman of Trump's Counsel of Economic Advisors, came out swinging. "One of the hypotheses that's been floating around about the economy lately is that the strong economy that we are seeing is just a continuation of recent trends. You know, since we are the nerds of the White House, we decided this was a testable hypothesis," Hassett said in a speech at a White House press briefing.

He then unveiled a series of charts showcasing a whole host of economic indicators, including small business optimism, nonresidential fixed investment, capital spending, durable goods orders, purchasing manager index, and new business creation. To test the hypothesis, Hassett said they looked at recent trends until Trump was elected and how those economic trends were expected to play out according to baseline. Then he compared how those trends performed in reality since Trump took office.

As for the findings, entrepreneurship is great again, with over one hundred fifty thousand more business applications being filed each quarter *over trend*. That isn't to say that there are one hundred fifty thousand new business applications being filed every quarter—it means there are one hundred fifty thousand more than projected being filed had they been filed at the same pace as under Obama.

Investment in small businesses is $300 billion higher than we would've seen had the trend Obama set continued. Before the election, only 10 percent of small business owners said that now would be a good time to expand—which tripled under Trump. Orders of capital goods (indicating future investment) were declining prior to the election but immediately rebounded. Blue-collar employment would've declined had it continued its prior trend. Instead, it's grown and broken that trend Obama set. Blue-collar employment is growing at the fastest rate since 1984.[5]

And as the economy booms, not only are the unemployed finding work, those who previously gave up looking for work are reentering the labor force. As they enter the labor force, they're easily finding jobs since there are more job openings today than unemployed people.[6]

Economically speaking, Barack Obama was one of our worst presidents, so it remains a mystery how the strongest economy since World War II could possibly be attributable to him. Who knows—maybe George W. Bush is to thank!

Did the Stimulus Work?

Is former president Barack Obama to thank for pulling us out of the worst financial crisis since the Great Depression? His trillion-dollar stimulus generated plenty of debate, and there's no question that we did rebound from recession under his administration, but how connected are the two, and how does his recovery compare to others in history?

It should've been a red flag to most economists when the Obama administration began inventing new economic terms to measure the stimulus's alleged success, such as how many jobs were being "saved or created" by it. Obama told us not long after passing the stimulus that it had created or saved one hundred fifty thousand jobs in June and would save or create another six hundred thousand by September.[1] How does one measure a "saved" job? Simple: create a baseline prediction (for example: predict the economy will lose a million jobs next month), and then if the economy were to only lose two hundred thousand jobs, Obama could claim he "saved" eight hundred thousand jobs. How convenient!

It's never a vote of confidence when the statistics are being tortured to prove a point, and when measured using conventional (i.e., real) statistics, the stimulus didn't live up to Obama's own hype.

The Stimulus Didn't Meet the Obama Administration's Own Predictions

Prior to passing the stimulus to find out what's in it (wrong bill, I know), the Obama administration predicted the unemployment rate would never top 8 percent with the stimulus passed. But in absence of the stimulus,

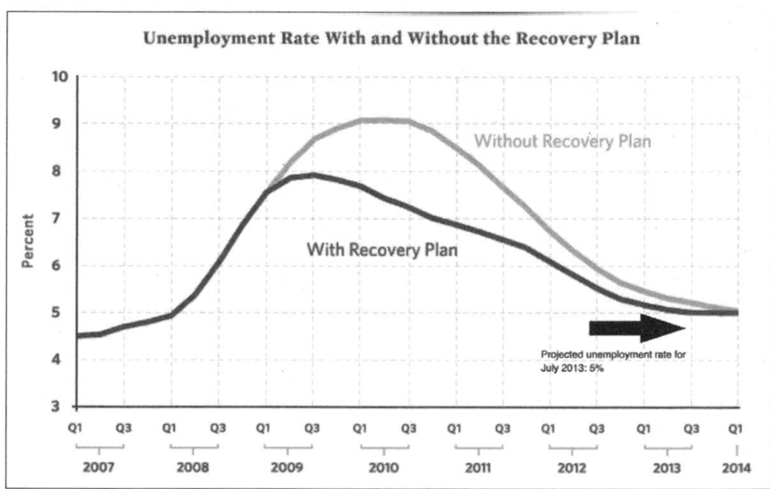

Source: White House

we were warned that unemployment would exceed 9 percent. Above are those projections graphically.[2]

Paul Krugman posted the graph to his blog in early January 2009, asking stimulus skeptics "is this enough?" to satisfy their doubts. "Kudos, by the way, to the administration-in-waiting for providing this—it will be a joy to argue policy with an administration that provides comprehensible, honest reports, not case studies in how to lie with statistics,"[3] Krugman added to yet another comment rendered hilarious by hindsight.

And now that enough time has passed to do a full comparison, here's what really happened (see chart next page):[4]

Not only did unemployment crack 8 percent, 9 percent, and 10 percent, the actual unemployment rate peaked higher than the worst-case unemployment rate that was predicted we'd suffer *without* the stimulus.

And if that wasn't bad enough…

Despite Failing, the Real Unemployment Rate Was Still Higher Than Reported

Despite unemployment being higher than Obama predicted it would be in absence of the stimulus, the true rate was still masked in large part

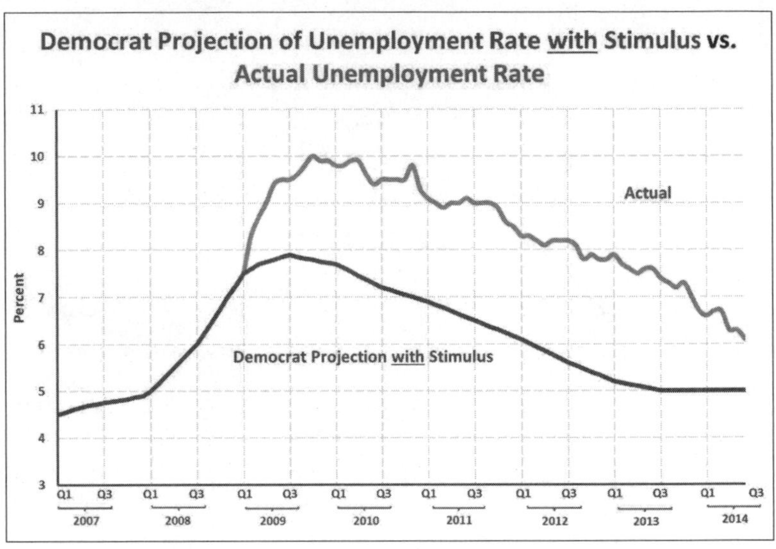

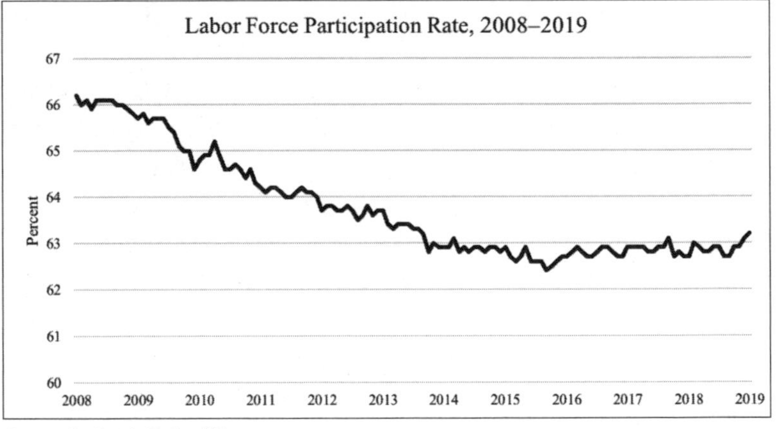

Source: St. Louis Federal Reserve

because the labor force participation rate declined under Obama. A person is only counted as unemployed if they're out of work and currently looking for work. But if an unemployed worker simply gives up looking, they're no longer counted as "unemployed" in the statistics, even though their situation remains unchanged.[5]

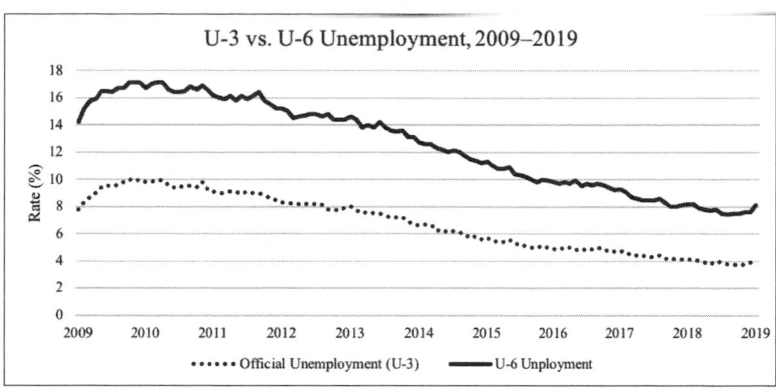

Source: St. Louis Federal Reserve

The headline unemployment rate you often see is the U-3 unemployment rate, which is simply the number of unemployed individuals as a percentage of the total labor force. A similar alternative measure, the U-6 unemployment rate, includes discouraged workers in the unemployment statistics, and you can see what a difference that makes charted.[6]

From Obama taking office to his departure, the number of Americans employed rose by 9.9 million—compared to 14.6 million who left the labor force. In other words, nearly 50 percent more left the labor force than became employed.[7] The labor force participation rate of those aged sixty-five and older increased during the Obama years, meaning this shrinkage in the labor force under his watch cannot be simply attributed to people leaving the labor force by retiring.[8]

The Speed of the Recovery

The fact that the economy recovered under Obama doesn't say much because all economies go through cycles. What is notable is the glacial pace at which the economy recovered. As Rex Sinquefield noted in *Forbes* magazine:

> *The Obama recovery of the last seven years remains the worst in postwar American history. Average GDP growth since the bottom of the recession in 2009 was barely above 2.1 percent per year. The average since 1949 is well above 4 percent per year during the previous 10 expansions.*[9]

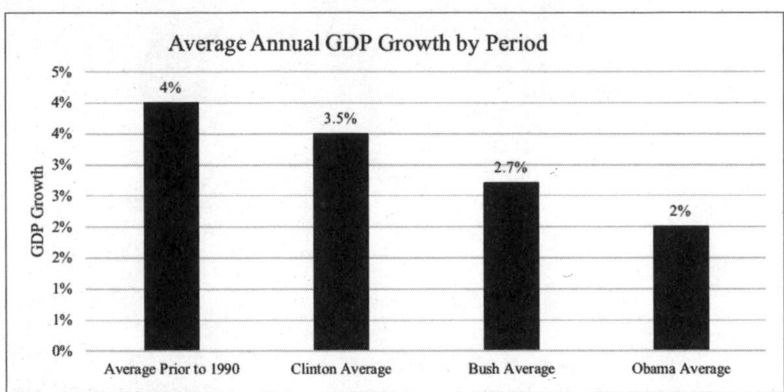

Source: CNN Business[10]

Had Obama's recovery kept pace with historical averages, incomes would've been 20 percent higher at the end his presidency than they were.[11]

How's that for a recovery?

Is Obama to Thank for the Trump Stock Market Surge?

Anyone who has checked their retirement accounts since Donald Trump's presidential victory already knows that the market went on a historic tear following the 2016 election, which continued uninterrupted throughout the following year. Even despite the turbulence of 2018, investors still came out massively ahead of where they were in November 2016.

Praise Be to Trump–or Obama?

The most common claim is that this current bull run has nothing to do with Donald Trump and is rather an extension of a run that began under Obama. In other words, we're supposed to believe that Trump was passed the baton and just ran the final one hundred meters. There is some element of truth to the claim in that the bull run did indeed begin under Obama, and by August 22, 2018, Trump had allowed it to become the longest bull run in American history.[1] To revisit the track-race analogy, while Trump is continuing a bull market, his final one hundred meters are outperforming the first three hundred.

As evidence to support their criticism of Trump's market performance, some critics (such as Paul Krugman) point to how European stock performance in 2017 mostly paralleled that of US markets. "Sure the markets surged in 2017" the argument goes, "but it was just part of a global economic recovery."

Paul Krugman tweeted that "since Trump seems to have decided that stocks are proof of his success, here's US verses euro stocks over the past year."[2] He tweeted a chart showing the performance of the Euro Stoxx 50 (an index of European stocks) closing out the year up 17.73 percent, close to the S&P 500 Index, which was up a higher but close 18.94 percent. Krugman's time frame on his chart was from October 2016 to October 2017.

Below is a similar chart comparing the S&P 500 to a Blackrock fund that tracks the EAFE (an index of developed market stocks, most of which are European). The date range is January 1, 2017, to December 31, 2017, and more or less paints an identical picture to Krugman's chart. It shows the EAFE rising 21 percent to the S&P's 19.4 percent. Both the S&P and EAFE pay roughly a 2 percent dividend, so that doesn't change the math in either direction.

As any finance undergrad would understand, however, this is hardly a slam dunk for Trump's critics.[3]

A Nobel laureate like Krugman really ought to know better when making such a claim because he's not accounting for how the value of the US dollar impacts foreign stock prices for domestic investors. For an American investor, the underlying assets in the index Krugman is citing are quoted in whatever domestic currency those companies reside in (so a British company's stock price would be quoted

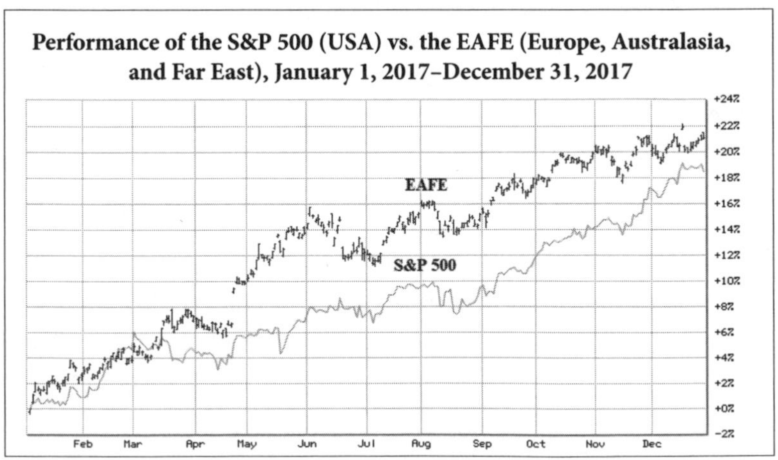

Performance of the S&P 500 (USA) vs. the EAFE (Europe, Australasia, and Far East), January 1, 2017–December 31, 2017

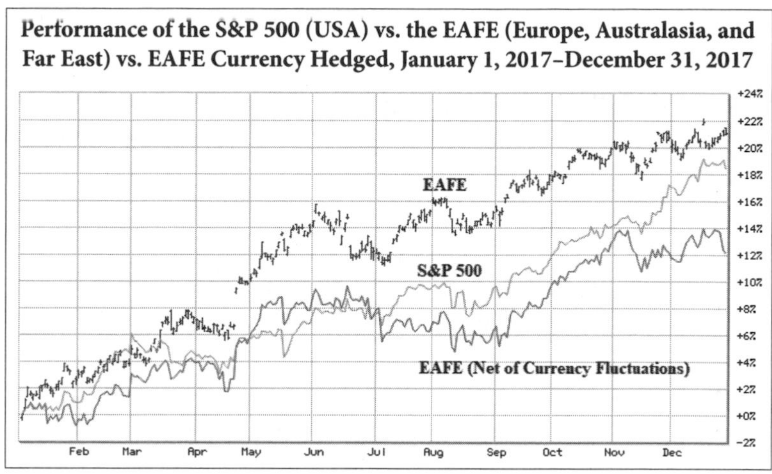

Performance of the S&P 500 (USA) vs. the EAFE (Europe, Australasia, and Far East) vs. EAFE Currency Hedged, January 1, 2017–December 31, 2017

in pounds, for instance). The value of foreign stocks to an American investor therefore *increase* when the relative value of a dollar *decreases*, as their foreign stocks (quoted in that foreign currency) will be worth more in terms of US dollars.

This is relevant because the US dollar declined 10 percent in 2017 (12.4 percent against the euro in particular), meaning that the foreign funds returns that Krugman is drawing attention to are significantly higher than they should be.[4]

This can be quantified and shown graphically because Blackrock also offers a "currency hedged" version of its EAFE fund (meaning it's not impacted by the dollar's fluctuations), and that one has lagged the S&P 500 massively, rising only 12.5 percent over the same period.

Furthermore, US stocks and international stocks completely diverged early into 2018. US markets were up between 5–7 percent halfway into the year, while international stocks were down by the same amount, on average. Though US markets did end up closing out 2018 at a loss, they still outperformed foreign markets (which lost even more value).

Hilariously Bad Pundit Predictions

In the face of those lecturing us about the "truth" about Trump's stock market, you must remember just how bad the predictions of Trump's market critics have been. On the night of the election, stock futures declined as it became evident that Trump would win the presidency, briefly confirming the fears of the Chicken Littles among us. Krugman famously wrote that night, "It really does now look like President Donald J. Trump, and markets are plunging. When might we expect them to recover?... If the question is when markets will recover, a first-pass answer is never."[5]

Nailed it.

Within days of Trump's victory the market began to roar, which should've silenced critics, but not CNN. "The big surge on November 7 snapped a nine-day losing streak for stocks that many attributed to Donald Trump's newfound momentum" columnist Paul R. La Monica wrote on November 14.[6] But, he warned, "several market strategists expressed concerns that the market is underestimating the possibility of Trump rattling the markets during his time in office." Another supposed threat to the markets? Trump's stance on immigration. "Trump's anti-immigration stance could also be a big problem for U.S. tech companies, which have attracted a lot of talented foreign workers due to the H1-B visa program. Will Trump seek to end that?" Ironically, technology stocks outperformed the market as a whole in 2017 and 2018.

La Monica concluded, "Now this isn't to say that the market definitely is due for a crash during the Trump administration. But experts think investors may now need to take a step back and remember that there still isn't a lot that the market knows about possible Trump policies."

The market knows a lot now—and it certainly likes what it sees.

US Outperformed International Markets Despite Declining in 2018

Volatility returned to the markets in 2018, with the Dow and S&P closing down 6 and 7 percent, respectively. Or as CNN put it, "2018 was the worst for stocks in 10 years."[7]

And they're right—but if we're to compare the US to the rest of the world, we again massively outperformed simply by not performing worse.[8]

2018 Global Equity Returns	
Country	% Return (Nominal)
Brazil	-0.5%
Russia	-0.7%
USA	-5.0%
Israel	-5.5%
Thailand	-5.5%
Malaysia	-6%
India	-7.3%
Norway	-8.6%
Taiwan	-8.9%
Switzerland	-9.1%
Indonesia	-9.2%
Singapore	-9.4%
Columbia	-11.5%
Australia	-12%
France	-12.8%
Poland	-12.9%
Japan	-12.9%
Sweden	-13.7%
United Kingdom	-14.2%
Nigeria	-14.3%
Denmark	-15.4%
Mexico	-15.5%
Spain	-16.2%
Canada	-17.2%
Italy	-17.8%
China	-18.9%
Chile	-19.7%
Germany	-22.2%
Ireland	-25.3%
Belgium	-26.9%
Austria	-27.4%
Greece	-36.8%
Turkey	-41.4%
Argentina	-50.8%

Source: MSCI

When only two countries in the entire world performed better than the US (and only performed better by performing “less poorly”), our “worst year in a decade” doesn’t look quite so bad after all.

Did Obama Deport More Illegal Aliens than Trump?

Has the number of deportations fallen off a cliff since President Donald Trump took office? You couldn't be faulted if you come to such a conclusion when the entire mainstream media seems to have bought the claim at face value, hook, line, and sinker, reporting that "Obama deported more people than Trump." *Bloomberg*, *Politico*, *The Economist*, NPR, and countless others have all reported on some variant of the claim.

To quote from a *Bloomberg* article published at the end of 2017, "President Donald Trump sent 26 percent fewer Mexicans back home this year through November than Barack Obama did in the same period in 2016."[1] Put numerically, one hundred fifty-two thousand Mexican nationals were deported from the US between January and November of 2017 (the statistics were released late December, hence ending the measurement in November). By contrast, there were two hundred five thousand deportations of Mexican nationals during the first eleven months of 2016. Note that the claim is only including Mexican illegal immigrants (which are half of all illegals).

I don't understand why some liberals think this claim is a slam dunk. Aren't they the ones against mass deportation? You'd think a drop in deportations would make liberal observers happy, but instead it's become an attack on Trump's supposed incompetence in enforcing a key tenant of his presidential platform.

The *Bloomberg* article does include this minor disclaimer, however, that "the decrease in removal numbers overall compared to fiscal year 2016 was primarily due to about 17 percent fewer migrants apprehended at the border." Apprehensions at the border fell to the lowest level since 1971 during Trump's first year in office, according to data from the US Border Patrol.[2]

In other words, because of Trump's rhetoric, fewer prospective illegals even bothered to approach the border in the first place (mainly due to Trump's strict rhetoric on immigration and beefing up the Border Patrol's budget). And here's the thing: Obama massively inflated "deportation" figures by counting "catch and releases" at the border as "deportations." As the *Los Angeles Times* revealed in 2014:

> *A closer examination shows that immigrants living illegally in most of the continental U.S. are less likely to be deported today than before Obama came to office, according to immigration data. Expulsions of people who are settled and working in the United States have fallen steadily since his first year in office and are down more than 40% since 2009 (through 2013).*[3]

And yet if you look at the Department of Homeland Security's deportation numbers during the same period (2009–2013) and took them at face value, you'd believe that deportations increased by roughly 11 percent.[4] Why? Because "on the other side of the ledger, the number of

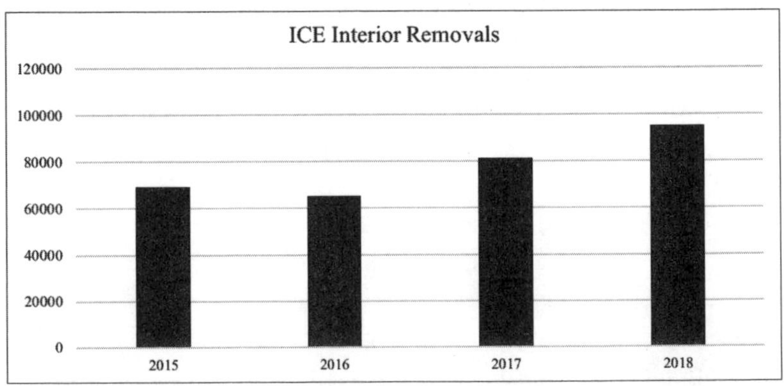

Source: ICE

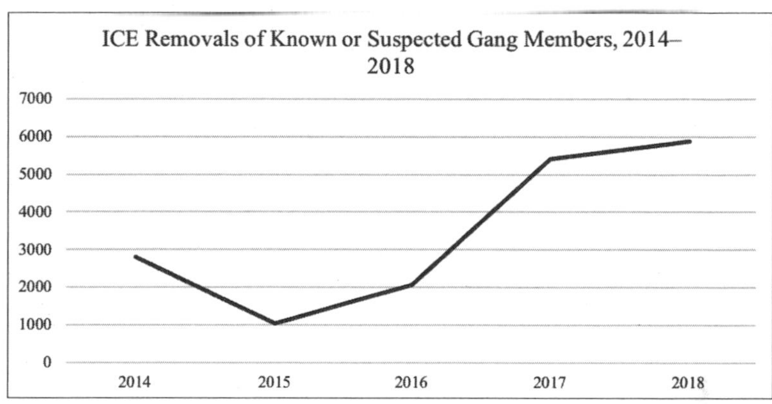

Source: ICE

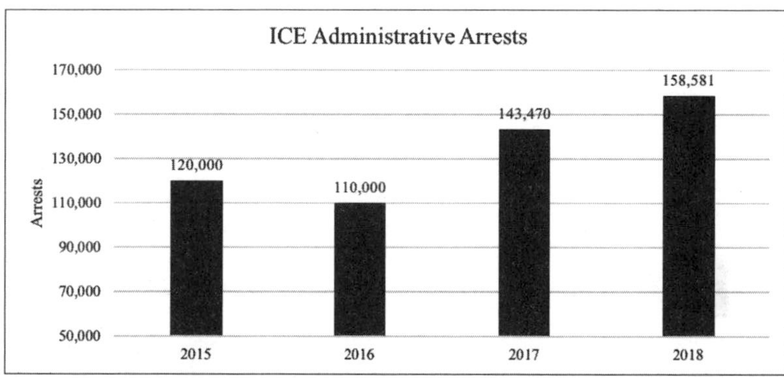

Source: ICE

people deported at or near the border has gone up—primarily as a result of changing who gets counted in the U.S. Immigration and Customs Enforcement agency's deportation statistics." Measuring deportations excluding those at the border, there was unquestionably an increase in deportations in 2017 (and then 2018).[5] Most of these "interior removals" are of illegals with a criminal record.[6]

Arrests of illegal immigrants (particularly criminal illegal immigrants) have surged, even though they had not been deported at the time the statistics were recorded.[7]

Absent redefining what a "deportation" is, deportations are indeed up in the administration that made combating illegal immigration a central part of its campaign platform.

No surprise there.

Has Trump "Foxified" the White House?

According to the *Washington Post*, the "Trump White House" is now the "Fox News White House." After former Fox News anchor Heather Nauert was selected by President Donald Trump to replace Nikki Haley as UN ambassador, *Post* columnist Philip Bump decried the "Foxification" of the White House.[1]

And Trump has indeed hired plenty of Fox News talent.

Former Fox News employees who work (or worked) for the Trump administration include National Security Adviser John Bolton, Trump legal team member Joseph E. diGenova, Director of Strategic Communications Mercedes Schlapp, former Deputy National Security Adviser K. T. McFarland, Assistant Secretary for Public Affairs for the Treasury Tony Sayegh, Communications Advisor Bill Shine, and almost Heather Nauert (who would withdraw her consideration). The only other network journalist Trump has hired was CNBC's Larry Kudlow.

Without any context for those six FNC hires, the *Washington Post*'s criticism is meaningless. After all, how many journalists did Barack Obama hire? The answer is nearly three times as many, and ironically, it was another writer at the *Washington Post* (Paul Farhi) who called foul on Obama's massive hiring of left-wing journalists back in 2013 following the hiring of *Time*'s Richard Stengel.

Although Farhi acknowledges that it's common for presidents to hire members of the press, he expressed concern at the time, because "Obama may be different in terms of the sheer number of ink-stained wretches and other news-media denizens that he has attracted." More specifically: "The pattern of Obama hires has periodically aroused suspicions about the media's allegedly cozy relationship with the president."[2]

As one may have noticed, Trump lacks such a cozy relationship with the press.

Obama hired at least twenty-three journalists, and hilariously, hired nearly as many solely from the *Washington Post* as Trump has hired exclusively from Fox. The list includes:[3]

- US Ambassador Samantha Power (*US News & World Report, Boston Globe, New Republic*)
- Speechwriter Desson Thomson (*Washington Post* movie critic and Clinton speechwriter)
- John Kerry staffer Glen Johnson (*Boston Globe* editor)
- Assistant Secretary of State for Public Affairs Douglas Frantz (*Los Angeles Times, New York Times*, and *Washington Post*)
- Press Secretary Jay Carney (*Time* magazine)
- State Department Undersecretary Richard Stengel (*Time* magazine managing editor)
- Senior Managing Director of the Office of Public Affairs Stephen Barr (*Washington Post*)
- VP Joe Biden's communications director Shailagh Murray (*Washington Post*)
- Counselor Rosa Brooks (*Los Angeles Times*)
- Senior Communications Adviser for HHS Roberta Baskin (Center for Public Integrity
- Department of Education Deputy Assistant Secretary for Communication David Hoff (*Education Week*)
- Department of Transportation spokeswoman Sasha Johnson (CNN)

- Department of Transportation communications director Jill Zuckman (MSNBC)
- Senior Policy Strategy for Science and Technology Rick Weiss (*Washington Post*, Center for American Progress)
- Communications Director for the Office of Health Reform Linda Douglass (CBS, ABC)
- The Treasury Department's Eric Dash (*New York Times*)
- The Treasury Department's Anthony Reyes (MSNBC)
- Obama speechwriter Aneesh Raman (CNN)
- Chief of Staff to the US China ambassador Jim Sciutto (CNN)
- The EPA's Kelly Zito (*San Francisco Chronicle*)
- Susan Rice speechwriter Warren Bass (*Washington Post*)
- The Justice Department's Beverley Lumpkin (Project on Government Oversight)
- The Defense Department's Geoff Morell (ABC)

One of those on the list, ABC's Geoff Morell, began working for the Defense Department in 2007 under George W. Bush and continued working in the Obama administration, so perhaps it would be appropriate to exclude him.

Regardless, there's still at least twenty-two journalists who went to work for Obama, while Trump is under fire for hiring six from Fox (or seven if you include Kudlow). Either way, Obama hired roughly three times as many journalists as Trump has, and of course, they were all journalists who previously cozied up to the administration in their work.

The only attempt I've seen for a rebuttal to this fact came from the *Washington Post*'s Erik Wemple, who argued that Obama's hiring was different because they weren't all from one network (Fox).[4] Amusingly, Obama almost hired as many people solely from the *Washington Post* as Trump did from Fox. It should be obvious to anyone who's channel surfed before that the reason Trump's journalist hires are from Fox is because there aren't any other mainstream right-wing networks to choose journalists from. You would think Wemple would be aware of that, given he's employed in a field (journalism) where only 7 percent of people are Republicans.[5]

Did Obama Pay Iran Ransom Money?

The Obama administration sent $1.7 billion cash to the government of Iran right around the time that five American hostages/prisoners were freed by the Iranian regime on January 17, 2016—and naturally one would assume those events were connected. President Trump made such a claim while on the campaign trail (and later as president) and was widely dismissed by the media and Obama himself for the "conspiracy" theory.

The Official Line of Defense

In response to allegations of paying ransom money, the Obama administration claimed the payment was a return of money for payments (plus interest) that Iran made to the US in 1979 for military equipment it did not receive. That $400 million went into a Foreign Military Sales trust fund, and that remained untouched since Jimmy Carter froze Iran's assets in 1979.

Obama personally stated in August 2016 that "we do not pay ransom. We didn't here, and we won't in the future." He went further, claiming that the payment was completely unrelated. "We announced these payments in January. Many months ago. They were not a secret," Obama said. "It wasn't a secret. We were completely open with everybody about it." John Kerry also denied that the payment and freed hostages were related.[1]

In summary, Obama's defense is that the cash payment was owed to Iran regardless ($400 million plus $1.3 billion in interest), so the freed prisoners are completely unconnected.

How well does that defense hold up?

The Fact that Payment Was in Cash Proves the Events Are Connected

Shady transactions have a tendency to be done in cash, and there's no exception here.

Paying Iran in cash makes no sense, and the explanation of former Obama Treasury Department official Paul Ahern makes even less sense. During congressional testimony about the payments, he claimed that "cash was the most reliable way to ensure Iran received the funds in a timely manner, and it was the method preferred by the relevant central banks."[2] The supposed logic here is that a wire transfer could be hard to make as there could be difficulties finding a global bank willing to complete such a transaction.

That apparently wasn't a concern back in 2015 on no fewer than two occasions.[3] In July of that year, when the US and Iran announced the nuclear agreement, the US paid Iran $948,000 through wire to settle an old claim over "architectural drawings and fossils." And again in April, the US wired Iran another $9 million to remove thirty-two metric tons of heavy water (which can help in the production of nuclear weapons).

So why is it relevant that Iran was paid in cash rather than a wire? Control.

Former Obama State Department official John Kirby openly admitted that the US held on to the initial $400 million cash payment until the American prisoners were far away from Iran to "retain maximum leverage" in the situation. Kirby denies that the payment could in any way be called a ransom payment, but he admitted that the payments were in exchange for them.[4] I'm unsure what kind of mental gymnastics Kirby is performing, but his statements are in direct conflict with Obama and Kerry's claim that the payment had no connection to the prisoners whatsoever.

The Payment Is Still Ransom—Even Though It Was Legitimately Owed to Iran Since 1979

During the time of the nuclear talks, the governments of the US and Iran were negotiating other random unrelated past grievances while they finally were at the table with one another. At least $400 million was owed to Iran (plus interest), and that longstanding dispute was settled in exchange for five hostages. The fact that this debt already existed does not change the fact that it was settled in a ransom-like scenario where an exchange for that debt was made. If you owed someone money and they kidnapped one of your loved ones and demanded a ransom equal to the amount they're owed, does it magically not become ransom? Of course not.

If this payment wasn't ransom, the US likely would've gone through a negotiating process to only pay Iran net of the $400 million in claims we have against Iran for violations of the "Victims of Trafficking and Violence Prevention Act."[5] And if there was no ransom, why the lying from Ahern, Obama, and Kerry?

Backing up my interpretation of events is the Iranian government acknowledging as much.

Iran Literally Calls the Payments Ransom

A month after the cash delivery, a state-run Iranian TV channel ran a thirteen-minute mini-documentary called "Rules of the Game," in which a narrator describes a "cash for hostages" deal with America.[6]

"The Iranians had a costly proposal for the swap: the release of seven Iranians imprisoned in America, 1.7 billion dollars, and clearance of the names of sixteen Iranians who, on the pretext of violating oppressive sanctions, had been placed on a list of those facing criminal prosecution in America," the narrator says. "But this was not all that Iran wanted. The removal of Bank Sepah from the sanctions list was also added to Iran's demands. All of this in exchange for the freedom of only four American nationals: a win-lose transaction in favor of the Islamic Republic of Iran and to the detriment of the American government."

Well, they got that right.

The narrator also boasts that the payment leaves Obama vulnerable to a Republican backlash if anyone found out about the exchange.

It looks like they got that right too.

A Caravan of Myths About Obamacare's "Repeal"

In passing his historic tax overhaul at the end of 2017, President Donald Trump included rules that ripped the heart out of Obamacare by repealing the individual mandate, which previously fined individuals who didn't purchase health insurance. "We have essentially repealed Obamacare," Trump said after the tax bill passed.

Health care is the number one issue that Democrats campaigned on in the 2018 midterms, so it's worth clarifying some myths about Trump and Obamacare given that they'll resurface again in 2020. Despite fear-mongering from liberals and Trump's claim that he "essentially repealed" Obamacare, Trump only repealed a single (albeit major) component of Obamacare: the individual mandate. That was the least-popular aspect of the law, and more popular components such as the Medicare expansion and the provision allowing young adults to stay on their parents' insurance until age twenty-six remained in effect.

That said, the alleged benefits of Obamacare have all been oversold, just as the consequences of its partial repeal have been exaggerated.

Obamacare Didn't Reduce Health Care Costs

The debate over the effects of repealing Obamacare (in part or full) overlooks the fact that Obamacare failed to live up to its promise of reducing health care costs. "I will sign a universal health care bill into law by the

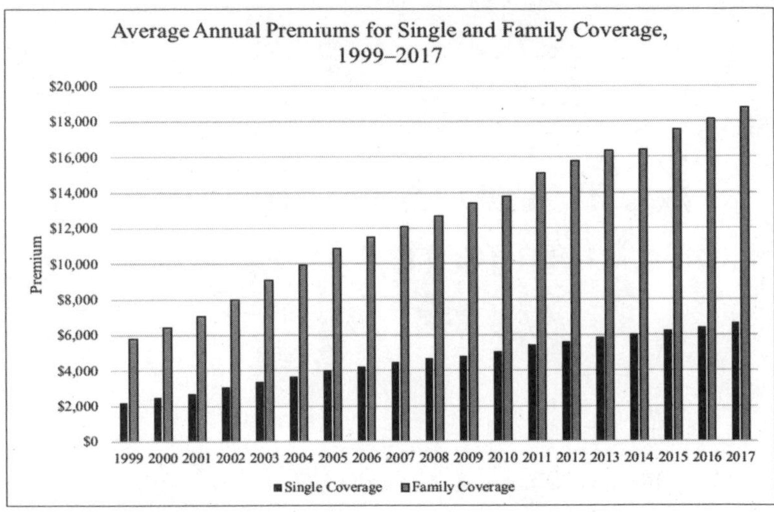

Source: Kaiser Family Foundation

end of my first term as president that will cover every American and cut the cost of a typical family's premium by up to $2,500 a year," Obama promised while out on the campaign trail in 2007.[1]

Clearly that did not happen. The average family coverage plan cost $16,351 in 2014 (the year Obamacare fully took effect) and rose to $18,764 by 2017 (a year in which the law was still in full effect despite Trump's presidency).[2]

Private Obamacare Insurance Is Glorified Catastrophic Insurance

Those who receive insurance through Obamacare exchanges are essentially covered with the equivalent of a catastrophic health care plan, as the deductibles render their insurance "insurance in name only" for most. The average "silver plan" has a $3,937 deductible, and "bronze plans" $5,873. Overall, the average deductible is roughly $4,000. Most purchase silver plans, which cover 70 percent of health expenses.[3]

Most Were Insured Through Medicaid

Has Obamacare succeeded in reducing the number of uninsured? Yes—but mostly through a program that's over a half-century old. To give some context on the pre-Obamacare statistics, at the beginning of 2008, a *Gallup* poll found that 14.6 percent of Americans did not have health insurance coverage. The uninsured rate rose to an all-time high of 18 percent in 2013 after Obamacare was passed but before people were required to have insurance.[4] That rate declined to 8.8 percent by 2017 (with 28.5 million uninsured), which was virtually unchanged from 2016.[5]

It must be noted that all statistics are inflated because illegal aliens are counted in population statistics (and thus drive up the uninsured rates). A Center for Immigration Studies study found that illegals accounted for roughly one in seven people without insurance in 2006. If that figure holds, the adjusted uninsured rates would be 12.5 percent in 2008, 15.4 percent in 2013, and 7.5 percent in 2017.[6]

Obamacare did indeed reduce the percentage of people uninsured, though nearly all the newly insured were insured by parts of the law that Trump did not touch.

The Department of Health and Human Services released a report at the end of 2016 claiming that twenty million were newly insured as a result of Obamacare (leading to the inevitable untrue headlines that twenty million would lose insurance without Obamacare). Of that twenty million, 5.8 million were insured through the subsidized individual market (through Obamacare exchanges), 2.3 million from the provision allowing young adults to stay on their parents' health plans until age twenty-six, and the remaining 11.9 million were insured through the Medicaid expansion.[7]

Still, the twenty million figure is an overstatement. Nearly five million of those now insured through Medicaid were already eligible for it before Obamacare, and some percentage of the 2.3 million who remained on their parents' plans would've otherwise purchased their own private plans.

If Trump were to take action to shut down the remaining Obamacare exchanges, that would simply be speeding up the inevitable, as nearly all exchanges have already failed. Only four Obamacare exchanges remain in 2018 after nineteen have failed.[8]

Surprisingly, insuring people through Medicare is cheaper than through Obama's faux-private insurance. Figures from the Congressional Budget Office show they plan to spend an average of $6,300 on each individual who purchases subsidized health insurance through Obamacare's exchanges in 2018. However, they're set to spend "only" roughly $4,900 for each Medicaid recipient who enrolled.[9] In other words, it would've been simpler and more cost-effective for Obama to have simply expanded an existing public health care program than to implement Obamacare.

Trump's Actions Can't "Take Away" Anyone's Health Care

Despite any hysterical rhetoric you've seen, there is no grand scheme to "take away" anyone's health care, and nothing Trump has done has come close to doing so.

You can only lose insurance through Trump's individual mandate repeal voluntarily if you stop purchasing insurance in absence of the penalty. Interestingly enough, there seems to be an ideological divide evident in those voluntarily ceasing to purchase insurance. Over the past two years, the uninsured rate among Republicans rose from 7.9 percent to 13.9 percent while it remained flat among Democrats at 9.1 percent.[10]

The Individual Mandate Repeal Saved Affected Families a Fortune

The fee for Obamacare's individual mandate, officially called the "Shared Responsibility Payment," charged those who didn't purchase insurance the higher of:

- 2.5 percent of a household's total income
- $695 per adult and $347.50 per child under 18, up to a maximum of $2,085, increasing every year by the rate of inflation
- 70 percent of households pay the penalty of $695 per uninsured adult and $347.50 per uninsured child because that's higher than 2.5 percent of their income[11]

While the purpose of the mandate and associated penalties is to incentivize people to purchase insurance, there are millions of people stuck in the middle who can't afford private insurance but aren't eligible for Medicaid, and then must pay a fine on top of that.

Assuming 3 percent inflation over a forty-seven-year period, the individual mandate would've cost most households affected $209,300 over their lifetimes.

Obamacare's "Repeal" Is Not Killing Forty Thousand-Plus People Per Year

Liberals have made it very clear they think a catastrophe would immediately occur if Obamacare were fully repealed (as opposed to the individual mandate repeal we got).

"Repealing the Affordable Care Act will kill more than 43,000 people annually" reported the *Washington Post*.[12] "Nearly 36,000 people could die every year" in absence of Obamacare, cautioned the far-left Think Progress.[13] Meanwhile, Bernie Sanders informed us that "when you throw twenty-three million people off of health insurance—people with cancer, people with heart disease, people with diabetes—thousands of people will die…there is study after study making this point."

Coming to those figures is relatively simple—just estimate differences in mortality between the insured and uninsured, and then multiply the difference by the number of expected newly uninsured. It's common sense, but it doesn't account for the fact that there's insurance, and then there's Obamacare insurance.

But first, let's consider the sources of the claims.

- The study that concluded with the "43,000 deaths" figure compared mortality in states that expanded Medicaid in the early 2000s and didn't estimate the health benefits of Medicaid (as most of those insured by Obamacare were insured by the Medicaid expansion). This study was conducted in part by David Himmelstein, founder of Physicians for a National Health Program.
- The "36,000 deaths" figure is from a *Think Progress* study that compared morality rates in Massachusetts before and after the enactment of Romneycare, on which Obamacare is based.

So what's wrong with the studies?

- The entire premise of the Himmelstein study is working under the assumption that Medicaid improves health outcomes—as it appeared to in the data from the early 2000s he's relying on. However, many studies dispute this. Most notable is the famous "Oregon Medicaid health experiment" that analyzed the 2008 Medicaid expansion in the state. The study concluded that Medicaid has "no statistically significant impact on physical health measures." The main benefit to recipients is that Medicaid acts as a financial cushion.[14]
- The *Think Progress* study assumes that thirty million people would lose coverage if Obamacare were repealed. In other words, the study assumes that roughly twice as many people would lose coverage than gained coverage as a result of Obamacare initially. Additionally, Massachusetts has among the highest quality medical care in the nation, so the state is an outlier in regard to health outcomes.[15]

But who cares what two studies say when they're in light of the objective fact that mortality rates have *increased* since the enactment of Obamacare? If you look at the death rate after excluding all external causes (such as drugs, alcohol, murder, suicide—anything where medical

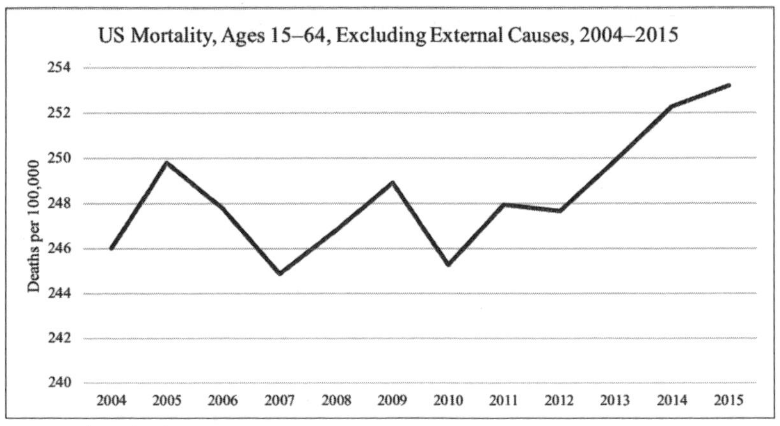

Source: The Federalist

intervention would be impossible), it increased from a rate of 247.4 per one hundred thousand people from 2004–2013, to 252.9 in 2014–2015.[16]

If we were to round up Himmelstein's study to forty-five thousand deaths, we'd expect the death rate to have dropped to 238 per one hundred thousand. Clearly, liberals are designing their studies about as well as their health care systems.

Obama Takes Credit for an Oil Production Boom He Did Everything to Prevent

It's ironic that after spending the entirety of his presidency blaming the state of the economy on George W. Bush, Barack Obama is finally taking credit for an economic boom once he's left. In light of oil prices recently tanking from $80 a barrel to around $50 (after rising earlier in the year [2018]), Obama tooted his own horn once again. Speaking at the Baker Institute for Public Policy in Houston, Texas, Obama said:

> *I was extraordinarily proud of the Paris Accords because, look I know we're in oil country and we need American energy. And by the way, American energy production, you wouldn't always know it, but it went up every year I was president. And you know that whole suddenly America's like the biggest oil producer...that was me, people.*[1]

But was it really? As president, Obama could directly control the levels of oil production on federal land but could only influence private oil production through regulation (or by failing to approve projects, including the Keystone XL pipeline). As is always the case in politics, Obama's claim is one that's "technically true" (that oil production rose under his presidency)[2] but extremely misleading (because it had nothing to do with him).

As is visible on the chart, US crude production soared over 50 percent since Trump took office.

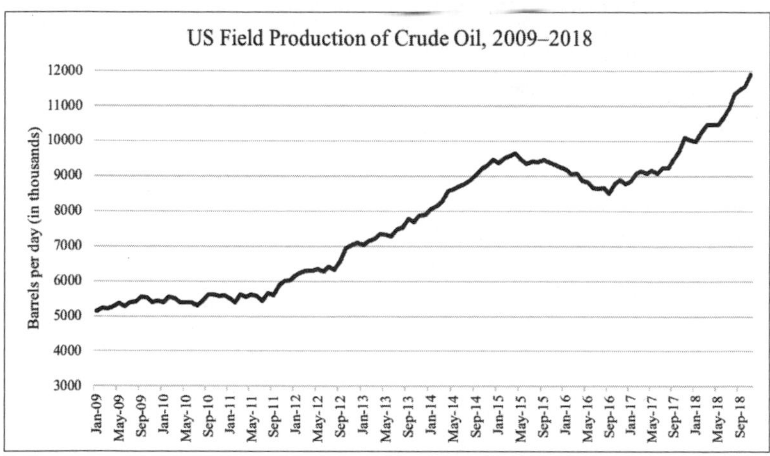

Source: US Energy Information Administration

Oil Production on Federal Land Tanked

As Obama exited office, domestic crude oil production had seen the largest nominal increase under any presidency, but where the growth in production occurred dispels any claim Obama can take credit for it.[3]

The figures through 2016 from the Bureau of Land Management (BLM) tell a story of rising oil production on private land and bottlenecked production on federal land. According to an analysis of the numbers from the Western Energy Alliance, major indicators of federal onshore and natural gas operations declined, including the number of leases, acres leased, permits approved, and wells being drilled.[4]

As a result, while private oil production increased 108 percent from 2009 to 2017, it increased less than 20 percent on federal lands. Though Obama was speaking about oil instead of natural gas, that energy source too suffered a massive decline in production on federal land.[5]

Oil and gas production on federal land is still far below their historical averages. Due to regulations passed under the Obama administration, the amount of time it takes the BLM to process a permit increased nearly 20 percent under Obama from 205 days to 242 days.[6]

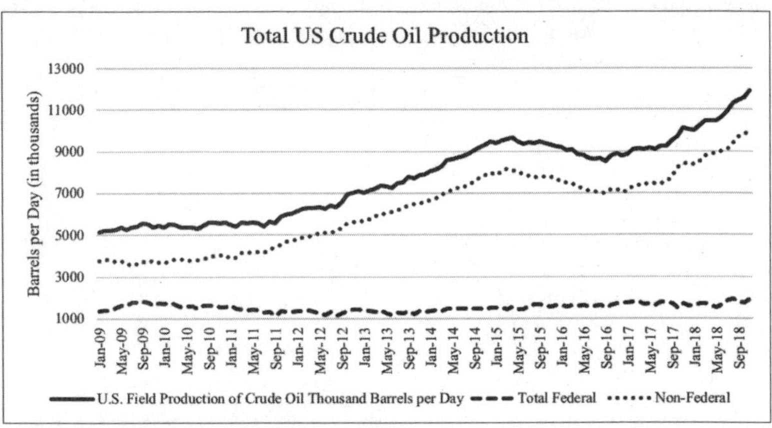

Source: US Energy Information Administration

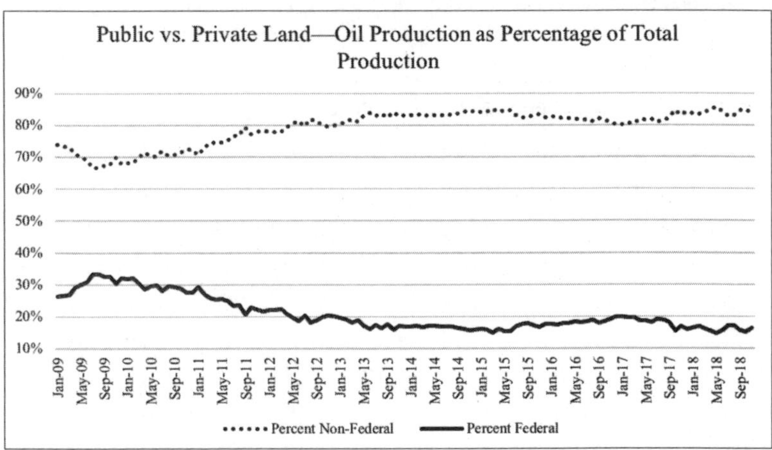

Source: US Energy Information Administration

The Energy Information Administration (EIA) Credits Technology, Not Obama, for the Oil Boom

The EIA credits technological improvements in drilling for oil, not Obama, for the increase in production. "U.S. crude oil production has increased significantly over the past 10 years, driven mainly by production from tight rock formations using horizontal drilling and hydraulic fracturing," according to the EIA.[7]

Obama released regulations in 2015 to reduce fracking on federal land, which Trump later shredded.[8]

What About When Oil Prices Fell Under Obama in 2015?

Oil prices suffered a rout in 2015 after beginning to teeter in late 2014, but that was a result of OPEC (primarily Saudi Arabia) starting a price war with the US. Two years into the price war, the Saudis had increased daily production from 9.75 million barrels per day to 10.5 million, bringing the price of oil below $50 and costing the Saudis themselves $525 million daily in lost revenue.[9]

It was a costly strategy attempting to crush America's shale industry but ended up only increasing the Saudis' oil market share by 1 percent after two years. It also inadvertently saved American consumers billions at the pump—but this was thanks to Saudi Arabia, not Obama.

Unlike Obama, Trump is Behind the Recent Price Drop

The recent oil price drop from $80 to $50 also can be attributed to the Saudis—but Trump can actually take credit for it.

In addition to the 50 percent surge in domestic crude production, according to CNBC, oil analysts are in agreement that Trump "hoodwinked" Saudi Arabia into pushing the global oil market into oversupply. "They got sort of tricked here," said John Kilduff, the manager of a hedge fund that specializes in energy-related investments. "The Russians and the Saudis in particular ramped up production, ramped up exports ahead of what was supposed to be severe sanctions on Iran, and when the administration gave the eight waivers to Iran's largest buyers, it undercut that whole equation," he continued.[10]

"So now we've tripped into an oversupply situation almost overnight because of the severe reaction by Russia and the Saudis to cover for Iran losses, which never materialized." The Saudis will eventually wise up and adjust output, but it's undeniable how clever Trump's move was.

Who Was Tougher on Russia—Trump or Obama?

Actions speak louder than media rhetoric, and that couldn't be truer when it comes to President Donald Trump's supposed romance with the Kremlin. It is amusing to note how randomly the left seems to create new villains, when as recently as the 2012 presidential election, showing any concern over Russia's global influence was laughable to Democrats.

A personal favorite example came from October 2012 when the Democratic Party's official Twitter account tweeted that "Romney, who calls Russia our 'No.1 geopolitical foe,' doesn't seem to realize it's the 21st century."[1] That came after a debate in which Obama said in response to Romney's criticisms of Russia that "the 1980s called" and they "want their foreign policy back."

Suddenly, not only are the Russians public enemy number one, they've supposedly been in cahoots with a Republican presidential candidate and now president. Vladimir Putin did admit that he preferred Donald Trump over Hillary Clinton in the 2016 election at the Helsinki Summit (leading some clueless liberals to cite this as "proof" of collusion), but those same liberals didn't notice (or care) that Putin also said he preferred Obama over Romney in 2012.[2]

It's not hard to see why. As the left-leaning Brookings Institution reminds us:[3]

- Obama turned a blind eye to Russia's war with Georgia in 2008.
- In 2009 Obama axed missile defense plans for Poland and the Czech Republic, which Russia interpreted as America retreating from the European continent. Russia then became more interventionist in Europe.
- Obama didn't utter a peep as Russia annexed Crimea and invaded eastern Ukraine in 2014.
- Obama ignored calls from Congress, foreign policy experts, and members of his own cabinet to provide lethal weapons to Ukraine.

Obama has also been criticized by his fellow Democrats for not doing enough in response to the alleged Russian hacking of the Democratic National Committee (which they later claimed didn't occur) or the alleged Russian hacking of Hillary Clinton's private email server (which we now know was done by the Chinese).

Perhaps Obama's biggest blunder with Russia was the failure of his attempted "Russia reset" in 2009, which began with Hillary Clinton literally traveling to Russia with a "reset button" that vaguely resembled one of those "Easy" buttons you'd see in a Staples commercial.[4] The word "reset" was misspelled on the button, and things only went downhill from there. US Ambassador to Russia Michael McFaul was the architect of the reset plan—and encouraged future administrations to not pursue the same policies that the Obama administration did.[5] Bill Clinton also deemed the attempted "reset" a failure.[6] US-Russia relations soon deteriorated following the attempted reset.

Unlike Obama, Trump hasn't been weak on Russia. Trump has said he's the "toughest on Russia," and while he's no stranger to hyperbole, there's no question that he was tougher than at least his predecessor.

Although Trump isn't shy to heap praise on Putin, you wouldn't think the two had a cozy relationship if you were to judge Trump only by the actions he's taken toward Russia as president.

- Trump did approve the sale of lethal weapons to Ukraine in December 2017.[7]

- On the annexation of Crimea, Sarah Huckabee Sanders stated, "We do not recognize Russia's attempt to annex Crimea. We agree to disagree with Russia on that front. And our Crimea sanctions against Russia will remain in place until Russia returns the peninsula to the Ukraine."[8]
- Trump has ordered missiles to be fired at Syrian military sites (after President Bashar al-Assad was accused of using chemical weapons on his own people), which have a strategic alliance with Russia. In response, Putin accused the US of "making the already catastrophic humanitarian situation in Syria even worse and bringing suffering to civilians with its strikes."[9]
- In August 2017, Trump signed into law CAATSA, the "Countering America's Adversaries Through Sanctions Act," which imposed sanctions on Iran, North Korea, and Russia. In the words of the geopolitical intelligence publisher Stratfor, "CAATSA demonstrates that the United States is more strident than ever in pushing other countries to reduce their defense and energy ties with Russia."[10]
- In March, following the poisoning of former KGB agent Sergei Skripal and his daughter (a crime believed to be committed by the Russian government), Trump expelled sixty Russian diplomats.
- In April, Trump imposed more sanctions on Russia following the indictments of thirteen Russians for "malicious cyber activities" earlier in March. Russia's stock market dropped 11 percent on the news. Shares of the Russian aluminum giant Rusal (which is the world's second-largest aluminum company) cratered 40 percent on the news.[11]

And what's the evidence that Trump has been weak on Russia? Trump saying some nice things about Putin and vice versa?

The two are respectful to one another despite politics—not because of them.

Who Was Worse Toward the Press—Trump or Obama?

When Jim Acosta's press pass was temporarily suspended by the White House, it ignited a firestorm of criticism and revived charges that President Donald Trump is at war with the media. Those in the media may want to remind themselves who exactly started that war.

While Trump's rhetoric toward the media has often been hostile, Trump hasn't interfered with journalists' actual work one iota relative to Obama.

The month before Trump took office, Pulitzer Prize-winning journalist James Risen wrote in the *New York Times* that "if Donald J. Trump decides as president to throw a whistle-blower in jail for trying to talk to a reporter, or gets the FBI to spy on a journalist, he will have one man to thank for bequeathing him such expansive power: Barack Obama."[1]

Risen would know—he fought efforts from the Department of Justice under both Obama and George W. Bush to compel him to identify sources from a 2006 book of his.

"The Most Transparent Administration in History"

The self-described "most transparent" administration in history was objectively the least.[2]

According to a report published during Obama's last year in office, his administration set a record for rejections of Freedom of Information Act

(FOIA) requests. The Obama administration either censored materials or rejected requests outright for access in a record 596,095 cases (77 percent of the time).[3] In just his last year in office alone, the Obama administration spent $36.2 million in legal fees fighting FOIA related lawsuits.

Prosecuting Journalists

Obama prosecuted more journalists under the Espionage Act than all other presidents combined. While many certainly deserved it (such as the artist formally known as Bradley Manning), are we to believe there were more acts of espionage from 2009 to 2016 than the rest of American history since the act was passed?

In total, thirteen people have been prosecuted under the Espionage Act for sharing classified information with journalists since 1945. Of those thirteen, eight were arrested while Obama was president.[4] Only one person has been prosecuted under the Espionage Act during Trump's presidency (a woman bizarrely named Reality Winner), which is entirely justified for the same reasons that Manning's charges were justified.

As Cleve R. Wootson Jr. puts it, "Trump rages about leakers. Obama quietly prosecuted them."[5]

Obama Would've Expelled Fox News If He Could've

Trump seemingly only wants a single person from the press pool expelled—Jim Acosta of CNN. Obama wanted all of Fox News gone.[6] As recently as September 2018, Obama said with a straight face that "it shouldn't be Democratic or Republican to say that we don't threaten the freedom of the press because they say things or publish stories we don't like. I complained plenty about Fox News, but you never heard me threaten to shut them down or call them enemies of the people."[7]

Obama may have not branded Fox News "enemies of the people," but he certainly treated them as if they were.

In 2009, Obama's White House intentionally excluded Chris Wallace from a round of interviews related to Obama's push for health care reform.

Later in the year, the administration attempted to block Fox reporters from interviewing pay czar Kenneth Feinberg and then lied about it. An internal White House email dated October 22, 2009, proves that the White House director of broadcast media told Treasury officials "we'd prefer if you skip Fox please."

Obama's communications director Anita Dunn publicly echoed the same sentiments at the time. "We're going to treat them [Fox News] the way we would treat an opponent. As they are undertaking a war against Barack Obama and the White House, we don't need to pretend that this is the way that legitimate news organizations behave."[8]

In 2012 Fox was excluded from a White House conference call related to the then recent attacks in Benghazi, Libya, that killed four Americans. Fox was also excluded from the CIA's briefing about the attack.

To again reference the Espionage Act, in 2012 Fox News's James Rosen (not to be confused with the aforementioned James Risen) was labeled a "criminal co-conspirator" under the Espionage Act because he used a State Department contractor as a source for a story. At least five of Rosen's phone lines were seized, and the FBI obtained a warrant to search his emails. The phone records of Rosen's parents were also seized.[9]

What's the Trumpian comparison? Calling people he doesn't like "fake news" and hurting Jim Acosta's feelings?

GUN CONTROL MYTHS

This entire section could probably be merged with "media myths," because it seems to be those in the media who talk about guns the most know the least about them.

For that reason, I've long believed that gun control opponents naturally have the upper hand in the gun control debate. You won't see anyone on our side claim a shooter was armed with an "AR-15 shotgun" (as CNN said of the Navy Yard shooter), think that the words "semiautomatic" and "automatic" are interchangeable, or think that "AR" stands for "assault rifle."

As fun as it is to poke fun at those sorts of liberals, it can hardly be all we rely on, as not every gun control advocate possesses the same lack of gun knowledge as your typical internet commenter.

Though seldom in the news cycle, you can guarantee that a gun control debate with follow for at least a week after any high-profile mass shooting. When it comes to proposing sweeping gun reform, Australia has been the left's go-to example of a country that supposedly got rid of all their guns and never saw a mass shooting again. As always seems to be the case when the media romanticizes another nation, the reality is hardly so simple, and an essay explaining the truth will dominate most of this chapter.

After debunking Australian gun control, the media's conventional wisdom that the US has the majority of the world's mass shootings is challenged, as are a half-dozen other anti-gun lies.

destroyed them. This program, the National Firearms Agreement (NFA), resulted in the stock of civilian firearms in the country being reduced by approximately 15 to 20 percent.

Did Gun Control Eliminate Australian Mass Public Shootings?

The case for Australian gun control is simple: in the eighteen years prior to the NFA (1979–1996), there were thirteen fatal mass shootings in Australia. And in the eighteen years after? Zero.

As you can see in the chart below, however, the cluster of mass shootings in 1979–1996 was something of a rarity. In fact, until 1979, the country essentially went the entire twentieth century without a single mass shooting before any significant change to their gun control laws were made.

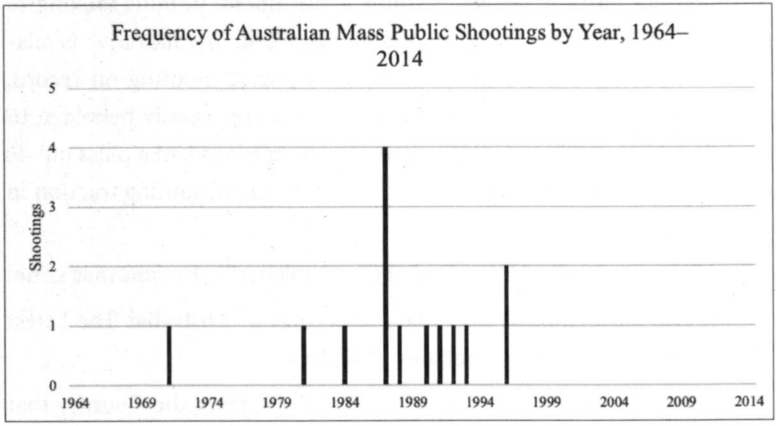

Source: The Conversation[5]

The smoking gun proving that Australia's lack of mass shootings isn't due to gun control is that most of Australia's mass public shootings were committed with guns not banned by the NFA that are still legal. A study by criminologist Gary Kleck found that just two of Australia's mass shootings in the eighteen years preceding the NFA were committed by firearms banned by the NFA.[6] So in other words, there are no laws in effect that could possibly have prevented all but two of Australia's mass shooting from happening again.

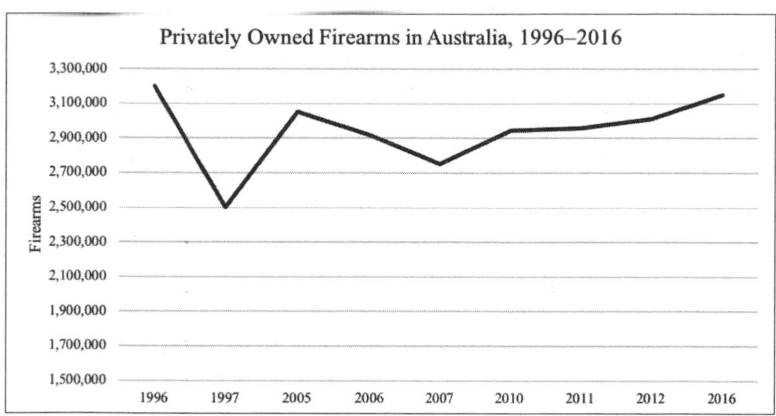

Source: GunPolicy.org

Additionally, all the guns destroyed from the NFA have now been offset by imports of still-legal firearms. The number of private guns in circulation in Australia today is roughly the same as before the Port Arthur massacre.[7] Note that another source has Australia's gun ownership in 2015 estimated at 3.5 million (or three hundred fifty thousand higher than charted).[8]

While there are more firearms in circulation in Australia today than before the NFA, there are roughly 23 percent fewer owned per capita (and the nature of the firearms owned has changed).[9]

A 2017 study by Gun Control Australia found that compliance with the NFA has been substantially weakened over the years, with not a single Australian state or territory in full compliance. Most states now allow children to fire guns, the ban on high-powered semiautomatic weapons has been diluted in some states, and the mandatory twenty-eight-day waiting period to purchase a gun has been relaxed in most states.[10]

Non-Gun Mass Killings Offset Mass Shootings

According to Kleck, mass murder by other means (knives, fire, car attack, and the like) where five or more were killed increased from zero incidents in the eighteen years before the NFA to six in the years following until 2017.[11]

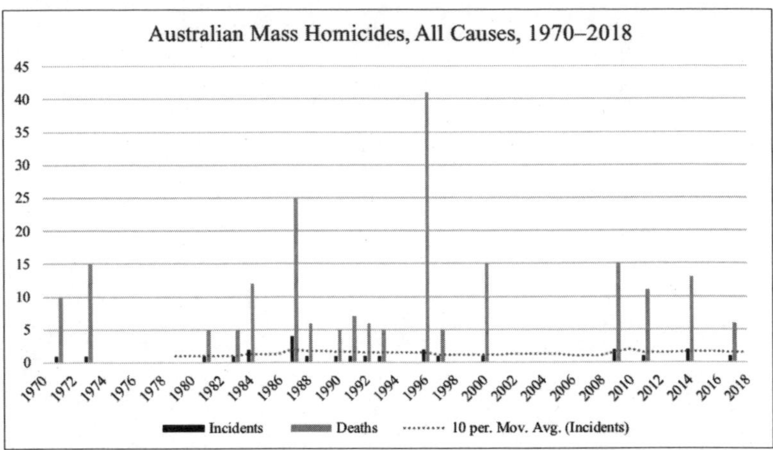

Source: Gun Facts. This chart includes a 2018 mass killing that was committed with a firearm, but it was a familicide, not a mass public shooting. I excluded it from the first chart of mass shootings in this essay for that reason.

Indeed, there's been no significant change in both the frequency of mass murders and deaths from mass murders relative to the size of Australia's population since the NFA.[12] In fact, there's been no change at all.

Mass Homicides in Australia Before/After NFA				
Incidents Per 1,000 Population			Deaths Per 1,000 Population	
22 Years	Total	Average	Total	Average
Before	0.13	0.08	0.13	0.08
After	0.09	0.1	0.09	0.1

Source: Gun Facts

Did Gun Violence Decline in Australia?

Gun violence fell like a rock in Australia following gun control (by roughly half in the two decades following it)—and it also happened to fall like a rock in America too, which implemented no such similar gun control measures. Everything is relative, and Australia's gun violence decline post-gun control occurred at a time when violence and crime was declining across the board in the developed world.

A 2016 American Medical Association study examined trends in firearm homicides and suicides before and after the adoption of gun control in Australia from the 1996 NFA and found no evidence of a statistically significant effect of gun control on the preexisting downward trend of the firearm homicide rate.[13]

Interestingly, unlike America where most homicides are committed with firearms (two-thirds), only about a quarter of Australia homicides were carried out with firearms prior to the NFA. Thus, it makes no sense to over-credit gun control for a decline in overall violence in Australia, when most of that violence wasn't committed with firearms.

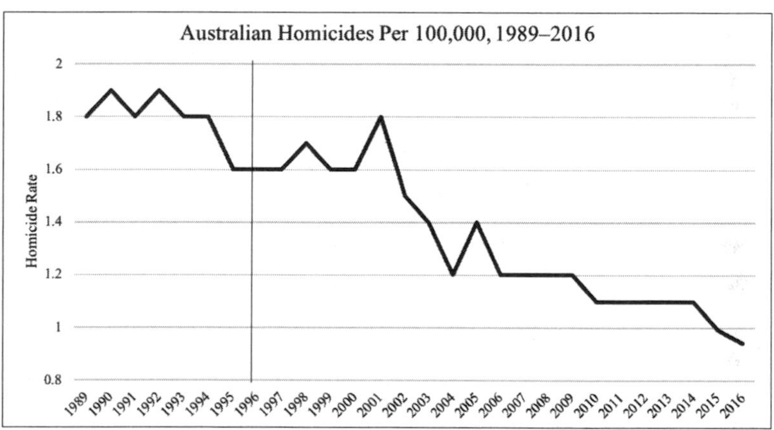

Source: Crime Statistics Australia

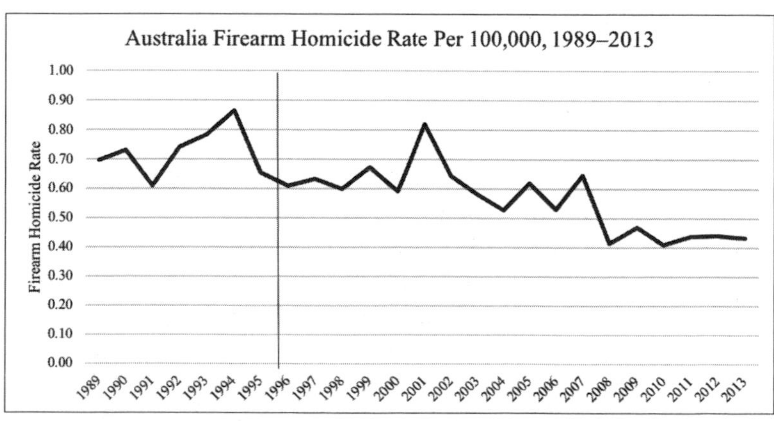

Sources: Crime Statistics Australia, Institut National d'Etudes Démographique[14]

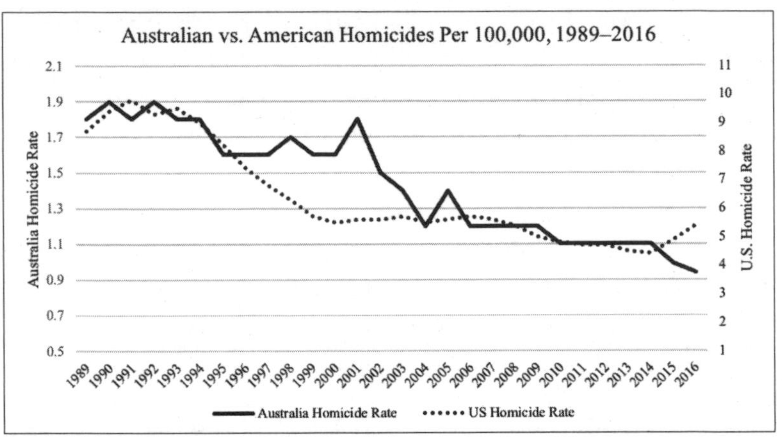

Sources: Crime Statistics Australia, FBI

Over a similar time period (1993–2014), gun homicides in America were cut by more than half. Keep in mind that the number of guns per capita in circulation increased by about 50 percent in America over this period.[15] The overall homicide rate fell faster (as a percent decline) in America than in Australia.[16]

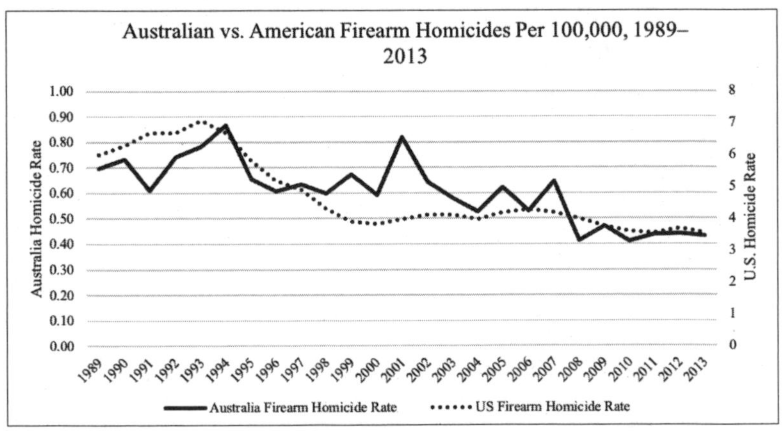

Sources: Crime Statistics Australia, FBI, CDC

Australian Gun Control Wouldn't Be Possible to Implement in America

Even if we were to take the claims of gun control advocates at face value, Australian gun control wouldn't be possible to implement in America for at least three major reasons.

1. **America has a whole lot of guns.** Resulting from the NFA, Australia confiscated six hundred fifty thousand weapons, or between 15 and 20 percent of all firearms in circulation at the time in 1996.[17] In America, a country with as many guns as people, this would require the government to confiscate fifty- to sixty-five million firearms.

   Remember when your liberal friend told you that it's impossible to deport our nation's eleven to fifteen million illegal immigrants? If that's impossible, then how in the world would collecting up to sixty-five million firearms be possible?

2. **Australia is an island.** Unlike the United States, Australia doesn't have a two-thousand-mile unsecured border with a neighboring third world nation. The US-Mexico border has been crossed illegally tens (if not hundreds) of millions of times. If we can't keep people and $60-plus billion in drugs every year from crossing the border, why would guns be the exception?[18]

3. **The Second Amendment would be impossible to repeal—and doing so wouldn't ban a single gun.** Any gun grabber bent on implementing any kind of mandatory gun buyback (aka confiscation) in America would immediately be challenged in the courts on Second Amendment grounds.

Nearly twelve thousand amendments have been proposed to the US Constitution, and yet we have only twenty-seven. Do you think there's a chance in hell an amendment repealing the Second would be twenty-eighth? The obvious answer is "no"—and that's just the first logistical challenge a gun grabber would need to overcome before coming up with a plan to round up hundreds of millions of firearms.

Australian ambassador to the US Joe Hockey helped craft the NFA while he served in parliament, but even he doesn't believe similar legislation would be a remedy for the US. In his words:

> *Australia and the United States are completely different situations, and it goes back to each of our foundings. America was born from a culture of self-defense. Australia was born from a culture of "the government will protect me." Australia wasn't born as a result of a brutal war. We weren't invaded. We weren't attacked. We weren't occupied. That makes an incredible difference, even today.*[19]

Attitudes in Australia have never been even close to as pro-gun as they are in America, so there was little resistance to their government's mandatory buyback. To make quite an understatement, the gun owners of America would react just a tad differently.

Does the US Lead the World in Mass Shootings?

One talking point following any mass public shooting is that such tragedies "simply don't happen" anywhere else in the world. Following the 2015 Charleston church shooting that killed nine, former president Barack Obama famously said that "this type of mass violence does not happen in other advanced countries. It doesn't happen in other places with this kind of frequency."

To support the claim, the White House released a statement citing research from criminologist Adam Lankford, which concluded the US has roughly 5 percent of the world's population but 31 percent of the world's mass shootings (with 90 of 292 mass shootings with four or more victims having occurred in the US).[1] The time frame was from 1966 to 2012 and put the blame on America's gun laws and gun culture. The study also found that American mass shootings tend to be carried out with multiple weapons, while mass shootings abroad tend to be carried out with a single weapon (though interestingly the average death toll per shooting is lower in the US despite that, with about 6.87 victims per incident in the US and 8.8 per incident abroad).

Countless publications cited the study as proof that mass shootings are a uniquely American problem, but a critical study found serious flaws in Lankford's research, concluding instead that despite having 4.6 percent of the world's population and 40 percent of the world's firearms, we in the

US experience just 2.88 percent of the world's mass shootings. According to the study, authored by John R. Lott Jr. and titled "How a Botched Study Fooled the World About the U.S. Share of Mass Public Shootings: U.S. Rate is Lower than Global Average":

> *Lankford claims to have "complete" data on such shooters in 171 countries. However, because he has neither identified the cases nor their location nor even a complete description on how he put the cases together, it is impossible to replicate his findings.*
>
> *It is particularly important that Lankford share his data because of the extreme difficulty in finding mass shooting cases in remote parts of the world going back to 1966. Lack of media coverage could easily lead to under-counting of foreign mass shootings, which would falsely lead to the conclusion that the U.S. has such a large share.* [2]

As was revealed, Lankford massively undercounted mass shootings abroad, giving the US an unjustly high share of the world's mass shootings in his findings. Lott's study used the same criteria for mass shootings as Lankford, though his researchers relied on a wide array of crime databases to search for mass shootings and hired people who spoke Chinese, French, Polish, Russian, Spanish, and other languages to scour international sources Lankford may have missed.

And Lankford missed a lot. Lott's list includes:

> *1,448 attacks and at least 3,081 shooters outside the United States over just the last 15 years of the period that Lankford examined (1998–2012). We find at least fifteen times more mass public shooters than Lankford in less than a third the number of years. Coding these events sometimes involves subjectivity. But even when we use coding choices that are most charitable to Lankford, his 31 percent estimate of the US's share of world mass public shooters is cut by over 95 percent. By our count, the US makes up less than 1.43% of the mass public shooters, 2.11% of their murders, and 2.88% of their attacks. All these are much less than the US's 4.6% share of the world population [emphasis mine]. Attacks in the US are not only less frequent than other countries, they are also much less deadly on average.*

In other words, the US has had 43 mass shootings from 1998 to 2012, compared with 1,448 in the rest of the world.

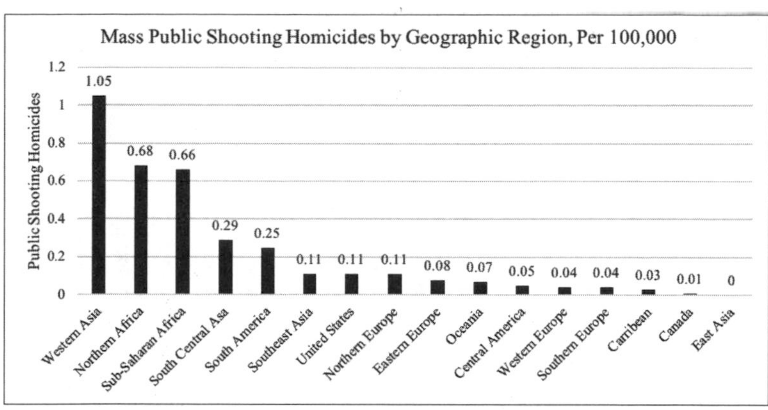

Source: John Lott, Crime Prevention Research Center

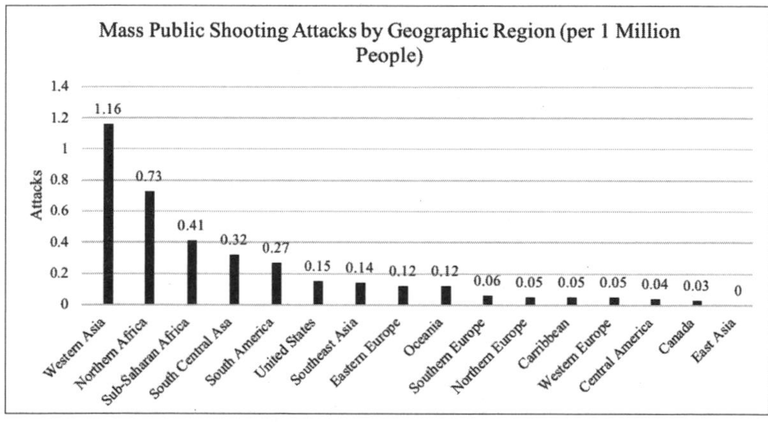

Source: John Lott, Crime Prevention Research Center

Though there's an impression that mass shootings are on the rise in the US, that's certainly not true relative to the rest of the world:

And aside from mass shootings, America is not a uniquely violent country despite widespread gun ownership. Americans commit just 3.7 percent of the world's murders, despite having 4.6 percent of the world's population and 40 percent of the world's firearms.[3]

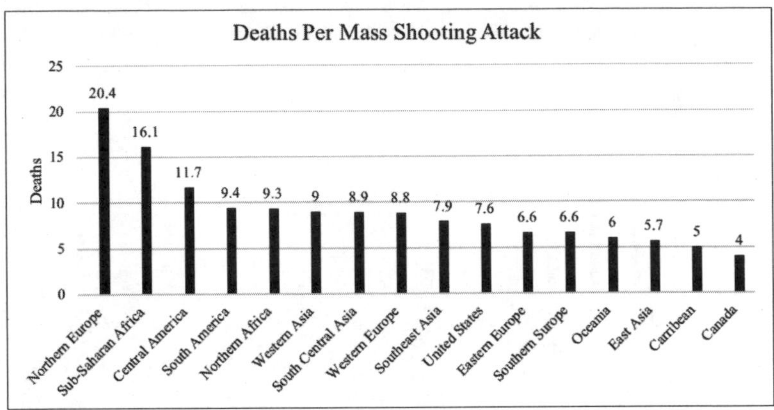

Deaths Per Mass Shooting Attack
Deaths
25
20
15
10
5
0
20.4
16.1
11.7
9.4
9.3
9
8.9
8.8
7.9
7.6
6.6
6.6
6
5.7
5
4
Northern Europe
Sub-Saharan Africa
Central America
South America
Northern Africa
Western Asia
South Central Asia
Western Europe
Southeast Asia
United States
Eastern Europe
Southern Surope
Oceania
East Asia
Carribean
Canada

Source: John Lott, Crime Prevention Research Center

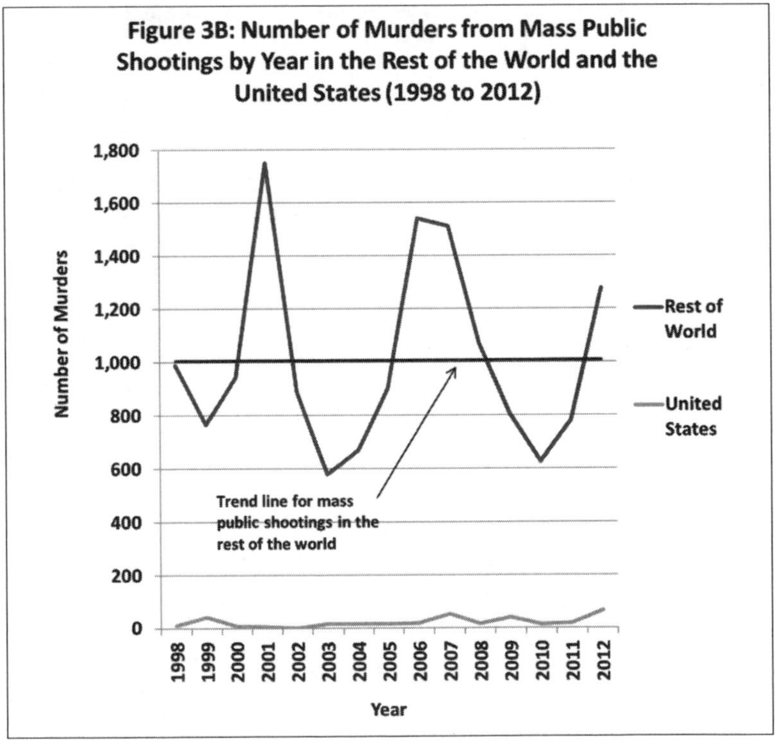

Figure 3B: Number of Murders from Mass Public Shootings by Year in the Rest of the World and the United States (1998 to 2012)
Number of Murders
1,800
1,600
1,400
1,200
1,000
800
600
400
200
0
Trend line for mass public shootings in the rest of the world
Rest of World
United States
1998
1999
2000
2001
2002
2003
2004
2005
2006
2007
2008
2009
2010
2011
2012
Year

Source: John Lott, Crime Prevention Research Center

Are Guns "Almost Never" Used in Self-Defense?

Did you know that you should never buy fire insurance? What's the point when most people won't ever see their house catch fire?

Such flawed logic ignores that the very point of insurance is to protect against low-probability events you don't expect to occur (or certainly hope they don't). While this is easy to understand in the context of insurance, some see things differently when it comes to self-defense.

An NPR story with the headline "How Often Do People Use Guns in Self-Defense?" gives the impression "almost never." Author Samantha Raphelson quotes Harvard researcher David Hemenway in stating that "the average person…has basically no chance in their lifetime ever to use a gun in self-defense."

Hemenway had conducted a study back in 2015, which found that "figures from the National Crime Victimization Survey (NCVS) show that people defended themselves with a gun in nearly 0.9 percent of crimes from 2007 to 2011."[1]

Apparently, we're supposed to disarm ourselves because Hemenway thinks it would be preferable if guns were used in self-defense 0 percent of the time. Not only that, we're supposed to disarm ourselves based on bogus statistics. As Reason magazine's Jacob Sullum noted:

> *The NCVS, unlike surveys that have generated higher defensive gun use (DGU) estimates, is not anonymous. Respondents have to supply their*

names and contact information, they are initially interviewed in person by a representative of the federal government, and they know the survey is commissioned by the Justice Department, a law enforcement agency. Hence it is plausible that some respondents remain silent about their DGUs because they worry that their actions could be legally questionable, given all the restrictions on where and when people may use firearms.[2]

The survey also doesn't ask people if they ever used a firearm in self-defense. It's up to them to describe if they did. In other words, it's up to you to voluntarily disclose to the government the time you pulled a gun on someone. Even if entirely justified, there are countless reasons why one would be hesitant to do so.

Other contradictory studies support the thesis that the NVCS is undercounting defensive gun use. According to James Agresti:

A 1994 survey conducted by Bill Clinton's CDC found that Americans use guns to frighten away intruders who are breaking into their homes about 500,000 times per year

Obama's CDC conducted a gun control study in 2013, finding that "Almost all national survey estimates indicate that defensive gun uses by victims are at least as common as offensive uses by criminals, with estimates of annual uses ranging from about 500,000 to more than 3 million…" The study also noted issues with the NVCS's estimates. "Some scholars point to a radically lower estimate of only 108,000 annual defensive uses based on the National Crime Victimization Survey," but this "estimate of 108,000 is difficult to interpret because respondents were not asked specifically about defensive gun use."[3]

And some other considerations:

- The Hemenway study found that it's rural dwellers who are most likely to use a gun in self-defense, but it's urban dwellers who experience the most violence—and the strictest gun control laws. This brings an old Michael Moore quote to mind, which he thought was an argument for gun control: "the vast majority of these guns are owned by people who live in safe parts of town or mostly in suburbs and rural areas, places where there are very few murders."[4]

- Most crimes occur outside the home. Thus, if Hemenway is concerned about guns not being used in self-defense enough, he should come out in support liberalizing concealed carry laws. Concealed carry permit holders commit infractions at lower rates than police, so anyone who believes only police should own firearms must add CCP holders to that list.[5]

Think that'll happen anytime soon? I won't keep my fingers crossed.

The State with the "Craziest Gun Laws" Is Also the Safest

Does progressive Vermont have the nation's craziest gun laws? That's certainly what liberals outside of the state seem to think.

One of their senators, Bernie Sanders, found himself under fire from his fellow candidates during the 2016 Democrat primary for the crime of having "only" a D- rating from the NRA. In particular, Sanders found himself defending a completely rational vote of his: when in 2005 he voted in favor of legislation granting gun manufacturers legal immunity from being sued by gun victims (just like how we don't hold General Motors liable for car fatalities).

Rival Hillary Clinton specifically attacked Vermont's lax gun laws as fueling gun problems in other states, but she never went into the specifics of Vermont's gun laws—or gun crime in the state. Among the criticisms Vermont has received from anti-gun groups includes:

- In 2009, the Brady Campaign to Prevent Gun Violence said that Vermont's gun laws are the "worst in the nation," which "lead to the illegal trade of firearms" and that they "put children at risk."[1]
- The Giffords Law Center to Prevent Gun Violence gives Vermont an "F" on its gun control scorecard.[2]
- Vermont gets a few honorable mentions in a *Washington Post* article on the "6 Craziest State Gun Laws," which reports that you can conceal and carry a firearm at age sixteen in the state without

a license. The state also has no minimum age to own a rifle or shotgun.[3]

- The Trace (a website started with funding by "Everytown for Gun Safety") chided Vermont as a "gun rights paradise," quoting one gun-rights activist as saying that "Vermont, for over 220 years, has never had permits, has never had registration, and has never had any serious gun control laws."[4]

Vermont sounds like a scene out of *Mad Max* when described by the anti-gun lobby, but the state's residents would probably laugh at the characterization. Vermont was the safest state in the nation in 2016[5] and the second safest in 2017,[6] and you'll have to keep your eyes peeled if you want to see any gun violence there.

According to the Vermont Department of Health, they had only seven gun homicides a year every year from 2011 to 2014.[7] In 2015 the state had twelve, but that fell back to seven in 2016. In a state of six hundred twenty thousand, that's a rate of 1.12 firearm homicides per one hundred thousand people in a typical year.

The FBI statistics report only two gun homicides in Vermont in 2012 and a firearm homicide rate of 0.3 per one hundred thousand.[8]

For comparison, gun-controlled Chicago had an average firearm homicide rate of 15.25 per one hundred thousand people from 2010 to 2015.[9]

What about the claims that Vermont's lax gun laws are fueling gun violence in other states? That's based off a 2013 ATF study that found that "adjusting for population, Vermont has the highest rate of guns traced and recovered in other states after being used for criminal activity." By "highest rate," they mean an entire 147 guns that left Vermont and were used in crimes across state lines—hardly an epidemic. The "rate" is only high because of Vermont's low population.[10]

It's no wonder liberals are quick to criticize Vermont's gun laws—but never seem to talk about Vermont's gun violence.

Is the AR-15 Uniquely Dangerous?

(Coauthored with Corey Iacono)

From Parkland, Florida, to Las Vegas, Nevada, the semiautomatic AR-15 rifle and its variants have seemingly become the weapons of choice for mass shooters in the United States.

According to the Pew Research Center, 81 percent of Democrats and even 50 percent of Republicans believe the federal government should ban "assault-style rifles" like the AR-15.[1] Given the massive amount of carnage AR-15s and similar rifles have caused, can we reasonably trust the public to own such weapons?

The AR-15 is the most popular rifle owned in America, and whether it poses a unique threat that other guns don't must be considered. We as a country already drew a line long ago prohibiting citizens from owning machine guns because their cause for harm was so disproportionate to any claimed benefits.

Is the AR-15 no different? A review of the statistics suggests otherwise.

Some Notes on the Data

The Centers for Disease Control and Prevention (CDC) and the FBI are the two authoritative sources for homicide statistics in the United States.[2] According to the Bureau of Justice Statistics (BJS), the CDC reports "produce more accurate homicide trends at the national level" because it captures less under-reporting than the FBI statistics.[3]

However, the homicide data recorded by the CDC includes all homicides committed by civilians *regardless of criminal intent*. The FBI data instead focuses on intentional homicides (i.e., murder) known to law enforcement and excludes nonnegligent homicide (i.e., manslaughter).

Because of this, in the BJS's words, the FBI data is "better suited for understanding the circumstances surrounding homicide incidents." This is especially true given that the FBI, but not the CDC, records the type of firearm used in a given homicide. For that reason, my analysis uses FBI statistics instead of the CDC's.

That said, there are two notable limitations of the FBI's statistics.

- First, the FBI reports do not look at "assault-style" rifles specifically, but rather murders involving *all* types of rifles, whether they are committed with an AR-15 or a hunting rifle.
- Second, each year there are a few thousand homicide cases where the type of firearm used goes unreported to the FBI. This means that some murders listed under "unknown firearm" may, in fact, be rifle murders.

To account for the second limitation, I extrapolated from the rifle's share of overall homicides when the type of firearm wasn't known. If 5 percent of gun homicides are committed with rifles, and there were one hundred firearm homicides where the type of firearm is unknown, I would count this as five rifle murders.

How Many Murders Involve Rifles Like the AR-15?

According to the FBI's data, *all* rifles, not just "assault-style rifles," constituted on average 340 homicides per year from 2007 through 2017. When we adjust these numbers to take under-reporting into account, that number rises to an average of 439 per year. This amounts to fewer than 5 percent of all firearm homicides.

Rifles make up a minority of gun violence and are used even less commonly in homicides than some non-firearm weapons. Between 2007

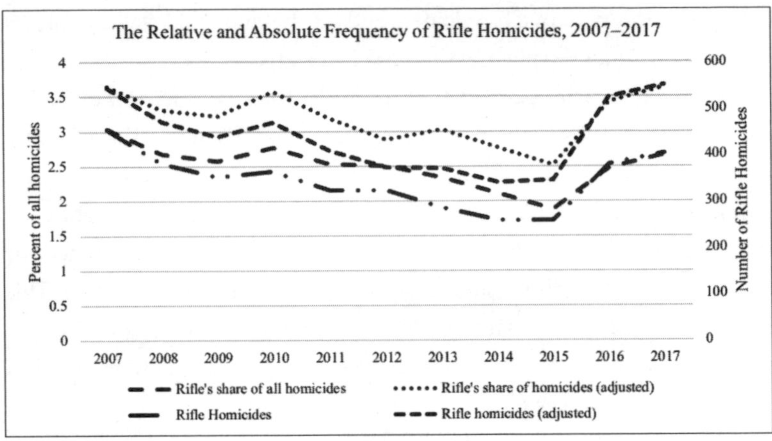

Source: FBI

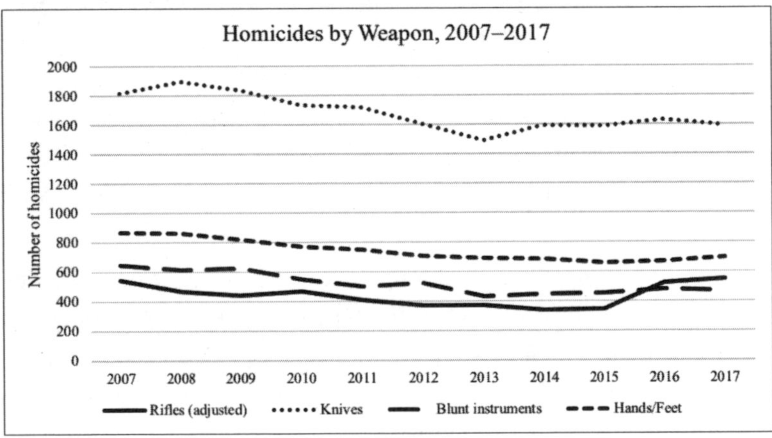

Source: FBI

and 2017, nearly one thousand seven hundred people were murdered with a knife or sharp object per year. That's almost four times the number of people murdered by an assailant with any sort of rifle.

In any given year, for every person murdered with a rifle, there are fifteen murdered with handguns, 1.7 with hands or fists, and 1.2 with blunt instruments. In fact, homicides with any sort of rifle represent a mere 3.2 percent of all homicides on average over the past decade.

Given that the FBI statistics pertain to *all* rifles, the homicide frequency of "assault-style" rifles like the AR-15 is necessarily lesser still, as such firearms compose a fraction of all the rifles used in crime.

According to a *New York Times* analysis, since 2007 [to February 2018], at least "173 people have been killed in mass shootings in the United States involving AR-15s."[4]

That's 173 over a span of a decade, with an average of 17 homicides per year. To put this in perspective, consider that at this rate it would take almost one hundred years of mass shootings with AR-15s to produce the same number of homicide victims that knives and sharp objects produce in one year.

With an average of 13,657 homicides per year during the 2007–2017 time frame, about one-tenth of one percent of homicides were produced by mass shootings involving AR-15s.

Conclusion

Mass shootings involving rifles like the AR-15 can produce dozens of victims at one time, and combined with extensive media coverage of these events, many people have been led to believe that such rifles pose a significant threat to public safety.

However, such shootings are extremely rare, and a look at the FBI data informs us that homicide with these types of rifles represents an extremely small fraction of overall homicide violence. Banning or confiscating such firearms from the civilian population would likely produce little to no reduction in violent crime rates in America.

Did the NRA Help Ban the CDC from Researching Gun Violence?

According to our liberal friends, the Centers for Disease Control and Prevention (CDC) is banned from researching gun violence and it's all thanks to the NRA.

In October 2017, following the massacre at Mandalay Bay in Las Vegas, the *Washington Post* ran an article titled "Why Gun Violence Research Has Been Shut Down for 20 Years." In it, author Todd Frankel writes that "in 1996, the Republican-majority Congress threatened to strip funding from the CDC unless it stopped funding research into firearm injuries and deaths. The National Rifle Association accused the CDC of promoting gun control. As a result, the CDC stopped funding gun-control research."[1]

What Frankel is referring to is the Dickey Amendment, named after Arkansas Republican Jay Dickey. It was as a result of his amendment that the CDC saw $2.6 million cut from its budget, the exact amount they had spent on gun control efforts. It's based off that chain of events that we see headlines like:

- "This Senator Wants to Revive Federal Research on Gun Violence, 22 Years After Congress Banned It"—*Mother Jones*[2]
- "Treat Gun Violence Like the Public Health Epidemic It Is and Lift Research Ban"—*Baltimore Sun*[3]

- "The CDC Can't Fund Gun Violence Research. What If That Changed?"—*Wired*[4]

But despite the budget cut, the CDC was never banned from researching gun violence or gun control by the Dickey Amendment. According to *The Federalist*'s David Harsanyi:

> *Absolutely nothing in the amendment prohibits the CDC from studying "gun violence." In response to this inconvenient fact, gun controllers will explain that while there isn't an outright ban, the Dickey amendment has a "chilling" effect on the study of gun violence. Unlikely is the notion that a $2.6 million cut in funding so horrified the agency that it was rendered powerless to pay for or conduct studies on gun violence. The CDC funding tripled from 1996 to 2010. The CDC's budget is over six billion dollars today.*[5]

I assume that the purpose of this talking point is to suggest that opponents of gun control fear having their beliefs debunked, but when Obama had the CDC study gun violence in 2013 (which you'd think would've prevented people from pushing this bogus narrative), it hardly came to the conclusions that Obama wanted. In fact, the study acknowledged that there could be millions of self-defensive gun uses each year.[6]

That's not the only study out of the CDC that could hardly be considered damning to those favoring gun rights. The CDC conducted a series of surveys on self-defensive gun use in 1996, 1997, and 1998, then proceeded to never release the findings or publicly acknowledge that it was researching the subject.

The question asked in the CDC survey addressed the use or threatened use of a firearm to deter a crime. "During the last 12 months, have you confronted another person with a firearm, even if you did not fire it, to protect yourself, your property, or someone else?"

Florida State University criminologist Gary Kleck recently got access to the surveys and after reviewing them discovered that they found "in an average year during 1996–1998, 2.46 million U.S. adults used a gun for self-defense."[7] At least two of those surveys were conducted in years that liberals claim the CDC was banned from conducting gun research.

Language clarifying that the Dickey Amendment does not prohibit the research of gun violence was signed into law by President Donald Trump on March 23 of 2018, though I'm sure the myth will still be around despite that.

Endnotes

Scandinavian Socialism

1 Valley News Editorial Board, "Closing the Gaps: Disparities That Threaten America," Sanders.gov, August 5, 2011, https://www.sanders.senate.gov/newsroom/must-read/close-the-gaps-disparities-that-threaten-america.

2 Jonathan Swan, "Sanders Defends Past Praise of Fidel Castro," *The Hill*, March 9, 2016, https://thehill.com/blogs/ballot-box/presidential-races/272485-sanders-defends-past-praise-of-fidel-castro.

3 "The World Factbook: Taxes and Other Revenues," Central Intelligence Agency, https://www.cia.gov/library/publications/resources/the-world-factbook/fields/225.html.

4 "Revenue Statistics 2018—The United States," OECD, https://www.oecd.org/tax/revenue-statistics-united-states.pdf

5 Erica York, "Summary of the Latest Federal Income Tax Data, 2017 Update," *Tax Foundation*, January 17, 2018, https://taxfoundation.org/summary-federal-income-tax-data-2017/.

6 "2018 Federal Tax Rates, Personal Exemptions, & Standard Deductions," IRS, https://www.irs.com/articles/2018-federal-tax-rates-personal-exemptions-and-standard-deductions.

7 "The Opportunity Costs of Socialism," White House (Council of Economic Advisers), October 2018, https://www.whitehouse.gov/wp-content/uploads/2018/10/The-Opportunity-Costs-of-Socialism.pdf, 30–31.

8 "Opportunity Costs of Socialism," 30.

9 "Opportunity Costs of Socialism," 31.

10 "Opportunity Costs of Socialism," 33–37.

11 "Opportunity Costs of Socialism," 36.

12 "Growing Unequal? Income Distribution and Poverty in OECD Countries," OECD Publishing, 2008, https://read.oecd-ilibrary.org/social-issues-migration-health/growing-unequal/how-much-redistribution-do

-governments-achieve-the-role-of-cash-transfers-and-household-taxes_9789264044197-6-en#page4.

13 "Sweden. Individual—Taxes on Personal Income," PwC, 2018, http://taxsummaries.pwc.com/ID/Sweden-Individual-Taxes-on-personal-income.

14 "Denmark. Individual—Taxes on Personal Income," PwC, 2018, http://taxsummaries.pwc.com/ID/Denmark-Individual-Taxes-on-personal-income.

15 "Norway. Individual—Taxes on Personal Income," PwC, 2018, http://taxsummaries.pwc.com/ID/Norway-Individual-Taxes-on-personal-income.

16 https://www.irs.com/articles/2018-federal-tax-rates-personal-exemptions-and-standard-deductions.

17 Jared Walczak and Scott Drenkard, "State and Local Sales Tax Rates 2018," *Tax Foundation*, February 13, 2018, https://taxfoundation.org/state-and-local-sales-tax-rates-2018/.

18 Glenn Phelps and Steve Crabtree, "Worldwide, Median Household Income About $10,000," *Gallup*, December 16, 2013, https://news.gallup.com/poll/166211/worldwide-median-household-income-000.aspx.

19 Information available through the American factfinder tool on the Census Bureau's website. https://factfinder.census.gov/faces/nav/jsf/pages/index.xhtml. The relevant information can be found by selecting "advanced search" and then searching "Norwegian," "Swedish," and "Danish" under the "Race/Ethnic Group" category. The relevant tables are titled "Selected Population Profile in the United States."

20 "American FactFinder."

21 "Median Household Income: 2012," US Census Bureau, Small Area Income and Poverty Estimates (SAIPE) Program, December 2013, https://www.census.gov/content/dam/Census/newsroom/releases/2013/cb13-214_maps.pdf.

22 Daniel J. Mitchell, "The Swedish Case for Limited Government," Foundation for Economic Education, October 26, 2016, https://fee.org/articles/the-swedish-case-for-limited-government/.

23 Warren Hoge, "Swedes Are Out Sick Longer, and Budget is Ailing," *New York Times*, September 14, 2002, https://www.nytimes.com/2002/09/24/world/swedes-are-out-sick-longer-and-budget-is-ailing.html.

24 Suzanne Daley, "Danes Rethink a Welfare State Ample to a Fault," *New York Times*, April 20, 2013, https://www.nytimes.com/2013/04/21/world/europe/danes-rethink-a-welfare-state-ample-to-a-fault.html.

25 Sveinung Sleire, "Scandinavia Leaves 20% on the Dole," *Business Report*, June 11, 2017, https://www.iol.co.za/business-report/scandinavia-leaves-20-on-the-dole-9601043.

26 Chris Matthews, "What the Left Gets Wrong About Scandinavia," *Fortune*, January 26, 2016, http://fortune.com/2016/01/26/democrat-bernie-sanders-scandinavia-socialism/.

27 Stefan Folster and Johan Kreicbergs, "Twenty Five Years of Swedish Reforms," Reform Institutet, March 5, 2014, http://www.reforminstitutet.se/wp/wp-content/uploads/2014/03/Twentyfiveyearsofreform140301.pdf.
28 "Central Government Debt, Total (% of GDP) for Sweden," St. Louis Federal Reserve, https://fred.stlouisfed.org/series/DEBTTLSEA188A.
29 Carmen M. Reinhart and Kenneth S. Rogoff, "Responding to Our Critics," *New York Times*, April 25, 2013, https://scholar.harvard.edu/files/rogoff/files/reinhart_rogoff_responding_to_our_critics.pdf.
30 Nima Sanandaji, "Scandinavian Unexceptionalism: Culture, Markets, and the Failure of Third-Way Socialism," Institute of Economic Affairs, http://www.iea.org.uk/sites/default/files/publications/files/Sanandajinima-interactive.pdf, 56.
31 Tyler Cowen, "Sweden Has Lots of Wealth Inequality," *Marginal Revolution* (blog), May 30, 2014, https://marginalrevolution.com/marginalrevolution/2014/05/wealth-inequality-in-sweden.html.
32 Cowen, "Lots of Wealth Inequality."
33 Sanders, Bernie. August 4, 2016. https://www.facebook.com/berniesanders/photos/it-is-insane-and-counter-productive-to-the-best-interests-of-our-country-and-our/1101555426566127/
34 "Education and Earnings," OECD, https://stats.oecd.org/Index.aspx?DataSetCode=EAG_EARNINGS.
35 "Education at a Glance 2018," OECD, https://www.oecd-ilibrary.org/education/education-at-a-glance-2018_eag-2018-en.
36 Rasmus Landerso and James J. Heckman, "The Scandinavian Fantasy: The Sources of Intergenerational Mobility in Denmark and the U.S.," National Bureau of Economic Research, July 2016, https://www.nber.org/papers/w22465.
37 Sanders, Bernie. August 4, 2016. https://www.facebook.com/berniesanders/photos/it-is-insane-and-counter-productive-to-the-best-interests-of-our-country-and-our/1101555426566127/
38 Christina Forsberg, "Repayment of Swedish Student Loan," Swedish Board for Study Support, June 2016, http://edpolicy.umich.edu/files/forsberg-swedish-loan-repayment-2016.pdf?fbclid=IwAR2Z4LB6Agr7flr-cLPKrYln_s-YEwcvL5A6AoVoRm2r2vK-_apoxnW22pe8.
39 "About the Norwegian State Educational Loan Fund," Lanekassen, updated November 12, 2018, https://www.lanekassen.no/nb-NO/Languages/About-the-Norwegian-State-Educational-Loan-Fund-/.
40 "Student Debt and the Class of 2015," Institute for College Access & Success, October 2016, https://ticas.org/sites/default/files/pub_files/classof2015.pdf.
41 Alex Usher, "Global Debt Patterns: An International Comparison of Student Loan Burdens and Repayment Conditions," Educational Policy Institute, September 2005, http://educationalpolicy.org/pdf/global_debt_patterns.pdf, 12.

42 Usher, "Global Debt Patterns," 14.
43 Claudia Allemani et al., "Global Surveillance of Trends in Cancer Survival 2000–14 (CONCORD-3): Analysis of Individual Records for 37 513 025 Patients Diagnosed with One of 18 Cancers from 322 Population-Based Registries in 71 Countries," *The Lancet* 391, no. 10125 (March 2018): 1023–1075, https://www.thelancet.com/action/showPdf?pii=S0140-6736%2817%2933326-3.
44 OECD, *Health at a Glance 2011: OECD Indicators*, (OECD Publishing, 2011), https://www.oecd.org/els/health-systems/49105858.pdf.
45 "2018 Index of Economic Freedom," The Heritage Foundation, February 2, 2018, https://www.heritage.org/international-economies/commentary/2018-index-economic-freedom.
46 James Gwartney et al., "Economic Freedom of the World: 2018 Annual Report," Fraser Institute, https://www.fraserinstitute.org/sites/default/files/economic-freedom-of-the-world-2018.pdf.
47 "Nordic Solutions and Challenges—a Danish Perspective," presented at the Harvard Kennedy School Institute of Politics, Youtube video, 1:09:39, October 30, 2015, https://www.youtube.com/watch?v=MgrJnXZ_WGo; relevant quote is at 8:07–8:45.
48 Carl Bildt (@CarlBildt), "Bernie Sanders was lucky to be able to get to the Soviet Union in 1988 and praise all its stunning socialist achievements before the entire system and empire collapsed under the weight of its own spectacular failures," Tweet, February 25, 2019, https://twitter.com/carlbildt/status/1100039769810235393

Socialist Damage Control on Venezuela

1 Rachelle Krygier, "'The Maduro Diet': A Photo Essay from Venezuela," *Americas Quarterly*, April 18, 2017, https://www.americasquarterly.org/content/maduro-diet-photo-essay-venezuela.
2 "Blaming Socialism, US Media Distorts Venezuela's Food Crisis," Telesur, February 23, 2017, https://www.telesurenglish.net/news/Blaming-Socialism-US-Media-Distorts-Venezuelas-Food-Crisis-20170223-0053.html.
3 Greg Depersio, "How Does the Price of Oil Affect Venezuela's Economy?" Investopedia, September 20, 2018, https://www.investopedia.com/ask/answers/032515/how-does-price-oil-affect-venezuelas-economy.asp.
4 "Saudi Arabia—Market Overview," Export.gov, last updated November 5, 2018, https://www.export.gov/article?id=Saudi-Arabia-Market-Overview.
5 Osmel Manzano and Jose Sebastian Scrofina, "Resource Revenue Management in Venezuela: A Consumption-Based Poverty Reduction Strategy," National Resource Governance Institute, March 2013, https://resourcegovernance.org/sites/default/files/Venezuela_Final.pdf.
6 "2018 Index of Economic Freedom: Saudi Arabia," The Heritage Foundation, https://www.heritage.org/index/country/saudiarabia.

7 Rafael Romo, "Food Shortages Worry Venezuelans," CNN, December 13, 2011, https://www.cnn.com/2011/12/13/world/americas/venezuela-food-shortages/index.html?no-st=9999999999.
8 "IMF Projects Venezuela Inflation Will Hit 1,000,000 Percent in 2018," *Reuters*, July 23, 2018, https://www.reuters.com/article/us-venezuela-economy/imf-projects-venezuela-inflation-will-hit-1000000-percent-in-2018-idUSKBN1KD2L9.
9 "Venezuela Crude Output Hits 28-Year-Low: OPEC," *Reuters*, November 13, 2017, https://www.reuters.com/article/us-venezuela-oil/venezuela-crude-output-hits-28-year-low-opec-idUSKBN1DD1QD.
10 Deisy Buitrago and Alexandra Ulmer, "Under Military Rule, Venezuela Oil Workers Quit in a Stampede," *Reuters*, April 17, 2018, https://www.reuters.com/article/us-venezuela-oil-workers-insight/under-military-rule-venezuela-oil-workers-quit-in-a-stampede-idUSKBN1HO0H9.
11 Sarah Birnbaum, "Understaffed and Overextended: How Venezuela's Oil Industry Fell Apart," Public Radio International, January 4, 2018, https://www.pri.org/stories/2018-01-04/understaffed-and-overextended-how-venezuela-s-oil-industry-fell-apart.
12 Mark Weisbrot, "Poverty Reduction in Venezuela: A Reality-Based View," *ReVista: Harvard Review of Latin America* (Fall 2008), https://revista.drclas.harvard.edu/book/poverty-reduction-venezuela.
13 Brooke Fowler, "Top 10 Facts About Poverty in Venezuela," The Borgen Project, September 7, 2018, https://borgenproject.org/top-10-facts-about-poverty-in-venezuela/.
14 Valley News Editorial Board, "Close the Gaps: Disparities That Threaten America," Sanders.gov, August 5, 2011, https://www.sanders.senate.gov/newsroom/must-read/close-the-gaps-disparities-that-threaten-america.
15 Michael Moore (@MMFlint), "Hugo Chávez declared the oil belonged to the ppl. He used the oil money to eliminate 75 percent of extreme poverty, provide free health & education 4 all," Tweet, March 5, 2013, https://twitter.com/MMFlint/status/309124649244057600.
16 John Stossel, "Chomsky's Venezuela Lesson," May 31, 2017, *Creators*, https://www.creators.com/read/john-stossel/05/17/chomskys-venezuela-lesson.
17 Jeremy Corbyn (@jeremycorbyn), "Thanks Hugo Chavez for showing that the poor matter and wealth can be shared. He made massive contributions to Venezuela & a very wide world," Tweet, March 5, 2013, https://twitter.com/jeremycorbyn/status/309065744954580992
18 Stossel, "Chomsky's Venezuela Lesson."

The Reagan Deficits

1 "Defending the Reagan Deficits," The Heritage Foundation, June 16, 2014, https://www.heritage.org/budget-and-spending/commentary/defending-the-reagan-deficits.

2 James Pethokoukis, "Did Reagan's Tax Cuts Cause Those Big 1980s Budget Deficits? Or Was It Paul Volcker's Inflation Fighting?" American Enterprise Institute, December 6, 2012, https://www.aei.org/publication/did-reagans-tax-cuts-cause-those-big-1980s-budget-deficits-or-was-it-paul-volckers-inflation-fighting.
3 Tim Sablik, "Recession of 1981–82," Federal Reserve History, November 22, 2013, https://www.federalreservehistory.org/essays/recession_of_1981_82.
4 Tim Worstall, "Reagan's Tax Cuts Didn't Blow Out the Deficit and the Debt—That Was Volcker and Interest Rates," *Forbes*, May 4, 2017, https://www.forbes.com/sites/timworstall/2017/05/04/reagans-tax-cuts-didnt-blow-out-the-deficit-and-the-debt-that-was-volcker-and-interest-rates/#7b7f1a474d6c.
5 Phil Gramm and Mike Solon, "Reagan Cut Taxes, Revenue Boomed," American Enterprise Institute, August 3, 2017, http://www.aei.org/publication/reagan-cut-taxes-revenue-boomed/.
6 Andrew Olivastro, "Tax Cuts Increase Federal Revenues," The Heritage Foundation, December 31, 2002, https://www.heritage.org/taxes/report/tax-cuts-increase-federal-revenues.

Red State Welfare

1 "Red States Are Welfare Queens," *Business Insider*, August 18, 2011, http://www.businessinsider.com/red-states-are-welfare-queens-2011-8.
2 Paul Krugman, "Moochers Against Welfare," *New York Times*, February 16, 2012, https://www.nytimes.com/2012/02/17/opinion/krugman-moochers-against-welfare.html.
3 As Vox Day notes, "For example, the 'blue' state of Maryland's five 'blue' counties possessed an average murder rate of 13.22 per 100,000 residents, which is nearly fifteen times higher than the 0.89 murder rate in Maryland's nineteen 'red' counties." For an extended analysis of crime in red vs. blue states and counties, see Vox Day, *The Irrational Atheist* (Dallas: BenBella Books, 2008), 67–73. Available free online at http://milobookclub.com/mart/TIA_free.pdf.
4 Tino Sanandaji, "Are Welfare Recipients Mostly Republican?" Wall Street Pit, February 25, 2012, http://wallstreetpit.com/89671-are-welfare-recipients-mostly-republican/.
5 "Long-Term Unemployed Survey," Kaiser Family Foundation and NPR, December 2011, https://www.npr.org/assets/news/2011/12/poll/topline.pdf.
6 Chuck DeVore, "Texas vs. California—Myth-Busting Time," SFGate, February 7, 2013, https://www.sfgate.com/opinion/openforum/article/Texas-vs-California-myth-busting-time-4257744.php.
7 Kyle Sammin, "Are Red States Tax Takers and Blue States Tax Makers?" *The Federalist*, November 17, 2017, http://thefederalist.com/2017/11/17/red-states-tax-takers-blue-states-tax-makers/.

Do We Need a $15 Minimum Wage…?

1 "Annual Update of the HHS Poverty Guidelines," Federal Register, January 18, 2018, https://www.federalregister.gov/documents/2018/01/18/2018-00814/annual-update-of-the-hhs-poverty-guidelines.

2 Preston Cooper, "Sorry, Bernie, Few Full-Time Workers Live in Poverty," *Economics 21*, October 13, 2016, https://economics21.org/html/sorry-bernie-few-full-time-workers-live-poverty-2094.html.

3 Ben Gitis, "Primer: Minimum Wage and Combating Poverty," *American Action Forum*, December 3, 2013, https://www.americanactionforum.org/research/primer-minimum-wage-and-combating-poverty/.

4 Walter J. Wessels, "The Effect of Minimum Wages on the Labor Force Participation Rate of Teenagers," Employment Policies Institute, June 2001, https://www.epionline.org/wp-content/studies/wessels_06-2001.pdf.

5 K.R., "Labor Force Participation Rate for 16 to 19 Year Olds," Facebook graphic, April 4, 2016, https://www.facebook.com/UnbiasedAmerica/photos/a.130184327167571.1073741828.123061011213236/468644506654883.

6 Ekaterina Jardim et al., "Minimum Wage Increases, Wages, and Low-Wage Employment: Evidence from Seattle," National Bureau of Economic Research, June 2017, https://evans.uw.edu/sites/default/files/NBER%20Working%20Paper.pdf.

7 Alana Bannan, "Seattle Fires Research Team That Proved Minimum Wage Hike Would Hurt Low Wage Workers," Red Alert Politics, July 6, 2017, http://redalertpolitics.com/2017/07/06/seattle-fires-research-team-proved-minimum-wage-hike-hurt-low-wage-workers/.

Does the US Lead the World in Child Poverty?

1 "Measuring Child Poverty: New League Tables of Child Poverty in the World's Rich Countries," UNICEF, https://www.unicef-irc.org/publications/pdf/rc10_eng.pdf.

2 "Real Median Personal Income in the United States," St. Louis Federal Reserve, https://fred.stlouisfed.org/series/MEPAINUSA672N.

3 "Computations for the 2016 Poverty Guidelines," US Department of Health and Human Services, April 25, 2016, https://aspe.hhs.gov/computations-2016-poverty-guidelines.

4 "Average Salary in European Union 2015," Renis Fischer, March 15, 2018, https://www.reinisfischer.com/average-salary-european-union-2015.

5 http://www.globalrichlist.com/.

6 Jeffrey S. Passel and D'Vera Cohn, "Unauthorized Immigrant Totals Rise in 7 States, Fall in 14," Pew Research Center: Hispanic Trends, November 18, 2014, http://www.pewhispanic.org/2014/11/18/unauthorized-immigrant-totals-rise-in-7-states-fall-in-14/.

7 "The Elephant in the Classroom: Mass Immigration's Impact on Public Education," FAIR, September 2016, https://www.fairus.org/issue/publications-resources/elephant-classroom-mass-immigrations-impact-public-education.
8 "Illegal Aliens: Extent of Welfare Benefits Received on Behalf of U.S. Citizen Children," Government Accountability Office, November 19, 1997, https://www.gao.gov/products/hehs-98-30.
9 Chris Conover, "How American Citizens Finance $18.5 Billion In Health Care for Unauthorized Immigrants," *Forbes*, February 26, 2018, https://www.forbes.com/sites/theapothecary/2018/02/26/how-american-citizens-finance-health-care-for-undocumented-immigrants.
10 Illegals cost an additional $0.9 billion from implicit subsidies due to the tax exemption that nonprofit hospitals receive.
11 Conover, "How American Citizens Finance."
12 Matt O'Brien and Spencer Raley, "The Fiscal Burden of Illegal Immigration on United States Taxpayers," FAIR, September 27, 2017, https://fairus.org/issue/publications-resources/fiscal-burden-illegal-immigration-united-states-taxpayers.
13 Jason Richwine, "The Fiscal Cost of Unlawful Immigrants and Amnesty to the U.S. Taxpayer," The Heritage Foundation, May 6, 2013, https://www.heritage.org/immigration/report/the-fiscal-cost-unlawful-immigrants-and-amnesty-the-us-taxpayer.
14 Linda Qiu, "How Much Do Undocumented Immigrants Pay in Taxes," *PolitiFact*, October 2, 2016, https://www.politifact.com/punditfact/statements/2016/oct/02/maria-teresa-kumar/how-much-do-undocumented-immigrants-pay-taxes/.
15 Lisa Christensen Gee, Matthew Gardner, and Meg Wiehe, "Undocumented Immigrants' State & Local Tax Contributions," Institute on Taxation and Economic Policy, February 2016, https://itep.org/wp-content/uploads/immigration2016.pdf.
16 Octavio Blanco, "Why Undocumented Immigrants Pay Taxes," CNN, April 19, 2017, https://money.cnn.com/2017/04/19/news/economy/undocumented-immigrant-taxes/index.html.
17 "Labor Force Statistics from the Current Population Survey from 2009 to 2019," Bureau of Labor Statistics, https://data.bls.gov/timeseries/LNS11000000.
18 "The Federal Budget in 2017: An Infographic," Congressional Budget Office, March 5, 2018, https://www.cbo.gov/publication/53624.
19 Paul Bedard, "Report: Illegal Immigration Costs $296 billion in Lost Taxes," *Washington Examiner*, September 1, 2017, https://www.washingtonexaminer.com/report-illegal-immigration-costs-296-billion-in-lost-taxes.
20 "Raise More Than a Quarter Trillion Dollars of Tax Revenue by Ending Tax Subsidies for Unauthorized Employment of Illegal Aliens," Center

for Immigration Studies, August 31, 2017, https://cis.org/Report/Raise-More-Quarter-Trillion-Dollars-Tax-Revenue-Ending-Tax-Subsidies-Unauthorized-Employment.

How Bill Clinton Faked the Clinton Surplus

1 William A. Niskanen and Stephen Moore, "Supply-Side Tax Cuts and the Truth about the Reagan Economic Record," Cato Institute, October 22, 1996, https://object.cato.org/pubs/pas/pa261.pdf.
2 J.D. Foster, "Tax Cuts, Not the Clinton Tax Hike, Produced the 1990s Boom," The Heritage Foundation, March 4, 2008, https://www.heritage.org/taxes/report/tax-cuts-not-the-clinton-tax-hike-produced-the-1990s-boom.
3 Craig Steiner, "The Clinton Surplus Myth," Townhall Finance, August 22, 2011, https://finance.townhall.com/columnists/craigsteiner/2011/08/22/the_clinton_surplus_myth.

Did We Used to Tax the Rich at 90 Percent?

1 "Bernie Sanders Asked If American Economy Is 'Moral,'" NBC News, May 26, 2015, https://www.nbcnews.com/business/economy/bernie-sanders-asks-if-american-economy-moral-n364541.
2 Krugman (@paulkrugman), "That 90% top rate in the 60s wasn't as crazy as modern context might make it seem. And remember, economy thrived," Tweet, September 5, 2017, https://twitter.com/paulkrugman/status/905041626002796545.
3 "Top Marginal Tax Rates 1916–2010," Visualizing Economics, April 14, 2011, http://visualizingeconomics.com/blog/2011/04/14/top-marginal-tax-rates-1916-2010.
4 Calculated using the consumer price index inflation calculator. See also Andrew Syrois, "The Good Ol' Days: When Tax Rates Were 90 Percent," Mises Institute, November 24, 2015, https://mises.org/library/good-ol-days-when-tax-rates-were-90-percent.
5 Jane G. Gravelle and Donald J. Marples, "Tax Rates and Economic Growth," Congressional Research Service, January 2, 2014, https://fas.org/sgp/crs/misc/R42111.pdf.
6 Scott Greenberg, "Taxes on the Rich Were Not That Much Higher in the 1950s," *Tax Foundation*, August 4, 2017, https://taxfoundation.org/taxes-rich-1950-not-high/.
7 "Federal Receipts as Percent of Gross Domestic Product," Federal Reserve Bank of St. Louis and US Office of Management and Budget, https://fred.stlouisfed.org/series/FYFRGDA188S and https://www.usgovernmentrevenue.com/revenue_chart_1903_2018USp_20s1li011mcn_10f.

Debunking Four Crazy Cortez Ideas

1 US Department of Labor, "Labor Force Statistics from the Current Population Survey," Bureau of Labor Statistics, January 2018, https://www.bls.gov/cps/cpsaat36.htm.
2 Daniel Bier, "In Government, Nobody Quits—And You Can't Get Fired," Foundation for Economic Education, October 2015, https://fee.org/articles/in-government-nobody-quits-and-you-cant-get-fired/.
3 Gideon Resnick, "House Democrats to Introduce Federal Jobs Guarantee Bill," *Daily Beast*, July 24, 2018, https://www.thedailybeast.com/house-democrats-to-introduce-federal-jobs-guarantee-bill.
4 BCL and Matt Palumbo, "Firearm Facts and Fallacies," *Being Classically Liberal*, June 19, 2014, https://beingclassicallyliberal.liberty.me/firearm-facts-and-fallacies/.
5 Christopher S. Koper, "Updated Assessment of the Federal Assault Weapons Ban: Impacts on Gun Markets and Gun Violence, 1994–2003," US Department of Justice, July 2004, https://www.ncjrs.gov/pdffiles1/nij/grants/204431.pdf.
6 Palumbo, "Is the CDC Banned from Researching Gun Control?" April 2018, *Dan Bongino Show*, podcast, https://bongino.com/is-the-cdc-banned-from-researching-gun-control/.
7 "Addressing the 'Chronic' Housing Shortage in South Africa," People's Environmental Planning, June 2016, http://pep.org.za/2016/06/02/addressing-the-chronic-housing-shortage-in-south-africa/.

California—Model for America?

1 "Robert Reich: Tax Experiment," YouTube video, 03:50, December 9, 2016, https://www.youtube.com/watch?v=1KKCXJ6WesU.
2 Michael Shellenberger, "Number One in Poverty, California Isn't Our Most Progressive State—It's Our Most Racist One," *Forbes*, May 31, 2018, https://www.forbes.com/sites/michaelshellenberger/2018/05/31/number-one-in-poverty-california-isnt-our-most-progressive-state-its-our-most-racist-one/#16e25c805cd9.
3 Tracy Elsen, "SF's Population Is Growing Way Faster Than Its Housing Stock," *Curbed San Francisco* (blog), February 4, 2015, https://sf.curbed.com/2015/2/4/9995388/sfs-population-is-growing-way-faster-than-its-housing-stock.
4 Trudi Renwick and Liana Fox, "The Supplemental Poverty Measure: 2015," US Census Bureau, September 2016, https://www.census.gov/content/dam/Census/library/publications/2016/demo/p60-258.pdf.
5 Steven Greenhut, "California's Infrastructure Is Crumbling (When It's Not Burning)," *R Street*, December 15, 2017, https://www.rstreet.org/2017/12/15/californias-infrastructure-is-crumbling-when-its-not-burning/.

6 Shellenberger, "California In Danger: Why the Dream Is Dying and How We Can Save It," Environmental Progress, February 2018, https://static1.squarespace.com/static/56a45d683b0be33df885def6/t/5a8468c453450aa5dede1cd9/1518627027648/California+in+Danger+%E2%80%94+Final+Proof.pdf, 24–25.
7 Shellenberger, "Number One in Poverty."
8 Shellenberger, "California in Danger," 17.
9 Shellenberger, "California in Danger," 39.
10 "2018 Report Card for California's Surface Transportation Infrastructure," Infrastructure Report Card, 2017, https://www.infrastructurereportcard.org/state-item/california/.
11 "Texas 2017 Report Card GPA: C-," Infrastructure Report Card, 2017, https://www.infrastructurereportcard.org/state-item/texas/.
12 Shellenberger, "California in Danger," 26.

Blue State vs. Red State Economic Performance

1 Stephen Moore, "Nearly 1,000 People Move from Blue States to Red States Every Day. Here's Why," Daily Signal, October 9, 2015, https://www.dailysignal.com/2015/10/09/nearly-1000-people-move-from-blue-states-to-red-states-every-day-heres-why/.
2 Arthur B. Laffer, Stephen Moore, and Jonathan Williams, *Rich States, Poor States*, 3rd ed. American Legislative Exchange Council, 2010, https://www.alec.org/app/uploads/2016/01/RSPS-3rd-Edition.pdf.
3 Laffer, Moore, and Williams, *Rich States, Poor States*, 11th ed. American Legislative Exchange Council, 2019, https://www.alec.org/app/uploads/2019/01/RSPS-11th-Edition-WEB-LOW-REZ.pdf, 18.
4 Brendan Kirby, "Study: Unfunded Debt 12 Times Higher in Democratic-Run States," *LifeZette*, September 19, 2017, https://www.lifezette.com/2017/09/study-unfunded-debt-15-times-higher-in-democratic-run-states/.

Blue State Inequality

1 Krugman, "Republican Class Warfare: The Next Generation," *New York Times*, November 13, 2017, https://www.nytimes.com/2017/11/13/opinion/republican-taxes-next-generation.html.
2 Molly A. Martin, "Income Inequality Across Family Structure Types," Columbia University, February 14, 2004, https://paa2004.princeton.edu/papers/41712.
3 Ron Haskins and Isabel Sawhill, *Creating an Opportunity Society*, The Brookings Institution, 2009, https://www.brookings.edu/wp-content/uploads/2016/07/CreatinganOpportunitySociety1.pdf.

4 Jeffrey M. Jones, "Red States Outnumber Blue for First Time in Gallup Tracking," *Gallup*, February 3, 2016, https://news.gallup.com/poll/188969/red-states-outnumber-blue-first-time-gallup-tracking.aspx.
5 "Guess How Much More Money the Top 1% Make than the Bottom 99%," HowMuch, September 26, 2018, https://howmuch.net/articles/income-inequality-by-state.
6 Caitlin Owens, "Blue Districts Have More Income Inequality Than Red Ones," *Axios*, June 6, 2018, https://www.axios.com/income-inequality-blue-red-districts-641c4e96-327c-4237-91a5-6613ad80cff5.html.
7 Estelle Sommeiller and Mark Price, "The New Gilded Age," Economic Policy Institute, July 19, 2018, https://www.epi.org/publication/the-new-gilded-age-income-inequality-in-the-u-s-by-state-metropolitan-area-and-county/.

Are 97 Percent of the Poorest Counties Really Republican?

1 Louis Jacobson, "Are 97 of the Nation's 100 Poorest Counties in Red States?" *PolitiFact*, July 39, 2014, https://www.politifact.com/truth-o-meter/statements/2014/jul/29/facebook-posts/are-97-nations-100-poorest-counties-red-states/. Unsurprisingly, *PolitiFact* unjustifiably rates the claim as "mostly true" when it's only "technically true."
2 Data accessible online at https://www.docdroid.net/nwl5/red-and-blue-counties.xlsx.
3 Data available at https://www.docdroid.net/nwl5/red-and-blue-counties.xlsx

Corporate Myths—Tax, Wages, and CEO Pay

1 Gravelle, "International Corporate Tax Rate Comparisons and Policy Implications," Congressional Research Service, January 6, 2014, https://fas.org/sgp/crs/misc/R41743.pdf.
2 Paul Caron, "Sullivan: Behind the GAO's 12.6% Effective Tax Rate," *TaxProf* (blog), July 15, 2013, https://taxprof.typepad.com/taxprof_blog/2013/07/sullivan-.html.
3 Andrew B. Lyon, "Another Look at Corporate Effective Tax Rates, 2004–2010," *Tax Notes* 141 no. 3 (October 21, 2013): 313-318.
4 "Paying Taxes in 2013: The Global Picture (English)," The World Bank, January 1, 2013, http://documents.worldbank.org/curated/en/749401468321850315/Paying-taxes-2013-the-global-picture.
5 Philip Dittmer, "U.S. Corporations Suffer High Effective Tax Rates by International Standards," *Tax Foundation* no. 196 (September 2011): 1-12, https://files.taxfoundation.org/legacy/docs/sr195.pdf.
6 Gravelle, "International Corporate Tax Rate Comparisons."
7 Hassett, Kevin A. and Aparna Mathur. "Report Card on Effective Corporate Tax Rates." American Enterprise Institute, February 9, 2011. http://www.aei.org/publication/report-card-on-effective-corporate-tax-rates/

8 Lyon, "Another Look."
9 Kimberly A. Clausing, "Corporate Inversions," Urban Brookings Tax Policy Center, August 20, 2014, https://www.taxpolicycenter.org/publications/corporate-inversions.
10 "The Budget and Economic Outlook: 2014 to 2024," Congressional Budget Office, February 2014, https://www.cbo.gov/sites/default/files/113th-congress-2013-2014/reports/45010-outlook2014feb0.pdf.
11 Kevin S. Markle and Douglas A. Shackelford, "Cross-Country Comparisons of Corporate Income Taxes," National Bureau of Economic Research, February 2011, https://www.nber.org/papers/w16839.pdf.
12 William McBride, "Don't Believe the Economists About 'Low' U.S. Corporate Taxes," *Real Clear Markets*, February 18, 2014, https://www.realclearmarkets.com/articles/2014/02/18/dont_believe_the_economists_about_low_us_corporate_taxes_100907.html.
13 Pat Garofalo, "Corporate Profits Hit Record High While Worker Wages Hit Record Low," *ThinkProgress*, December 3, 2012, https://thinkprogress.org/corporate-profits-hit-record-high-while-worker-wages-hit-record-low-7f5f0626f239/.
14 "Donald Boudreaux and Liya Palagshvili, "The Myth of the Great Wages Decoupling," *Wall Street Journal*, March 6, 2014, https://www.wsj.com/articles/donald-boudreaux-and-liya-palagashvili-the-myth-of-the-great-wages-decoupling-1394151793.
15 "National Income," Federal Reserve Bank of St. Louis, March 28, 2019, https://fred.stlouisfed.org/series/A032RC1A027NBEA; National Income: Compensation of Employees, Federal Reserve Bank of St. Louis, March 28, 2019, https://fred.stlouisfed.org/series/A033RC1A027NBEA; and National Income: Corporate Profits with IVA and CCAdj: Profits after Tax with IVA and CCAdj, Federal Reserve Bank of St. Louis, March 28, 2019, https://fred.stlouisfed.org/series/A551RC1A027NBEA.
16 John Hood, "Lower Taxes, Higher Growth: Scholarly Research Reveals Economic Benefits of Fiscal Restraint," *Spotlight* no. 452, April 15, 2014, http://www.johnlocke.org/acrobat/spotlights/Spotlight452LowerTaxesHigherGrowth.pdf.
17 Daphne Chen, Shi Qi, and Don E. Schlagenhauf, "Corporate Income Tax, Legal Form of Organization, and Employment," Federal Reserve Bank of St. Louis, July 2014, http://research.stlouisfed.org/wp/2014/2014-018.pdf.
18 J. Entin, Stephen. "Labor Bears Much of the Cost of the Corporate Tax." Tax Foundation, October 24, 2017. https://taxfoundation.org/labor-bears-corporate-tax/
19 William M. Gentry, "A Review of the Evidence on the Incidence of the Corporate Income Tax," US Department of the Treasury, Office of Tax Analysis, December 2007, https://www.treasury.gov/resource-center/tax-policy/tax-analysis/Documents/WP-101.pdf.

20 Arnold C. Harberger, "The ABCs of Corporation Tax Incidence: Insights into the Open-Economy Case," chap. 2 in Tax Policy and Economic Growth (Washington, DC: American Council for Capital Formation, 1995), 51–73.

21 Kevin A. Hassett and Aparna Mathur, "Taxes and Wages," American Enterprise Institute, June 2006, http://www.aei.org/wp-content/uploads/2011/10/20060706_TaxesandWages.pdf.

22 Wiji Arulampalam, Michael P. Devereux, and Giorgia Maffini, "The Direct Incidence of Corporate Income Tax on Wages," Forshungsinstitut zur Zukunft der Arbeit Institute for the Study of Labor, October 2010, http://ftp.iza.org/dp5293.pdf.

23 R. Alison Felix, "Passing the Burden: Corporate Tax Incidence in Open Economies," Regional Research Working Paper, Federal Reserve Bank of Kansas City Regional Research, October 2007, http://www.kc.frb.org/Publicat/RegionalRWP/RRWP07-01.pdf.

24 Laurence Kotlikoff et al., "Simulating the Elimination of the U.S. Corporate Income Tax," National Bureau of Economic Research, December 2013, http://www.kotlikoff.net/sites/default/files/CorporateTaxPaper_Current.pdf.

25 Michael Schuyler, "Growth Dividend from a Lower Corporate Tax Rate," *Tax Foundation*, March 12, 2013, http://taxfoundation.org/article/growth-dividend-lower-corporate-tax-rate.

26 Gordon Gray, Douglas Holtz-Eakin, and Cameron Smith, "Macroeconomic Impacts of Corporate Tax Reform," American Action Forum, September 2012, http://americanactionforum.org/sites/default/files/Corporate%20Tax%209-26-12%20Final.pdf.

27 Barack Obama, "Remarks by the President on Economic Mobility," The White House, December 4, 2013, http://www.whitehouse.gov/the-press-office/2013/12/04/remarks-president-economic-mobility.

28 "Terms and Data Sources," AFL-CIO, https://aflcio.org/paywatch/terms-and-data-sources.

29 Lawrence Mishel and Jessica Schleder, "CEO Pay Remains High Relative to the Pay of Typical Workers and High-Wage Earners," Economic Policy Institute, July 20, 2017, https://www.epi.org/files/pdf/130354.pdf.

30 Krugman, *The Conscience of a Liberal* (New York: Norton, 2009), 42.

31 Reich, "Raise Taxes on Companies with CEO-to-Worker Pay Ratios," *Berkeley Blog* (blog), April 22, 2014, https://blogs.berkeley.edu/2014/04/22/corporate-taxes-to-match-ceo-to-worker-pay-ratio/.

32 "Occupational Employment and Wages, May 2017: 11-1011 Chief Executives," Bureau of Labor Statistics, March 30, 2018, https://www.bls.gov/oes/2017/may/oes111011.htm.

33 Lucian Bebchuk and Yaniv Grinstein, "The Growth of Executive Pay," *Oxford Review of Economic Policy* 21, no. 2 (2005): 283–303, http://www.law.harvard.edu/faculty/bebchuk/pdfs/Bebchuk-Grinstein.Growth-of-Pay.pdf.

34 Krugman, *The Conscience of a Liberal.*

35 Xavier Gabaix and Augustin Landier, "Why Has CEO Pay Increased So Much?" *Quarterly Journal of Economics* 123, no. 1 (July 2006): 49–100, https://www.nber.org/papers/w12365.
36 Based on the closing price of McDonald's on February 7, 2018, which gives the stock a market capitalization of $135.1 billion.

The Problem with Warren's Wealth Tax

1 Alan Cole, "The Math Problem That Could Sink the Bernie/AOC Agenda," *National Review*, January 30, 2019, https://www.nationalreview.com/2019/01/bernie-sanders-alexandria-ocasio-cortez-fiscal-policies-unworkable/.
2 Cole, "The Math Problem."
3 Naomi Jagoda, "Warren Stakes Out 2020 Ground with Wealth-Tax Proposal," *The Hill*, January 27, 2019, https://thehill.com/policy/finance/427075-warren-courts-progressives-with-wealth-tax-proposal.
4 Schuyler, "The Impact of Piketty's Wealth Tax on the Poor, the Rich, and the Middle Class," *Tax Foundation* no. 225 (October 2014), https://files.taxfoundation.org/legacy/docs/TaxFoundation_SR225.pdf.

Did Trump Cause a Surge in Hate Crimes?

1 Devlin Barrett, "Hate Crimes Rose 17 Percent Last Year, According to New FBI Data," *Washington Post*, November 13, 2018, https://www.washingtonpost.com/world/national-security/hate-crimes-rose-17-percent-last-year-according-to-new-fbi-data/2018/11/13/e0dcf13e-e754-11e8-b8dc-66cca409c180_story.html.
2 The Editorial board, "Hate Crimes Are Increasing Alongside Trump's Rhetoric," *St. Louis Post-Dispatch*, November 18, 2017, https://www.stltoday.com/opinion/editorial/editorial-hate-crimes-are-increasing-alongside-trump-s-rhetoric/.
3 Sarah Ravani, "FBI Hate Crimes in US, CA Surge in First Year of Trump's Presidency," *The San Francisco Chronicle*, November 14, 2018, https://www.sfchronicle.com/crime/article/FBI-Hate-crimes-in-U-S-CA-surge-in-first-year-13389522.php.
4 Sommer Brokaw, "FBI: Surge in Hate Crimes in 2017 the Largest Since 9/11," *United Press International*, November 13, 2018, https://www.upi.com/FBI-Surge-in-hate-crimes-in-2017-the-largest-since-911/7061542126116/.
5 "2017 Hate Crime Statistics Released: Report Shows More Departments Reporting Hate Crime Statistics," Federal Bureau of Investigation, November 13, 2018, https://www.fbi.gov/news/stories/2017-hate-crime-statistics-released-111318.
6 Daniel Engber, "The FBI Says Hate Crimes Are Soaring. It Actually Has No Idea," *Slate*, November 14, 2018, https://slate.com/technology/2018/11/hate-crimes-fbi-data-insufficient.html.

7 Data for 1995–2017 can be found at "FBI Uniform Crime Reports: Hate Crime," https://ucr.fbi.gov/hate-crime.
8 "About Hate Crime Statistics, 2016," FBI, https://ucr.fbi.gov/hate-crime/2016; and "About Hate Crime Statistics, 2017," FBI, https://ucr.fbi.gov/hate-crime/2017.
9 "2017 Hate Crime Statistics: Offenders," FBI, https://ucr.fbi.gov/hate-crime/2017/topic-pages/offenders.
10 As for the remainder, 7.5 percent were groups made up of individuals of various races, 0.8 percent (49 offenders) were American Indian or Alaska Native, 0.7 percent (42 offenders) were Asian, 3 offenders were Native Hawaiian or Other Pacific Islander, and 19.1 percent were unknown.
11 See the explainer under the heading "Ethnicity" in "2017 Hate Crime Statistics: Offenders."
12 "Population," United States Census Bureau, https://www.census.gov/topics/population.html.

Apartments and the Minumum Wage...

1 "Out of Reach: The High Cost of Housing," National Low-Income Housing Coalition, 2018, https://nlihc.org/sites/default/files/oor/OOR_2018.pdf.
2 Tracy Jan, "A Minimum-Wage Worker Can't Afford a 2-Bedroom Apartment Anywhere in the U.S.," *Washington Post*, June 13, 2018, https://www.washingtonpost.com/news/wonk/wp/2018/06/13/a-minimum-wage-worker-cant-afford-a-2-bedroom-apartment-anywhere-in-the-u-s/.
3 Hillary Hoffower and Andy Kiersz, "A Minimum-Wage Worker Needs 2 Full-Time Jobs to Afford a One-Bedroom Apartment in Most of the US," *Business Insider*, June 14, 2018, https://www.businessinsider.com/minimum-wage-worker-cant-afford-one-bedroom-rent-us-2018-6.
4 Kate Gibson, "Minimum Wage Doesn't Cover Rent Anywhere in the U.S.," *CBS News*, June 14, 2018, https://www.cbsnews.com/news/minimum-wage-doesnt-cover-the-rent-anywhere-in-the-u-s/.
5 "New Report Answers the Question 'How Much Do You Have to Earn to Afford a Modest Home in the U.S.?'" National Low-Income Housing Coalition, June 13, 2018, https://nlihc.org/press/releases/10895.
6 Robert Rector, "Poverty in the U.S.—We Spend Much More Per Person on Social Welfare Than Europe Does," The Heritage Foundation, September 28, 2015, https://www.heritage.org/poverty-and-inequality/commentary/poverty-the-us-we-spend-much-more-person-social-welfare-europe.

Are Federal Employees Underpaid?

1 Gregory Korte, "Trump Freezes Federal Worker Pay, Citing 'Serious Economic Conditions,'" *USA Today*, August 30, 2018, https://www.usatoday.com/story/news/politics/2018/08/30/federal-pay-freeze-trump-cancels-2-1-percent-pay-raise-federal-workers-citing-budget-deficit/1145355002/.

2 Elijah Cummings (@RepCummings), Twitter, August 30, 2018, https://twitter.com/RepCummings/status/1035250312087588864.

3 National Black Worker (@NBWCP), Actions like these worsen the multi-dimensional jobs crisis already faced by Black workers," Twitter, September 11, 2018, https://twitter.com/NBWCP/status/1039544047914901505.

4 James D. Agresti, "Most Federal Employees Are Paid More Than Their Private-Sector Counterparts," *Just Facts Daily*, September 4, 2018, https://www.justfactsdaily.com/most-federal-employees-are-paid-more-than-their-private-sector-counterparts/.

5 "Comparing the Compensation of Federal and Private-Sector Employees, 2011 to 2015," Congressional Budget Office, April 2017, https://www.cbo.gov/system/files/115th-congress-2017-2018/reports/52637-federalprivate-pay.pdf.

6 Hilda L. Solis and Keith Hall, "National Compensation Survey: Occupational Earnings in the United States, 2010," Bureau of Labor Statistics, May 2011, https://www.bls.gov/ncs/ncswage2010.pdf.

7 Rachel Greszler, "Why It Is Time to Reform Compensation for Federal Employees," The Heritage Foundation, July 27, 2016, https://www.heritage.org/jobs-and-labor/report/why-it-time-reform-compensation-federal-employees.

8 Chris Edwards, "Federal Bureaucrats Are Paid 78% More than Private Sector Workers," Foundation for Economic Education, October 6, 2015, https://fee.org/articles/federal-bureaucrats-are-paid-78-more-than-private-sector-workers/.

9 Eric Yoder, "Federal Salaries Lag Behind Private Sector by 35 Percent on Average, Pay Council Says," *Washington Post*, November 9, 2015, https://www.washingtonpost.com/news/federal-eye/wp/2015/11/09/federal-salaries-lag-private-sector-by-35-percent-on-average-pay-council-says/?noredirect=on.

10 Erich Wagner, "Feds Make 32 Percent Less than Private Sector Counterparts, Salary Council Says," *Government Executive*, April 11, 2018, https://www.govexec.com/pay-benefits/2018/04/feds-make-nearly-32-percent-less-private-sector-counterparts-salary-council-says/147381/.

11 Andrew Biggs, "Are Federal Employees Really Underpaid by 34 Percent?" *Forbes*, November 1, 2016, https://www.forbes.com/sites/andrewbiggs/2016/11/01/are-federal-employees-really-underpaid-by-34-percent.

12 "Results of Studies on Federal Pay Varied Due to Differing Methodologies," Government Accountability Office, June 2012, https://www.gao.gov/assets/600/591817.pdf.

13 US Bureau of Labor Statistics, "Quits: Total Private," Federal Reserve Bank of St. Louis, April 9, 2019, https://fred.stlouisfed.org/series/JTS1000QUR.

14 US Bureau of Labor Statistics, Total Separations: Government," Federal Reserve Bank of St. Louis, April 9, 2019, https://fred.stlouisfed.org/series/JTS9000TSR.

15 Erica Werner and Lisa Rein, "Congressional Republicans Tentatively Agree to Raise Federal Worker Pay, Rebuffing Trump," *Washington Post*, October 4, 2018, https://www.washingtonpost.com/business/economy/congressional-republicans-tentatively-agree-to-raise-federal-worker-pay-rebuffing-trump/2018/10/04/2befe952-bcf2-11e8-8792-78719177250f_story.html?utm_term=.10b4382a2227.

Does the Fourteenth Amendment Protect Birthright Citizenship?

1 Michael Anton, "Birthright Citizenship: A Response to My Critics," Claremont CRB, July 22, 2018, https://www.claremont.org/crb/basicpage/birthright-citizenship-a-response-to-my-critics/.
2 P.A. Madison, "Defining Natural-Born Citizen," *The Federalist Blog* (blog), November 18, 2008, http://www.federalistblog.us/2008/11/natural-born_citizen_defined/comment-page-1/.
3 Thomas Cooley, *The General Principles in the Constitutional Law in the United States of America*, (Boston: Little, Brown, and Company, 1880), https://www.constitution.org/cmt/tmc/pcl.htm.
4 Will Ricciardella, "Citizenship—It Shouldn't Exist in the First Place," *The Daily Caller*, October 31, 2018, https://dailycaller.com/2018/10/31/donald-trump-right-birthright-citizenship/.

Has the GOP Gone Extreme?

1 David A. Love, "The Strange Collection of Extremists Running for Office as Republicans," CNN, May 4, 2018, https://www.cnn.com/2018/05/04/opinions/strange-collection-of-extremists-running-as-republicans-opinion-love/index.html.
2 Doug Saunders, "The Real Reason Donald Trump Got Elected? We Have a White Extremism Problem," *The Globe and Mail*, November 12, 2016, https://www.theglobeandmail.com/news/world/us-politics/the-real-reason-donald-trump-got-elected-we-have-a-white-extremism-problem/article32817625/.
3 Heather Cox Richardson, "A Political Historian Explains Why Republicans' Shift to the Extreme Right Could Backfire," *Quartz*, November 14, 2016, https://qz.com/831432/a-political-historian-explains-why-republicans-shift-to-alt-right-nationalism-could-backfire/.
4 Lee Drutman, "Yes, the Republican Party Has Become Pathological. But Why?" *Vox*, September 22, 2017, https://www.vox.com/polyarchy/2017/9/22/16345194/republican-party-pathological.
5 Jonah Goldberg, "The Myth of the Good Conservative," *National Review*, June 15, 2012, https://www.nationalreview.com/2012/06/myth-good-conservative-jonah-goldberg/.

6 James Joyner, "No Longer the 'Party of Eisenhower and Reagan,'" *The Atlantic*, January 12, 2013, https://www.theatlantic.com/international/archive/2013/01/no-longer-the-party-of-eisenhower-and-reagan/267092/.

7 Caroll Doherty, Jocelyn Kiley, and Bridget Johnson, "The Partisan Divide on Political Values Grows Even Wider," Pew Research Center, October 5, 2017, http://assets.pewresearch.org/wp-content/uploads/sites/5/2017/10/05162647/10-05-2017-Political-landscape-release.pdf.

8 "Far-Left Candidates Did Poorly in the Democratic Primaries," *The Economist*, September 20, 2018, https://www.economist.com/united-states/2018/09/20/far-left-candidates-did-poorly-in-the-democratic-primaries.

9 Cas Mudde, "Democrats Are Losing Millennial Vote and Need to Change Message," *The Guardian*, June 24, 2018, https://www.theguardian.com/commentisfree/2018/jun/24/democrats-losing-millennial-vote-change-message.

10 Mudde, "Democrats are Losing."

11 Marc J. Hetherington and Jonathan Weiler, *Prius or Pickup? How the Answers to Four Simple Questions Explain Americas Great Divide* (New York: Houghton Mifflin Harcourt, 2018), 129.

Is the American Dream Dead?

1 Mark R. Rank, "From Rags to Riches to Rags," *New York Times*, April 18, 2014, https://www.nytimes.com/2014/04/20/opinion/sunday/from-rags-to-riches-to-rags.html?smid=pl-share&_r=0.

2 Thomas Sowell, "Numbers Games," *Creators*, November 6, 2011, https://www.creators.com/read/thomas-sowell/11/11/numbers-games.

3 "Household Disposable Income and Inequality in the UK Household Disposable Income and Inequality in the UK: Financial Year Ending 2017," Office for National Statistics, January 10, 2018, https://www.ons.gov.uk/peoplepopulationandcommunity/personalandhouseholdfinances/incomeandwealth/bulletins/householddisposableincomeandinequality/financialyearending2017.

4 "Household Income Quintiles: 1967 to 2015," Tax Policy Center, May 3, 2017, https://www.taxpolicycenter.org/statistics/household-income-quintiles.

5 "Mobility, Measured: America Is No Less Socially Mobile Than It Was a Generation Ago," *The Economist*, February 1, 2014, https://www.economist.com/united-states/2014/02/01/mobility-measured.

Is the Senate Rigged Toward Republicans?

1 Amanda Marcotte (@AmandaMarcotte), Twitter, November 7, 2018, https://twitter.com/AmandaMarcotte/status/1060175360095064064.

2 Mikel Jollett (@Mikel_Jollett), Twitter, November 7, 2018, https://twitter.com/Mikel_Jollett/status/1060153314166358017.

3 Wikipedia, s.v. "2018 United States Senate Election in California," last modified April 11, 2019, 07:29, https://en.wikipedia.org/wiki/2018_United_States_Senate_election_in_California.
4 Wikipedia, s.v. "Party Divisions of the United States Congresses," last modified March 30, 2019, 21:08, https://en.wikipedia.org/wiki/Party_divisions_of_United_States_Congresses.

How to Lie with Statistics...

1 Amy Sherman, "Fact-Checking Cory Booker's Statistic on Attacks by White Nationalist Hate Groups," *PolitiFact*, January 18, 2018, https://www.politifact.com/truth-o-meter/statements/2018/jan/18/cory-booker/fact-checking-cory-bookers-statistic-attacks-white/.
2 "Combating Violent Extremism: Actions Needed to Define Strategy and Assess Progress of Federal Efforts," Government Accountability Office, April 2017, https://www.gao.gov/assets/690/683984.pdf.
3 Helen Davison, "Oregon College Shooting: He Asked 'Are You Christian?' Then He Shot and Killed Them," *The Guardian*, October 2, 2015, https://www.theguardian.com/us-news/2015/oct/02/oregon-college-shooting-he-asked-are-you-christian-then-he-shot-and-killed-them.
4 Matthew Herman, "Global Militant Attacks Caused Fewer Fatalities in 2017," IHS Markit, January 18, 2018, https://ihsmarkit.com/research-analysis/global-militant-attacks-caused-fewer-fatalities-in-2017.html.
5 Mark Wilson, "Nigeria's Boko Haram Attacks in Numbers—as Lethal as Ever," *BBC News*, January 25, 2018, https://www.bbc.com/news/world-africa-42735414.

The Real Reason the Kansas Tax Cuts Failed

1 Jim Tankersley, "Kansas Tried a Tax Plan Similar to Trump's. It Failed," *New York Times*, October 10, 2017, https://www.nytimes.com/2017/10/10/us/politics/kansas-tried-a-tax-plan-similar-to-trumps-it-failed.html.
2 Dominic Rushe, "Kansas's Ravaged Economy a Cautionary Tale as Trump Plans Huge Tax Cuts for Rich," *The Guardian*, December 10, 2017, https://www.theguardian.com/us-news/2017/dec/10/donald-trump-kansas-failed-tax-cuts.
3 Patrick Caldwell, "Trickle-Down Economics Has Ruined the Kansas Economy," *Mother Jones*, May 4, 2016, https://www.motherjones.com/politics/2016/05/sam-brownback-kansas-tax-cuts-trickle-down/.
4 Chris Cillizza, "How the Grand Conservative Experiment Failed in Kansas," CNN, June 10, 2017, https://www.cnn.com/2017/06/09/politics/sam-brownback-kansas/index.html.
5 Jeremy Hobson, "As Trump Proposes Tax Cuts, Kansas Deals with Aftermath of Experiment," NPR, October 25, 2017, https://www.npr.org/2017

/10/25/560040131/as-trump-proposes-tax-cuts-kansas-deals-with-aftermath-of-experiment.

6 Jeremy Scott, "Kansas Shows How Not to Design a Tax Cut, Not That All Tax Cuts at Bad," *Forbes*, June 9, 2017, https://www.forbes.com/sites/taxanalysts/2017/06/09/kansas-shows-how-not-to-design-a-tax-cut-not-that-all-tax-cuts-are-bad/.

7 Scott Drenkard and Joseph Bishop-Henchman, "Testimony: Reexamining Kansas Pass-Through Carve-Out," *Tax Foundation*, January 19, 2017, https://taxfoundation.org/testimony-reexamining-kansas-pass-through-carve-out/.

8 Bryan Lowry and Kelsey Ryan, "Fact Check: Brownback on the Kansas Economy," *Wichita Eagle*, October 28, 2016, https://www.kansas.com/news/politics-government/article111182802.html.

9 Colorado, Missouri, and Nebraska are not in the top ten.

10 "Kansas: State Profile and Energy Estimates," US Energy Information Administration, last modified March 21, 2019, https://www.eia.gov/state/analysis.php?sid=KS.

11 Jonathan Williams and Dave Trabert, "Why the Left and Others Fear Fundamental State Tax Reform," *Investor's Business Daily*, April 11, 2016, https://www.investors.com/politics/commentary/why-the-left-and-others-fear-fundamental-state-tax-reform/.

Who Has Stricter Immigration Laws...

1 Sean Collins Walsh, "Trump Immigration Crackdown Targets Central Americans Seeking Asylum," *Austin American-Statesman*, December 21, 2017, https://www.statesman.com/NEWS/20171221/Trump-immigration-crackdown-targets-Central-Americans-seeking-asylum.

2 "Continued Rise in Asylum Denials Rates: Impact on Representation and Nationality," TRACImmigration, December 13, 2016, http://trac.syr.edu/immigration/reports/448/.

3 Laura V. Gonzalez-Murphy and Rey Koslowski, "Understanding Mexico's Changing Immigration Laws," Wilson Center, March 2011, https://www.wilsoncenter.org/sites/default/files/GONZALEZ%20%2526%20KOSLOWSKI.pdf.

4 Tal Kopan, "Activists Say Mexico Deports Too Many Migrants, Not Too Few," CNN, April 2, 2018, https://www.cnn.com/2018/04/02/politics/mexico-immigrants-deportations/index.html.

5 Clay Boggs, "Mexico's Southern Border Plan: More Deportations and Widespread Human Rights Violations," WOLA, March 19, 2015, https://www.wola.org/analysis/mexicos-southern-border-plan-more-deportations-and-widespread-human-rights-violations/.

6 "Informe Sobre La Problemática De Niñas, Niños Y Adolescentes Centroamericanos En Contexto De Migración Internacional No Acompañados En Su

Tránsito Por México, Y Con Necesidades De Protección Internacional," CNDH Mexico, October 2016, http://www.cndh.org.mx/sites/all/doc/Informes/Especiales/Informe_NNACMNA.pdf.

7 "Mexico: Migration Authorities Unlawfully Turning Back Thousands of Central Americans to Possible Death," Amnesty International, January 23, 2018, https://www.amnesty.org/en/latest/news/2018/01/mexico-migration-authorities-unlawfully-turning-back-thousands-of-central-americans-to-possible-death/.

8 James Fredrick, "Mexico Deploys a Formidable Deportation Force Near Its Own Southern Border," NPR, May 7, 2018, https://www.npr.org/sections/parallels/2018/05/07/607700928/mexico-deploys-a-formidable-deportation-force-near-its-own-southern-border.

No, Trump Did Not Kick Immigrants Out of the Army

1 Martha Mendoza and Garance Burke, "AP NewsBreak: US Army Quietly Discharging Immigrant Recruits," *AP News*, July 6, 2018, https://www.apnews.com/38334c4d061e493fb108bd975b5a1a5d.

2 Scott Dworkin (@funder), Twitter, July 5, 2018, https://t.co/rPufaRuCpY.

3 Ana Navarro (@ananavarro), Twitter, July 5, 2018, https://t.co/flOf9nlDtm.

4 Gavin Newsom (@GavinNewsom), Twitter, July 6, 2018, https://t.co/T6iqtPljV5.

5 John Noonan (@noonanjo), Twitter, July 6, 2018, https://twitter.com/noonanjo/status/1015222212708782080?ref_src=twsrc%5Etfw.

6 Noonan (@noonanjo), Tweet, July 6, 2018, https://twitter.com/noonanjo/status/1015224166973411329?ref_src=twsrc%5Etfw.

7 Noonan (@noonanjo), Tweet, July 6, 2018, https://twitter.com/noonanjo/status/1015225568734928896?ref_src=twsrc%5Etfw.

8 Jeff Schogol, "No, President Trump Is Not Purging the Military of Immigrants," *Task and Purpose,* July 6, 2018, https://taskandpurpose.com/trump-purging-military-immigrants-mavni.

9 Dianna Cahn, "Army Loosens Restrictions on Privileges for Noncitizen Recruits in MAVNI Program," *Stars and Stripes*, April 26, 2018, https://www.stripes.com/army-loosens-restrictions-on-privileges-for-noncitizen-recruits-in-mavni-program-1.524101.

10 Amanda Prestigiacomo, "CBS Military Expert Pushes Back on AP's Army Immigration Recruit Story," *Daily Wire*, July 6, 2018, https://www.dailywire.com/news/32701/cbs-military-expert-pushes-back-aps-army-immigrant-amanda-prestigiacomo.

Do Illegal Aliens Really Commit Fewer Crimes?

1 James D. Agresti, "Illegal Immigrants Are Far More Likely to Commit Serious Crimes Than the U.S. Public," *Just Facts Daily*, June 29, 2018, https://www.

justfactsdaily.com/illegal-immigrants-far-more-likely-to-commit-serious-crimes-than-us-public/.

2 "2015 Yearbook of Immigration Statistics," Department of Homeland Security (Office of Immigration Statistics), December 2016, https://www.dhs.gov/sites/default/files/publications/Yearbook_Immigration_Statistics_2015.pdf.

3 Passel and Cohn, "20 Metro Areas Are Home to Six-In-Ten Unauthorized Immigrants in U.S.," Pew Research Center, February 9, 2017, http://www.pewresearch.org/fact-tank/2017/02/09/us-metro-areas-unauthorized-immigrants/.

4 "Percent of Offenses Cleared by Arrest of Exceptional Means by Population Group, 2015," FBI, 2015, https://ucr.fbi.gov/crime-in-the-u.s/2015/crime-in-the-u.s.-2015/tables/table-25.

5 Martin Kaste, "How Many Crimes Do Your Police 'Clear'? Now You Can Find Out," NPR, March 30, 2015, https://www.npr.org/2015/03/30/395799413/how-many-crimes-do-your-police-clear-now-you-can-find-out.

6 John R. Lott Jr., "Undocumented Immigrants, U.S. Citizens, and Convicted Criminals in Arizona," February 10, 2018, https://ssrn.com/abstract=3099992.

7 "Latest Data: Immigration and Customers Enforcement Detainers," TRACImmigration, data through April 2018, https://trac.syr.edu/phptools/immigration/detain/.

8 "Estimates of the Lawful Permanent Resident Population in the United States," Department of Homeland Security, last modified March 13, 2019, https://www.dhs.gov/immigration-statistics/population-estimates/LPR.

9 Lott, "UPDATED: Responding to Cato's and Others' Attacks on Our Research Regarding Crime by Illegal Immigrants," Crime Prevention Research Center, February 6, 2018, https://crimeresearch.org/2018/02/responding-catos-attacks-research-regarding-crime-illegal-immigrants/.

10 "Criminal Alien Statistics: Information on Incarcerations, Arrests, and Costs," Government Accountability Office, March 2011, https://www.gao.gov/assets/320/316959.pdf.

Trump's Tax Cuts Didn't All Go "to the Rich"

1 David Cicilline, "Cicilline Statement on Republicans' Tax Proposal," Ciccilline.house.gov, November 2, 2017, https://cicilline.house.gov/press-release/cicilline-statement-republicans%E2%80%99-tax-proposal.

2 "Distributional Analysis of the Conference Agreement for the Tax Cuts and Jobs Act," Tax Policy Center, December 18, 2017, https://www.taxpolicycenter.org/publications/distributional-analysis-conference-agreement-tax-cuts-and-jobs-act/full.

3 Naomi Jagoda, "Cruz Offers Bill to Cement Individual Tax Cuts," *The Hill*, January 8, 2018, https://thehill.com/policy/finance/368000-cruz-offers-bill-to-cement-individual-tax-cuts.

4 The Associated Press, "House Passes GOP Bill to Make New Tax Cuts Permanent," CNBC, September 28, 2018, https://www.cnbc.com/2018/09/28/house-passes-gop-bill-to-make-new-tax-cuts-permanent.html.

Tax Refund Confusion

1 Democratic Coalition (@TheDemCoalition),"Many people are seeing an increase in taxes due to the bill eliminating many of the deductions that were used by middle-class families in order to lower the amount of taxes they were required to pay," February 8, 2019, https://twitter.com/TheDemCoalition/status/1093986158693019649.
2 Victoria Cavaliere, "Average Tax Refund Down 8% So Far This Season," CNN, February 10, 2019, https://www.cnn.com/2019/02/09/politics/tax-code-early-returns-data/index.html.
3 "Federal Tax Withholding: Treasury and IRS Should Document the Roles and Responsibilities for Updating Annual Withholding Tables," GAO, July 2018, https://www.gao.gov/assets/700/693582.pdf.
4 Donna Borak, "Average Tax Refunds Up $40 for 2019," CNN, February 28, 2019, https://www.cnn.com/2019/02/28/economy/irs-refunds-tax-law/index.html.
5 Robert Bellafiore, "Who Benefits from the State and Local Tax Deduction?" *Tax Foundation*, October 5, 2018, https://taxfoundation.org/salt-deduction-benefit/.
6 Frank Sammartino and Kim S. Reuben, "Revisiting the State and Local Tax Deduction," Tax Policy Center, March 31, 2016, https://www.taxpolicycenter.org/publications/revisiting-state-and-local-tax-deduction.
7 Sammartino, Philip Stallworth, and David Weiner, "The Effect of the TCJA Individual Income Tax Provisions Across Income Groups and Across the States," Tax Policy Center, March 28, 2018, https://www.taxpolicycenter.org/publications/effect-tcja-individual-income-tax-provisions-across-income-groups-and-across-states/full.
8 Madland et al., "Under President Trump, Workers Continue to Struggle."
9 Jones, "Trump's Economic Scorecard: Higher Inflation."
10 US Bureau of Labor Statistics, Average Hourly Earnings of All Employees: Total Private."
11 Goldstein, "Baby Boom Retirements Are Holding Back Average Pay Growth."
12 "The Good News on Wage Growth," Federal Reserve Bank of San Francisco, August 14, 2017, https://www.frbsf.org/our-district/about/sf-fed-blog/wage-growth-good-news.
13 "Revisiting Wage Growth," Federal Reserve Bank of San Francisco, August 16, 2018, https://www.frbsf.org/our-district/about/sf-fed-blog/revisiting-wage-growth-august-2018/.

14 US Bureau of Labor Statistics, Average Hourly Earnings of All Employees: Total Private [CES0500000003], Federal Reserve Bank of St. Louis, https://fred.stlouisfed.org/series/CES0500000003.

A New Wage Gap Myth…

1 Anna North, "You've Heard That Women Make 80 Cents to Men's Dollar. A New Report Says It's Much Worse Than That," *Vox*, November 28, 2018, https://www.vox.com/policy-and-politics/2018/11/28/18116388/gender-pay-gap-real-equal.
2 Karin Agness Lips, "New Report: Men Work Longer Hours Than Women," *Forbes*, June 30, 2016, https://www.forbes.com/sites/karinagness/2016/06/30/new-report-men-work-longer-hours-than-women.
3 Kimberlee Leonard, "Is 32 Hours Legally Full-Time?" *Chron*, June 30, 2018, https://smallbusiness.chron.com/32-hours-legally-fulltime-11399.html.
4 Sarah Kliff, "A Stunning Chart Shows the True Cause of the Gender Wage Gap," *Vox*, February 19, 2018, https://www.vox.com/2018/2/19/17018380/gender-wage-gap-childcare-penalty.

Is There a Sports Wage Gap Too?

1 Brit McCandless, "They're Just Putting a Ceiling on Us," CBS News, November 21, 2016, https://www.cbsnews.com/news/team-usa-women-soccer-captains-on-equal-pay-60-minutes-overtime/.
2 Tony Manfred, "FIFA Made an Insane Amount of Money Off of Brazil's $15 billion World Cup," *Business Insider*, March 20, 2018, https://www.businessinsider.com/fifa-brazil-world-cup-revenue-2015-3.
3 Drew Harwell, "Why Hardly Anyone Sponsored the Most-Watched Soccer Match in U.S. History," *Washington Post*, July 6, 2015, https://www.washingtonpost.com/news/wonk/wp/2015/07/06/the-sad-gender-economics-of-the-womens-world-cup/.
4 Jeff Carlisle, "Average MLS Salary Goes Up, with Surprising Value Available Leaguewide," ESPN, May 19, 2016, http://www.espn.com/soccer/major-league-soccer/19/blog/post/2876311/average-mls-salary-goes-upwith-surprising-value-available-league-wide.
5 Jamie Goldberg, "National Women's Soccer League Makes Modest Increase to Salary Cap, Does Away with Amateur Player Rule," *The Oregonian*, https://www.oregonlive.com/portland-thorns/2018/03/national_womens_soccer_league_17.html.
6 Wikipedia, s.v. "National Women's Soccer League Attendance," last modified March 26, 2019, 03:31, https://en.wikipedia.org/wiki/National_Women%27s_Soccer_League_attendance.

Is There a Gender Debt gap?

1 "Women's Student Debt Crisis in the United States," American Association of University Women, May 2018, https://www.aauw.org/research/deeper-in-debt/.
2 Mark J. Perry, "Women Earned Majority of Doctoral Degrees in 2016 for 8th Straight Year and Outnumber Men in Grad School 135 to 100," American Enterprise Institute, September 28, 2017, http://www.aei.org/publication/women-earned-majority-of-doctoral-degrees-in-2016-for-8th-straight-year-and-outnumber-men-in-grad-school-135-to-100/.
3 Perry, "Highest-Paying College Majors, Gender Composition of Students Earning Degrees in Those Fields and the Gender Gap," American Enterprise Institute, October 19, 2016, http://www.aei.org/publication/highest-paying-college-majors-gender-composition-of-students-earning-degrees-in-those-fields-and-the-gender-pay-gap/.
4 Jaison R. Abel and Richard Deitz, "When Women Out-Earn Men," *Liberty Street Economics* (New York Federal Reserve), August 5, 2015, https://libertystreeteconomics.newyorkfed.org/2015/08/when-women-out-earn-men.html.

The Pink Tax—Another Feminist Figment?

1 Anna Bessendorf, "From Cradle to Cane: The Cost of Being a Female Consumer: A Study of Gender Pricing in New York City," NYC Department of Consumer Affairs, December 2015, https://www1.nyc.gov/assets/dca/downloads/pdf/partners/Study-of-Gender-Pricing-in-NYC.pdf.
2 "His-Counts and Her-Charges. When Is Price Discrimination Just Discrimination?" *The Economist*, May 24, 2012, https://www.economist.com/blogs/freeexchange/2012/05/prices.
3 "Why You Should Never Share Your Razor," Gilette Venus, https://www.gillettevenus.com/en-us/womens-shaving-guide/facts-and-myths/sharing-razors.
4 https://en.wikipedia.org/wiki/Gillette_Mach3.
5 R. Manzano Antón, G. Martínez Navarro, and D. Gavilán Bouzas, "Gender Identity, Consumption and Price Discrimination," *Revista Latina de Comunicación Social* 73 (2018): 385–400, http://www.revistalatinacs.org/073paper/1261/20en.html.

Is Obama to Thanks for the Trump Economy?

1 See "Did the Stimulus Work?"
2 Kimberly Amadeo, "US Economic Outlook for 2019 and Beyond," *The Balance*, January 1, 2019, https://www.thebalance.com/us-economic-outlook-3305669.

3 "It's Official: Trump Tax Cuts Are Boosting Growth and Mostly Paying for Themselves," *Investor's Business Daily*, April 10, 2018, https://www.investors.com/politics/editorials/trump-tax-cuts-revenues-deficits-paying-for-themselves/.
4 Ben Leubsdorf, "Economists Credit Trump as Tailwind for U.S. Growth, Hiring and Stocks," *Wall Street Journal*, January 11, 2018, https://www.wsj.com/articles/economists-credit-trump-as-tailwind-for-u-s-growth-hiring-and-stocks-1515682893.
5 Hassett's slides can be found at "Economic Update: Council of Economic Advisers," White House, September 10, 2018, https://www.whitehouse.gov/wp-content/uploads/2018/09/Press-Briefing-9.10.18-CEA_Final.pdf.
6 Eric Morath, "Job Openings Exceed Unemployed Americans Again in July as Employers Feel the Pinch," *Wall Street Journal*, September 11, 2018, https://www.wsj.com/articles/job-openings-exceed-unemployed-americans-again-in-july-as-employers-feel-the-pinch-1536691533.

Did the Stimulus Work?

1 Matt Kelley, "Obama Advisers: 1M Jobs Saved or Created," ABC News, September 10, 2009, https://abcnews.go.com/Business/obama-advisers-1m-jobs-saved-created/story?id=8543908.
2 Christina Romer and Jared Bernstein, "The Job Impact of the American Recovery and Reinvestment Plan," Council of Economic Advisers, January 9, 2009, https://www.economy.com/mark-zandi/documents/The_Job_Impact_of_the_American_Recovery_and_Reinvestment_Plan.pdf.
3 Krugman, "Romer and Bernstein on Stimulus," *New York Times*, January 10, 2009, https://krugman.blogs.nytimes.com/2009/01/10/romer-and-bernstein-on-stimulus/.
4 "Democrats' $1 Trillion Stimulus Didn't Reduce Unemployment Like They Promised," House Ways and Means Committee, July 17, 2014. https://gop-waysandmeans.house.gov/reason-15-democrats-1-trillion-stimulus-didnt-reduce-unemployment-like-they-promised/
5 US Bureau of Labor Statistics, "Civilian Labor Force Participation Rate," Federal Reserve Bank of St. Louis, April 5, 2019, https://fred.stlouisfed.org/series/CIVPART.
6 US Bureau of Labor Statistics, "Total Unemployed, Plus All Marginally Attached Workers Plus Total Employed Part Time for Economic Reasons," Federal Reserve Bank of St. Louis, April 5, 2019, https://fred.stlouisfed.org/series/UNRATE
7 Ali Meyer, "Obama Economy: 9.9 Million More Employed, but 14.6 Million Left Labor Force," *Washington Free Beacon*, January 9, 2017, https://freebeacon.com/issues/obama-economy-9-9-million-employed-14-6-million-left-labor-force/.

8 "Civilian Labor Force Participation Rate, by Age, Sex, Race, and Ethnicity," table 3.3, covering years 1996, 2006, 2016, and projected 2026 (in percent), Bureau of Labor Statistics, https://www.bls.gov/emp/tables/civilian-labor-force-participation-rate.htm

9 Rex Sinquefield, "Obama and the Dem's Dismal Recovery," *Forbes*, November 29, 2016, https://www.forbes.com/sites/rexsinquefield/2016/11/29/obama-and-the-dems-dismal-recovery/#541aa5d8cb0e.

10 Heather Long and Tami Luhby, "Yes, This Is the Slowest U.S. Recovery since WWII," *CNN Business,* October 5, 2016, https://money.cnn.com/2016/10/05/news/economy/us-recovery-slowest-since-wwii.

11 Long and Luhby, "Yes, This Is the Slowest."

Is Obama to Thank for the Trump Stock Market Surge?

1 Eshe Nelson, "It's Official: We're in the Longest Bull Market Ever," *Quartz,* August 22, 2018, https://qz.com/1364993/its-official-were-in-the-longest-bull-market-ever/.

2 Krugman (@paulkrugman), Tweet, October 11, 2017, https://twitter.com/paulkrugman/status/918102629066125312.

3 This may literally be the only time I've ever used my finance degree.

4 Nelson, "The US Dollar Just Had Its Worst Year in More Than a Decade, and 2018 Will Bring More of the Same," *Quartz*, December 30, 2017, https://qz.com/1164158/the-us-dollar-just-had-its-worst-year-in-more-than-a-decade-and-2018-will-bring-more-of-the-same/.

5 Krugman, "The Economic Fallout," *New York Times*, November 7, 2016, https://www.nytimes.com/interactive/projects/cp/opinion/election-night-2016/paul-krugman-the-economic-fallout.

6 R. La Monica, Paul. "The Trump market rally: too far, too fast." CNN, November 14, 2016. https://money.cnn.com/2016/11/14/investing/stock-market-record-high-donald-trump/index.html

7 Chris Isidore, "2018 Was the Worst for Stocks in 10 Years," CNN, December 31, 2018, https://www.cnn.com/2018/12/31/investing/dow-stock-market-today/index.html.

8 Charlie Bilello, "2018: The Year in Charts," Pension Partners (blog), January 3, 2019, https://pensionpartners.com/2018-the-year-in-charts/.

Did Obama Deport More Illegals than Trump?

1 Nacha Cattan, "Trump Sends Fewer Mexicans Home Despite Deportation Talk," *Bloomberg*, December 27, 2017, https://www.bloomberg.com/news/articles/2017-12-27/trump-sends-fewer-mexicans-back-home-despite-deportation-talk.

2 "United States Border Patrol. Nationwide Illegal Alien Apprehensions Fiscal Years 1925–2018," US Border Patrol, https://www.cbp.gov/sites/default/files/assets/documents/2019-Mar/bp-total-apps-fy1925-fy2018.pdf.

3 Brian Bennett, "High Deportation Figures Are Misleading," *Los Angeles Times*, April 1, 2014, https://www.latimes.com/nation/la-na-obama-deportations-20140402-story.html.

4 Ana Gonzalez-Barrera and Mark Hugo Lopez, "U.S. Immigrant Deportations Fall to Lowest Level Since 2007," Pew Research Center, December 16, 2016, http://www.pewresearch.org/fact-tank/2016/12/16/u-s-immigrant-deportations-fall-to-lowest-level-since-2007/.

5 Miriam Valverde, "Have Deportations Increased Under Donald Trump? Here's What the Data Shows," *PolitiFact*, December 19, 2017, https://www.politifact.com/truth-o-meter/article/2017/dec/19/have-deportations-increased-under-donald-trump-her/.

6 In 2015, 83 percent of illegals deported after residing in the US had a criminal record. The figure was 92 percent during Obama's last two years in office.

7 "ICE Statistics," US Immigration and Customs Enforcement, last updated December 14, 2018, https://www.ice.gov/statistics.

Has Trump "Foxified" the White House?

1 Philip Bump, "The Foxificaiton of the Trump White House, Visualized," *Washington Post*, December 7, 2018, https://www.washingtonpost.com/politics/2018/12/07/foxification-trump-white-house-visualized/.

2 Paul Farhi and Billy Kenber, "*Time*'s Stengel Latest in Long Line of Reporters Who Jumped to Jobs in Obama Administration," *Washington Post*, September 25, 2013, https://www.washingtonpost.com/lifestyle/style/times-stengel-latest-in-long-line-of-reporters-who-jumped-to-jobs-in-obama-administration/2013/09/25/3937c1fa-2244-11e3-b73c-aab60bf735d0_story.html.

3 Elspeth Reeve, "Rick Stengel Is at Least the 24th Journalist to Work for the Obama Administration," *The Atlantic*, September 12, 2013, https://www.theatlantic.com/politics/archive/2013/09/rick-stengel-least-24-journalist-go-work-obama-administration/310928/. Note, despite the headline, that the article does not list twenty-four journalists, hence the discrepancy between my twenty-three-name list and the headline's claimed twenty-four.

4 Erik Wemple (@ErikWemple), Tweet, December 7, 2018, https://twitter.com/ErikWemple/status/1071121427334598656.

5 Cillizza, "Just 7 Percent of Journalists Are Republicans. That's Far Fewer Than Even a Decade Ago," *Washington Post*, May 6, 2014, https://www.washingtonpost.com/news/the-fix/wp/2014/05/06/just-7-percent-of-journalists-are-republicans-thats-far-less-than-even-a-decade-ago/.

Did Obama Pay Iran Ransom Money?

1 Stephen Collinson, Elise Labott, and Kevin Liptak, "Obama on Iran Payment: 'We Do Not Pay Ransom,'" CNN, August 5, 2016, https://www.cnn.com/2016/08/04/politics/iran-400-million-kerry-rejects-ransom/index.html.
2 "Cash Transfer to Iran," C-SPAN, video, 3:28:36, September 8, 2016, https://www.c-span.org/video/?414929-1/hearing-focuses-payments-iran.
3 Louis Nelson, "U.S. Wire Payments to Iran Undercut Obama," *Politico*, September 18, 2016, https://www.politico.com/story/2016/09/us-iran-payments-wire-transfer-228324.
4 Nelson, "State Dept. Confirms $400 Million Iran Payment Conditioned on Prisoner Release," *Politico*, August 18, 2016, https://www.politico.com/story/2016/08/iran-payment-hostage-release-227170.
5 Rick Richman, "No, We Didn't 'Owe' Iran That $1.7 Billion Ransom Payment," *New York Post*, September 8, 2016, https://nypost.com/2016/09/08/no-we-didnt-owe-iran-that-1-7-billion-ransom-payment/.
6 George Maschke, "English Transcript of the Iranian Television Documentary Program 'Rules of the Game,'" George Maschke's Home Page (blog), February 17, 2016, https://georgemaschke.net/2016/02/17/english-transcript-of-the-iranian-television-documentary-program-rules-of-the-game-%D9%82%D8%A7%D8%B9%D8%AF%D9%87-%D8%A8%D8%A7%D8%B2%DB%8C/.

A Caravan of Myths About Obamacare's "Repeal"

1 Barack Obama, "Cut the cost of a typical family's health insurance premium by up to $2,500 a year," *PolitiFact*, comment made on June 23, 2007, https://www.politifact.com/truth-o-meter/promises/obameter/promise/521/cut-cost-typical-familys-health-insurance-premium-/.
2 "2017 Employer Health Benefits Survey," Kaiser Family Foundation, September 19, 2017, https://www.kff.org/report-section/ehbs-2017-section-1-cost-of-health-insurance/.
3 Dan Mangan, "Obamacare Plans Get More Restrictive and Deductibles Get Pricier in 2018," CNBC, November 30, 2017, https://www.cnbc.com/2017/11/30/obamacare-plans-get-narrower-and-deductibles-get-pricier-in-2018.html.
4 Brad Tuttle, "Here's What Happened to Health Care Costs in America in the Obama Years," *CNN Money*, October 4, 2016, http://time.com/money/4503325/obama-health-care-costs-obamacare/.
5 Katie Keith, "Two New Federal Surveys Show Stable Uninsured Rate," *Health Affairs*, September 13, 2018, https://www.healthaffairs.org/do/10.1377/hblog20180913.896261/full/.

6 Steven A. Camarota, "Facts on Immigration and Health Insurance," Center for Immigration Studies, August 30, 2009, https://cis.org/Fact-Sheet/Facts-Immigration-and-Health-Insurance.
7 Tara O'Neill Hayes, "How Many Are Newly Insured as a Result of the ACA?" American Action Forum, January 4, 2017, https://www.americanactionforum.org/insight/20-million/.
8 Ali Meyer, "19th Obamacare Co-Op Folds, Leaving Only 4 Operating in 2018," *Washington Free Beacon*, June 27, 2017, http://freebeacon.com/issues/19th-obamacare-co-op-folds-leaving-4-operating-2018/.
9 "Federal Subsidies for Health Insurance Coverage for People Under Age 65: Tables from CBO's Spring 2018 Projections," Congressional Budget Office, May 2018, https://www.cbo.gov/system/files?file=2018-06/51298-2018-05-health-insurance.pdf.
10 Nathaniel Weixel, "Poll Finds 4M Lost Health Insurance in Last Two Years," *The Hill*, May 1, 2018, https://thehill.com/policy/healthcare/health-insurance/385680-poll-uninsured-rate-is-climbing.
11 "ObamaCare Individual Mandate," Obamacare Facts, August 7, 2014, last updated November 16, 2018, https://obamacarefacts.com/obamacare-individual-mandate/.
12 David Himmelstein and Steffie Woolhandler, "Repealing the Affordable Care Act Will Kill More Than 43,000 People Annually," *Washington Post*, January 23, 2017, https://www.washingtonpost.com/posteverything/wp/2017/01/23/repealing-the-affordable-care-act-will-kill-more-than-43000-people-annually/?utm_term=.69b0e22c6bf8.
13 Ian Millhiser, "Here's How Many People Could Die Every Year If Obamacare Is Repealed," *Think Progress*, December 7, 2016, https://thinkprogress.org/heres-how-many-people-could-die-every-year-if-obamacare-is-repealed-ae4bf3e100a2/.
14 Katherine Baicker et al., "The Oregon Experiment—Effects of Medicaid on Clinical Outcomes," *New England Journal of Medicine* 368, no. 18 (May 2, 2013): 1713–1722, https://www.nejm.org/doi/full/10.1056/NEJMsa1212321.
15 Max Bloom, "No, Obamacare Repeal Will Not Kill Tens of Thousands," *National Review*, June 26, 2017, https://www.nationalreview.com/2017/06/obamacare-repeal-will-not-kill-thousands/.
16 Brian Frankie, "Running the Numbers on Mortality Rates Suggests Obamacare Could Be Killing People," *The Federalist*, April 25, 2017, http://thefederalist.com/2017/04/25/running-numbers-mortality-rates-suggests-obamacare-killing-people/.

Obama Takes Credit for an Oil Production Boom…

1 "Obama on Oil Production," C-SPAN, November 29, 2018, video, 1:44, https://www.c-span.org/video/?c4763205/obama-oil-production.

2 "U.S. Field Production of Crude Oil," US Energy Information Administration, January 31, 2019, https://www.eia.gov/dnav/pet/hist/LeafHandler.ashx?n=PET&s=MCRFPUS2&f=M.
3 Robert Rapier, "The Irony of President Obama's Oil Legacy," *Forbes*, January 15, 2016, https://www.forbes.com/sites/rrapier/2016/01/15/president-obamas-petroleum-legacy/.
4 Valeria Richardson, "Obama's Energy Legacy: Oil, Natural Gas Production on Federal Lands Tanked," *Washington Times*, March 15, 2017, https://www.washingtontimes.com/news/2017/mar/15/oil-gas-production-federal-land-tanked-under-obama/.
5 "Oil and Gas Production on Federal Land Falls Far Below Historic Norms," Institute for Energy Research, November 26, 2018, https://www.instituteforenergyresearch.org/fossil-fuels/oil-and-gas-production-on-federal-land-falls-far-below-historic-norms/.
6 "Oil and Gas Production on Federal Land."
7 "U.S. Production of Crude Oil Grew 5% in 2017, Likely Leading to Record 2018 Production," US Energy Information Administration, April 4, 2018, https://www.eia.gov/todayinenergy/detail.php?id=35632.
8 Josh Siegel, "Trump Administration to Repeal Obama Fracking Rule Friday," *Washington Examiner*, December 28, 2017, https://www.washingtonexaminer.com/trump-administration-to-repeal-obama-fracking-rule-friday.
9 Tracy Johnson, "Saudis Came Out Ahead in the Oil Price War, but Everyone Lost," CBC, October 17, 2016, https://www.cbc.ca/news/business/oil-price-market-share-war-winners-and-losers-1.3804008.
10 Tom DiChristopher, "'Duped,' 'Tricked' and 'Snookered': Oil Analysts Say Trump Fooled Saudis into Tanking Crude Prices," CNBC, November 15, 2018, https://web.archive.org/web/20181220081217/https://www.cnbc.com/2018/11/15/trump-duped-saudis-into-tanking-oil-prices-analysts-say.html.

Who Was Tougher on Russia—Trump or Obama?

1 The Democrats (@TheDemocrats), October 22, 2012, Tweet, https://twitter.com/TheDemocrats/status/260497619862835201.
2 James Marson and Lukas I. Alpert, "Putin on U.S. Vote: Obama 'Genuine,' Romney 'Mistaken,'" September 6, 2012, *Wall Street Journal*, https://www.wsj.com/articles/SB10000872396390443589304577635113013597198.
3 Benjamin Haddad and Alina Polyakova, "Don't Rehabilitate Obama on Russia," Brookings Institution, March 5, 2018, https://www.brookings.edu/blog/order-from-chaos/2018/03/05/dont-rehabilitate-obama-on-russia/.
4 Jacqueline Thomsen, "Trump Resurfaces Clinton's 2009 Reset Button Gaffe with Russia," *The Hill*, November 11, 2017, https://thehill.com/homenews/administration/359963-trump-resurfaces-clintons-2009-reset-button-gaffe-with-russia.

5 Oliver Knox, "Russia 'Reset' Architect to Next President: Don't Try That Again," *Yahoo!*, May 27, 2015, https://www.yahoo.com/news/russia-reset-architect-to-next-president-dont-120051660936.html.
6 "Off Message? Bill Clinton Claims Hillary's Failed Russian Reset," GOP, January 4, 2016, https://gop.com/off-message-bill-clinton-slams-hillarys-failed-russia-reset.
7 Josh Rogin, "Trump Administration Approves Lethal Arms Sales to Ukraine," *Washington Post*, December 20, 2017, https://www.washingtonpost.com/news/josh-rogin/wp/2017/12/20/trump-administration-approves-lethal-arms-sales-to-ukraine/?noredirect=on.
8 Jordan Fabian, "White House: US, Russia 'Agree to Disagree' on Crimea," *The Hill*, July 2, 2018, https://thehill.com/homenews/administration/395252-white-house-us-russia-agree-to-disagree-on-crimea.
9 Zachary Fryer-Biggs, "Russia Defiant After Syria Bombing, Warns of 'Consequences,'" *Vox*, April 14, 2018, https://www.vox.com/2018/4/14/17237742/syria-bombing-russia-response-trump-putin-iran.
10 "With CAATSA, the U.S. Is Trying to Make Russia Hurt," *Stratfor Worldview*, May 28, 2018, https://worldview.stratfor.com/article/caatsa-us-trying-make-russia-hurt.
11 Natasha Turak, "US Sanctions Are Finally Proving a 'Major Game Changer' for Russia," CNBC, April 10, 2018, https://www.cnbc.com/2018/04/10/us-moscow-sanctions-finally-proving-a-major-game-changer-for-russia.html.

Who Was Worse Toward the Press—Trump or Obama?

1 James Risen, "If Donald Trump Targets Journalists, Thank Obama," *New York Times*, December 30, 2016, https://www.nytimes.com/2016/12/30/opinion/sunday/if-donald-trump-targets-journalists-thank-obama.html.
2 Jonathan Easley, "Obama Says His Is 'Most Transparent Administration' Ever," *The Hill*, February 14, 2013, https://thehill.com/blogs/blog-briefing-room/news/283335-obama-this-is-the-most-transparent-administration-in-history.
3 Ted Bridis, "In Obama's Final Year, U.S. Spent $36 Million in FOIA Lawsuits," PBS, March 14, 2017, https://www.pbs.org/newshour/nation/obamas-final-year-u-s-spent-36-million-foia-lawsuits.
4 Cleve R. Wootson Jr., "Trump Rages About Leakers. Obama Quietly Prosecuted Them," *Washington Post*, June 8, 2017, https://www.washingtonpost.com/news/the-fix/wp/2017/06/08/trump-rages-about-leakers-obama-quietly-prosecuted-them.
5 Wootson, "Trump Rages."
6 Becket Adams, "Obama, Whose Administration Prosecuted and Spied on Reporters, Claims Trump Is Very Bad for Criticizing Newsrooms," *Washington*

Examiner, September 7, 2018, https://www.washingtonexaminer.com/opinion/obama-whose-administration-prosecuted-and-spied-on-reporters-claims-trump-is-very-bad-for-criticizing-newsrooms.

7 Carlos Garcia, "Obama Says He Never Attacked the Press and Gets a Scathing History Lesson," *The Blaze*, September 7, 2018, https://www.theblaze.com/news/2018/09/07/obama-says-he-never-attacked-the-press-and-gets-a-scathing-history-lesson.

8 Brian Stelter, "Fox's Volley with Obama Intensifying," *New York Times*, October 11, 2009, https://www.nytimes.com/2009/10/12/business/media/12fox.html.

9 Adams, "Obama Claims Trump Is Very Bad for Criticizing Newsrooms."

Australian Gun Control Facts and Fallacies

1 Clifton Leaf, "How Australia All But Ended Gun Violence," *Fortune*, February 20, 2018, http://fortune.com/2018/02/20/australia-gun-control-success/.

2 Will Oremus, "Did Gun Control Stop Mass Shootings in Australia? The Latest Research Says Yes—Probably," *Slate*, October 3, 2017, https://slate.com/news-and-politics/2017/10/did-gun-control-stop-mass-shootings-in-australia-probably.html.

3 Alexander Bisley, "How America Can Stop Mass Shootings, From the Country that Already Did," *GQ*, November 9, 2017, https://www.gq.com/story/rob-borbidge-australia-gun-control-interview.

4 Jacqueline Howard, "Australia's Mass Shootings Dropped to Zero After Gun Reforms," June 23, 2016, https://www.cnn.com/2016/06/23/health/australia-gun-law-reform-study/index.html.

5 Samara McPhedran, "Regulating People—Not Just Guns—Might Explain Australia's Decline in Mass Shootings," *The Conversation*, July 26, 2015, https://theconversation.com/regulating-people-not-just-guns-might-explain-australias-decline-in-mass-shootings-44770.

6 Gary Kleck, "Did Australia's Ban on Semiauto Firearms Really Reduce Violence? A Critique of the Chapman et al. (2016) Study," January 12, 2018, available at SSRN: https://ssrn.com/abstract=3086324, 18.

7 "Australia—Gun Facts, Figures, and the Law," GunPolicy.org, https://www.gunpolicy.org/firearms/region/australia.

8 Belinda Grant, "Australians Now Own MORE Guns Than They Did Before the 1996 Port Arthur Massacre—As It's Revealed We Imported a Record Number of Firearms Last Year," Daily Mail, April 27, 2016, https://www.dailymail.co.uk/news/article-3562714/Australians-guns-did-1996-Port-Arthur-massacre-revealed-country-imported-record-number-firearms-year.html.

9 In 1996, 17.6 percent of Australians owned guns, which fell to 13.58 percent after the NFA. The figure peaked as high as 15 percent in 2005 and was 13.7 percent in 2016.

10 Nick O'Malley, "Australia's Tough Gun Laws Have Been Weakened by the States, New Report," *Sydney Morning Herald*, October 4, 2017, https://www.smh.com.au/world/australias-tough-gun-laws-have-been-weakened-by-the-states-new-report-20171004-gyuc42.html.
11 Kleck, p. 25.
12 "Auditing Australia," Gun Facts, March 29, 2016, http://www.gunfacts.info/blog/auditing-australia/. My chart differs slightly from this data, as I excluded a 2018 familicide that they counted as a mass shooting.
13 Simon Chapman, Philip Alpers, and Michael Jones, "Association Between Gun Law Reforms and Intentional Firearm Deaths in Australia, 1979–2013," JAMA 316, no. 3 (2016): 291–299, http://jamanetwork.com/journals/jama/fullarticle/2530362.
14 Crime Statistics Australia only had the raw figures for firearm homicides (http://www.crimestats.aic.gov.au/NHMP/1_trends/), so adjustments were made per 100,000 based on population statistics obtained by Ined (https://www.ined.fr/en/everything_about_population/data/online-databases/developed-countries-database/).
15 Kyle Becker, "13 Charts Put America's Gun Violence in Perspective," *Independent Journal Review*, January 8, 2016, https://ijr.com/10-charts-that-put-obamas-gun-violence-town-hall-in-perspective/.
16 "Auditing Australia."
17 Mark Antonio Wright, "Australia's 1996 Gun Confiscation Didn't Work—and It Wouldn't Work in America," *National Review*, October 2, 2015, https://www.nationalreview.com/2015/10/australia-gun-control-obama-america/.
18 Joseph J. Kolb, "Mexican Official: Cartels Send $64B in Drugs into US Annually," Fox News, February 13, 2017, https://www.foxnews.com/us/mexican-official-cartels-send-64b-in-drugs-into-us-annually.
19 Molly McCluskey, "Australia's Ambassador Says His Country's Gun Laws Can't Save America," *Pacific Standard*, February 9, 2018, https://psmag.com/news/australia-ambassador-gun-laws.

Does the US Lead the World in Mass Shootings?

1 Adam Lankford, "Public Mass Shooters and Firearms: A Cross-National Study of 171 Countries," Violence and Victims 31, no. 2 (2016): 187–199, https://crimeresearch.org/wp-content/uploads/2018/06/Lankford-Public-Mass-Shooters-Firearms.pdf.
2 John R. Lott Jr., "How a Botched Study Fooled the World About the U.S. Share of Mass Public Shootings: U.S. Rate is Lower than Global Average," August 25, 2018, available at SSRN: https://ssrn.com/abstract=3238736.
3 "The Country with 40% of the World's Firearms Commits Less Than 4% of the World's Homicides," Facebook, Unbiased America, August 4, 2018, https://www.facebook.com/UnbiasedAmerica/posts/863758190476844.

Are Guns Almost Never Used in Self-Defense?

1 Samantha Raphelson, "How Often Do People Use Guns in Self-Defense?" NPR, April 13, 2018, https://www.npr.org/2018/04/13/602143823/how-often-do-people-use-guns-in-self-defense.
2 Jacob Sullum, "A Survey Not Designed to Measure Defensive Gun Use Finds Little of It," *Reason*, September 7, 2015, http://reason.com/blog/2015/09/07/a-survey-thats-not-designed-to-measure-d.
3 James Agresti, "Gun Control: Crime and Self Defense," Just Facts, https://www.justfacts.com/guncontrol.asp.
4 Jack Coleman, "Michael Moore Flummoxed by Link Between More Guns, Less Crime," NewsBusters, January 19, 2011, https://www.newsbusters.org/blogs/nb/jack-coleman/2011/01/19/michael-moore-flummoxed-link-between-more-guns-less-crime.
5 Aaron Bandler, "Report: Concealed Carry Permit Holders Are the Most Law-Abiding People in the Country," *Daily Wire*, August 10, 2016, https://www.dailywire.com/news/8255/report-concealed-carry-permit-holders-are-most-law-aaron-bandler.

The State with the Craziest Gun Laws Is Also the Safest

1 Bob Audette, "Brady Campaign Says Vermont Gun Laws Worst in Nation," Benningon Banner, February 9, 2009, https://www.benningtonbanner.com/stories/brady-campaign-says-vermont-gun-laws-worst-in-nation,126287.
2 "Annual Gun Law Scorecard," Giffords Law Center to Prevent Gun Violence, https://lawcenter.giffords.org/scorecard/.
3 Dylan Matthews, "The 6 Craziest State Gun Laws," *Washington Post*, December 16, 2012, https://www.washingtonpost.com/news/wonk/wp/2012/12/16/the-6-craziest-state-gun-laws/?utm_term=.9f35c395181f.
4 Eric Benson, "Vermont's Long, Strange Trip to Gun-Rights Paradise," *The Trace*, July 9, 2015, https://www.thetrace.org/2015/07/vermont-gun-rights-constitutional-carry/.
5 Thomas C. Frohlich, "Vermont Ranks No. 1 on Safest States List," *Burlington Free Press*, November 14, 2016, https://www.burlingtonfreepress.com/story/news/2016/11/14/vt-ranks-no-1-safest-states-list/93799588/.
6 Megan Trimble, "The 10 Safest States in America," *US News & World Report*, February 27, 2018, https://www.usnews.com/news/best-states/slideshows/10-safest-states-in-america.
7 Annie Russell, Henry Epp, and Liam Elder-Connors, "Gunshots: Vermont Gun Deaths, 2011–2016," Vermont Public Radio, http://projects.vpr.net/gunshots-vermont-gun-data.
8 Mona Chaliabi, "US Gun-Crime Map: Interactive," *The Guardian*, September 17, 2013, https://www.theguardian.com/news/datablog/interactive/2013/sep/17/us-gun-crime-map.

9 Francesca Mirabile, "Chicago Isn't Even Close to Being the Gun Violence Capital of the United States," The Trace, October 21, 2016, https://www.thetrace.org/2016/10/chicago-gun-violence-per-capita-rate/.

10 Katie Jickling, "More Vermont Guns Traced Out-of-State Crime," *Bennington Banner,* June 26, 2014, https://www.benningtonbanner.com/stories/more-vermont-guns-traced-to-out-of-state-crime,322498.

Is the AR-15 Uniquely Dangerous?

1 John Gramlich, "7 Facts About Guns in the U.S.," Pew Research Center, December 27, 2018, http://www.pewresearch.org/fact-tank/2018/12/27/facts-about-guns-in-united-states/.

2 "Assault or Homicide," National Center for Health Statistics, https://www.cdc.gov/nchs/fastats/homicide.htm; and "Crime in the U.S.," FBI, https://ucr.fbi.gov/crime-in-the-u.s.

3 "The Nation's Two Measures of Homicide," U.S. Bureau of Justice Statistics, July 2014, https://www.bjs.gov/content/pub/pdf/ntmh.pdf.

4 C. J. Chivers et al., "With AR-15s, Mass Shooters Attack with the Rifle Firepower Typically Used by Infantry Troops," *New York Times*, February 28, 2018, https://www.nytimes.com/interactive/2018/02/28/us/ar-15-rifle-mass-shootings.html.

Did the NRA Help Ban the CDC from Researching Gun Violence?

1 Todd C. Frankel, "Why Gun Violence Research Has Been Shut Down for 20 Years," *Washington Post,* October 4, 2017, https://www.washingtonpost.com/news/wonk/wp/2017/10/04/gun-violence-research-has-been-shut-down-for-20-years.

2 Edwin Rios, "This Senator Wants to Revive Federal Research on Gun Violence, 22 Years After Congress Banned It," February 21, 2018, *Mother Jones*, https://www.motherjones.com/politics/2018/02/the-government-banned-gun-violence-research-22-years-ago-this-senator-wants-to-put-an-end-to-it/.

3 Alexandra Sowa, "Treat Gun Violence Like the Public Health Epidemic It Is and Life Research Ban," *The Baltimore Sun*, February 22, 2018, https://www.baltimoresun.com/news/opinion/oped/bs-ed-op-0223-gun-research-20180222-story.html.

4 Eric Niiler, "The CDC Can't Fund Gun Research. What If That Changed?" *Wired*, March 7, 2018, https://www.wired.com/story/what-if-the-cdc-could-fund-gun-research/.

5 David Harsanyi, "No, Government Isn't 'Banned' from Studying Gun Violence," *The Federalist*, March 9, 2018, http://thefederalist.com/2018/03/09/no-government-isnt-banned-from-studying-gun-violence/.

6 "Priorities for Research to Reduce the Threat of Firearm-Related Violence," the National Academies Press, 2013, https://www.nap.edu/read/18319/chapter/3.

7 Brian Doherty, "CDC, in Surveys It Never Bothered Making Public, Provides More Evidence That Plenty of Americans Innocently Defend Themselves with Guns," *Reason*, April 20, 2018, https://reason.com/blog/2018/04/20/cdc-provides-more-evidence-that-plenty-o.